The Enterprise of Reading Differently:

The Novels of Shashi Deshpande in Postcolonial Arguments

The Novels of Shashi Deshpande in Postcolonial Arguments

Mrinalini Sebastian

Prestige

Published by
Prestige Books
New Delhi 110 058
Ph. 011-25507139
email: prestigebooks@gmail.com
website: asiabookclub.com

Associate Office
60/29-45 Parramatta Road,
Concord, NSW 2137
Australia

ISBN: 81-7551-078-1

Rs. 600

Printed at Chaman Offset Press, New Delhi 110 002

Contents

Said, Imperialism and Culture

Bhabha and Ambivalence in Postcolonial Discourse

Spivak and the Teacher of Literature

The Question of Location and Other Perspectives

Chapter Four

Postcolonial Arguments and the Novels of Shashi Deshpande

Chapter Five

For

Akka, Mama and Claudine Akka

Preface

In her book, *The Rhetoric of English India* (Chicago: University of Chicago Press, 1992), Sara Suleri claims that the "postcolonial condition is neither territorially bound nor more the property of one people than of the other: instead, its inevitably retroactive narrative allows for the inclusion both of its colonial past and of the function of criticism at the present time as necessary corollaries to the telling of its stories." (pp. 21-22) This book too starts off with the understanding that the colonial past is inextricably linked to the present in a postcolonial society. It uses the arguments of some postcolonial critics to read the novels of a contemporary Indian writer and at the same time offers a critique of the postcolonial discourse.

Although the title of this book has two parts, the emphasis is more on the first part because, in my opinion, postcolonial discourse is basically an act of rereading. It offers us different perspectives on various issues related to colonialism, and, of these, one of the most important is the rereading of the binary: centre—periphery. It appears as though the rejection of any such binary, initially, requires a deconstructive appraisal of it. This is what the three prominent postcolonial thinkers Edward Said, Homi K. Bhabha and Gayatri Chakravorty Spivak have done in their early contributions to this discourse.

Most of the postcolonial critics are greatly influenced by postmodern and poststructuralist thinking, and are, therefore, not in favour of any universal theory of postcolonialism. Difference, contingency, hybridity, are the themes which often figure in postcolonial discussions, and the earlier anti-colonial positions which were structured around issues of identity and nationality do not necessarily have a place in such arguments. The discursive field which we now term postcolonialism defies any systematising effort because it is wrought with differences of opinion and differences in approaches. But, in my view, these differences are characteristic of the field. Discordant notes are to be taken as a distinctive feature of postcolonial discourse.

If we accept this position, it will not be difficult to move on to the next set of arguments that I use in this work. I have attempted to bring 'postcolonial discussions to crisis' by way of reading it differently. This different reading is done when I use some of the arguments of the postcolonial critics to discuss the major novels of Shashi Deshpande, an Indian novelist who writes in English. I have borrowed the term 'bringing to crisis' from Spivak who seems to acknowledge this as a productive activity:

> What I mean by crisis is the moment at which you feel that your presuppositions of an enterprise are disproved by the enterprise itself. These are not necessarily moments of weakness. It seems to me that this is the only serious way in which crisis can become productive, when one feels for example, that the women's movement challenges the project of feminism. ("Negotiating the Structures of Violence," *The Post-Colonial Critic: Interviews, Strategies, Dialogues*, ed. Sarah Harasym, New York, Routledge, 1990, p. 139).

I claim that the major arguments of Said, Bhabha and Spivak are linked to the question of location and that they should be analysed in connection with the various parameters that define any context. Very often power relations between the colonisers and the colonised supported the hierarchy that existed within the colonised society. None of the postcolonial critics presented in this work deny the involvement of the elite of the colonised world in the process of colonisation. However, the very fact that long-accepted binaries are questioned now, gives us the opportunity to problematise the very space in which postcolonial discourse is evolving. It is around the question of location that the most interesting postcolonial discussions are set.

Even in this work the binary between theory and practice is dismantled by way of a juxtaposition. If the first part of the work introduces the term 'postcolonialism' and analyses the theoretical positions of some of the major postcolonial critics, the second part which looks like the 'practical' part actually poses a challenge to the first part of the work. The part which discusses the novels of Shashi Deshpande shows how some of the arguments of the post-colonial critics lose their priority in a context where multiculturalism is a way of life—forced or otherwise—and not an option. Though the book makes an effort to trace some of the major steps that give rise to postcolonial discourse. I must admit that two important contributions in this field have been left out. These are Ania Loomba's *Colonialism/ Postcolonialism* (London: Routledge. 1998) and Bart Moore-Gilbert's *Postcolonial Theory: Contexts, Practices, Politics* (London: Verso. 1997). Both take different approaches to the terms 'postcolonialism' and 'postcolonial theory.' These two publications came out after the initial work for this book was completed. Bart Moore-Gilbert's *Postcolonial Theory* is especially useful because it gives detailed analysis of the contributions of Said, Spivak and Bhabha to this discursive field. In addition. it shows that the practice of postcolonial criticism. which has a much older tradition. is not really alien to the theory of postcolonial discourse. There are points of contact and convergence even when critics like Aijaz Ahmed may not accept many postcolonial theorists and their mode of arguing from within the western academic centres.

What I try to show in this work is that unless we problematise the location of these 'postcolonial academicians,' we will find it difficult to make use of their valuable contribution in our own postcolonial academic contexts. I have attempted to demonstrate that we could read cultural artefacts like novels in a postcolonial manner. I have consciously selected a novelist who does not thematise the issues of nation, colonialism, neocolonialism, cultural identity, differences, or borders. I have resisted the tendency to produce a counter-canon by selecting the works of a novelist who does not get the kind of attention that an Arundathi Roy gets in the international scenario The postcolonial discourse provides us with arguments which can be used as tools for reading novels, even when these novels do not deal with the more obvious 'postcolonial themes.' The novels of Shashi Deshpande do not deal with issues of cultural difference and cultural conflicts, even when the narrative mode is realistic. The protagonist, in almost every case, is an educated, middle-class, Brahmin woman, who is confronted by a crisis in her life. Many of her protagonists are writers and the novels themselves offer the readers a view of the complex process by which these protagonists try to come to terms with the crises in their lives. The endings are indeterminate and do not offer any clear 'solutions' to the crises, even though many critical interpretations which are available talk about the 'self/realisation' of the woman in these novels.

Among other things, my readings of these texts in a 'postcolonial' manner, reveal the following details:

a) Novels of Shashi Deshpande defy the traditional categorisation of 'realist' fiction. The very fact that her protagonists are similar and that her plot lines are also similar suggests that she is reinscribing a particular representation of a woman from a particular background, and makes it look like a subverted mode of testimonial writing.
b) Even though there is no universally acknowledged methodology of reading colonial/postcolonial texts, we could try using Said's contrapuntal reading, Bhabha's idea of hybridity and cultural difference and Spivak's method of raising the issue of the gendered subaltern as tools for reading the novels of Shashi Deshpande.
c) If, like Said, we read Deshpande's novels paying attention to the women characters who appear as marginal figures in narration, along with those interpretations which focus only on the protagonists, we see that Said's use of the binary 'here' and 'there' is present in this particularised, culturally specific postcolonial world of the women presented in these novels. I have in mind here Said's discussion of the novels of Jane Austen. However, we could extend his arguments by saying that not only was Austen's 'here' supported by the presence of the colonies 'there,' but also the world of the intelligent, thinking-writing women of Shashi Deshpande's 'here' are supported by the marginal domestic women who enable the liberal-educated women to think and write.
d) If we try to use Bhabha's concepts of hybridity, cultural dif-

ference and ambiguity, we are initially faced with resistance put up by the structure of the novels. The novels generally represent a culturally closed world where very little transaction takes place across the boundaries. In the case of *Roots and Shadows* we see how a story about the ancestral house and of the traditional household controlled by a Brahmin widow demands that we not only give up our stereotypical views about Brahmin widows, but also allows us to see her as the prototype-agent who symbolically accepts cultural difference by bequeathing her property to the niece who is married to someone from outside the community.

e) If we try to make use of Spivak's idea of the 'subaltern woman,' we are confronted by the fact that even in Spivak, there is no specific description of this term. This is one more instance where Spivak is being cautious neither to typify, nor to simplify. However, what Spivak does not seem to remind her readers of, nor show through her own representations of stories or anecdotes, is the fact that in the numerously different contexts which a country like India contains, it is possible for a woman to be an oppressor as well as victim simultaneously. Who is the subaltern woman in Deshpande's *The Binding Vine*? Is it the woman who was forced to marry a man whom she did not wish to marry? Is it the young girl who is raped, tortured and is in a state of speechlessness because she is in a coma? Is it the working woman, who, even to show her concern for the suffering women must depend on the maid servant who in turn, looks after her children? Or is it the maid servant because she is economically dependent on the career woman?

Taking the specific instance of a novelist and her works, I have arrived at the following conclusions. My justifications for considering these conclusions important are based on Spivak's own observation that every case which proves the contrary makes any generalisation impossible. My conclusions are as follows:

i) There is a tendency among the three prominent critics that I mention above to relate to and to theorise on the basis of their migratory experience or experiences as teachers of multicultural courses in the Euro-American academy.

ii) Already there are voices to be heard, which call for more specified representation of the postcolonial spaces and postcolonial academies because of the difference in 'residence' amongst the postcolonial intellectuals.

iii) The tendency to privilege the migratory experience can be questioned only by choosing a specific cultural context, where movement of this kind is not possible even if one wanted to, where postcolonial concerns can still be of importance in teasing out the complex power relations which cut across borders of class, caste and gender.

iv) There is already a sort of counter-canon of postcolonial authors and their works. To uphold one set of authors and to ignore other writers, who, as I show, could also be read postcolonially, is to negate the purpose of postcolonial discourse. I have tried to include one more discordant note which questions as well as supports the project of postcolonial discourse.

Acknowledgements

This book is the result of research done during 1993-1997 when we were staying in Hamburg, Germany. I look back at these years as one of the most challenging years of my life. The difficult task of keeping alive my interest in postcolonial discourse in an unfamiliar academic context could be achieved only because there were many, who, through many different ways, transformed the unfamiliar space into a familiar location.

I am grateful to Hamburg University for sensitizing me to issues realated to the politics of location. It was only due to the unprejudiced interest of Professor Dr. Bettina Friedl of the Department of English Language and Culture, Hamburg University, that I could pursue my research goals. For her scholarly guidance, challenging comments and meticulous reading, I am grateful. I am thankful to Professor Dr. Joseph C. Schoepp, also of Hamburg University, for his valuable critique and suggestions.

Life in Hamburg was made pleasant by the international community at Missionsakademie, Hamburg. But for the interest taken by its Directors of Study, Dr. Dietrich Werner, Frau Barbara Maubach and Dr. Erhard Kamphausen, I would not have started this project. I am indebted to them for all the help I received from them. The kindness shown by Dr. Amèlè Ekuè, Hilde Benz-Werner, Doris Kamphausen, Monika Bak, Ingrid Kunze, Frau Kaptanogulu, Frau Reichardt and others at the Missionsakademie cannot be forgotten. The scholars residing at Missionsakademie and their families have shown us what it means to live in dialogue with peoples of different cultures. They became our family and stood by us when our own parents were far away.

I also owe a word of gratitude to the group of friends who

constantly kept in touch with us. Their friendship encouraged me and their concern inspired me. Of these many friends I am especially thankful to Helga Schwalm, Ulrike Erichsen, Frace Bettina Kratz, Frau Lore and Herr Gert Potyka, Christiane and Joachem Wietzke, Frau Edeltraut and Dr. Gerhard Wehmeier.

Anne-Marie and Jacques Rossel and their sister Claudine Rossel (the Akka, Mama and Claudine Akka of the dedication) have not only been grandparents to us but also staunch supporters of my decision to venture into academic research. Our cold winters were spent in the warmth of their home in Pully, near Lausanne in Switzerland. They have shown me that growing old does not put brakes on one's desire to learn and question. I am grateful to them for their love, for their ability to extend undemanding friendship to others, for the material as well as emotional support I received from them and for their faith in the vibrancy of life.

Our two famlilies have always been supportive. I thank my parents-in-law Hannah and David K. Sebastian for their love and trust and for the many newspaper clippings and novels that they sent me. My parents, Wilhelmina and J.R.G. Amanna, have encouraged me and goaded me to go on with the work even during the most difficult moments. I shall always be grateful to them for their faith in me, for the pride they take in my work and for what they mean to me.

The final touch for the book was given while I was teaching at Sheshadripuram College, Bangalore. To my students, my colleagues and to the Principal, I owe a word of thanks. Our family has become a part of the community living at the United Theological College, Bangalore. I am grateful to this communitiy for encouraging me in many different ways. In the last phase of the work when our computer let us down, it was the Clarke family which came forward to help me out. I thank Prema and Sathi Clarke and their children Avinash and Ashwin for their friendship and for their interest in my work.

Our children Neeraj and Saagarika have proved to me that unfettered reasearch is a luxury. Their demanding love however, has never led them into trivializing their parents' work. I marvel at their ability to cope with many displacements—geographical, cultural—in their young lives, and thank them for making our own life so lively and interesting.

I went to Germany officially as "the accompanying wife" of a research scholar. In spite of his busy life, my husband Kiran dreamed, along with me, of this kind of work. He took interest in it as though it were his own work. He has been a critic, an editor and a research companion. His irrepressible enthusiasm, his ability to react intensely to everything in life and his immense capacity for love, has prevented me from being complacent about life. Without him this book would not have seen the light of day.

I thank Dr. Lalsangkima Pachuau of UTC for his help in transferring the material on to an appropriate computer diskette.

Finally, it is because of the keen interest taken by Professor R.K Dhawan and Ms. D. Renu of Prestige Books, that the book has come out in this form. I acknowledge their help with gratitude.

Chapter One

Introduction

> One of the most absurd aspects of this quest for national authenticity is that—as far as India is concerned, anyway—it is completely fallacious to suppose that there is such a thing as a pure, unalloyed tradition from which to draw. The only people who seriously believe this are religious extremists. The rest of us understand that the very essence of Indian culture is that we possess a mixed tradition, a mélange of elements as disparate as ancient Mughal and contemporary Coca-Cola American.
>
> Salman Rushdie,
> "'Commonwealth Literature' Does Not Exist,"
> *Imaginary Homelands: Essays and Criticism 1981-1991*

> The force of colonial and postcolonial discourse as a theoretical and cultural intervention in our contemporary moment represents the urgent need to contest singularities of difference and to articulate diverse 'subjects' of differentiation.
>
> Homi K. Bhabha,
> "The Other Question: Stereotype, Discrimination and the Discourse of Colonialism," *The Location of Culture*

Setting the Parameters

It is true that one hardly hears about 'Commonwealth Literature' nowadays, even though never before has there been such an interest in the subject of colonial and postcolonial discourses as in the contemporary arena of cultural, anthropological and literary theoretical studies. This interest could be partly attributed to the achievement of many postcolonial intellectuals who have managed to break into the European and the North-American academic circles and partly to the postmodern concern for many of the issues related to Enlightenment and to the era of colonialism. Most of the postcolonial critics have tried to reconstruct the colonial period from a different perspective and many have atempted to undermine the assumed authority and unity of the colonial power. These critics, who have been greatly influenced by postmodern and poststructuralist thinking, are not promoting any universal theory of postcoloniality. Instead, this discursive field appears to be characteristically marked by the presence of many discordant notes. Difference, contingency, hybridity are the terms which often figure in postcolonial discussions.

This is a study which acknowledges the inescapable implications of the colonial past to the present in a postcolonial society and has attempted to give a critique of the postcolonial discourse using some of its own arguments. However, the difficulty in defining and specifying the term 'postcolonial' makes it necessary that parameters be set before any one aspect of postcolonial discourse is taken into consideration. If publication lists are any indication, the current interest in postcolonialism has almost taken the shape of an academic fashion. It has also empowered many postcolonial critics who have used the tool of 'difference' by giving them visibility as well as acclaim. The celebration of difference has also given rise to questions about the "emerging dominant."[1]

The privileging of 'difference' is also related to a demand that postcolonial intellectuals represent the Third World, 'the developing world,' the ex-colonies, to the rest of the world. Gayatri Chakravorty Spivak, a prominent postcolonial critic of Indian origin, questions this privileging of difference. She is sceptical of the demand that she speak as a Third World representative in the Western Academic circles.[2] Rather than restrict herself to the role of being a representative she chooses to take up the role of a teacher because

> In the field of ethno-cultural politics, the post-colonial teacher can help to develop . . . vigilance rather than continue pathetically to dramatize victimage or assert a spurious identity.

> She says 'no' to the 'moral luck' of the culture of imperialism while recognizing that she must inhabit it. indeed invest it, to criticize it.[3]

This work is also about 'difference.' However, it takes Spivak's concern for being vigilant seriously and tries not to 'dramatize victimage' or 'assert spurious identity.' Dramatizing victimage and asserting the identity of the postcolonial subject have been the stances adopted by the anti-colonial discourses. These rather essentializing methods have been replaced in contemporary discussions of colonialism by attempts to renarrate, reread and reinvestigate the past as well as the present of the colonial project.

Apart from Spivak, Edward Said and Homi K. Bhabha have been identified in this work as the important contributors to postcolonial discussions. All three of them have grappled with the binary centre-periphery, even though none of them endorses it. A rejection of the hierarchical opposites centre and periphery requires that we make a deconstructive appraisal of it. That is why Spivak speaks of 'inhabiting' and 'investing' in the culture of imperialism in order to criticize it.

Homi Bhabha approaches the binary from a different angle. He finds that the image of being powerful and authoritarian was projected by the centre in order to cover its own fears and he uses texts from the colonial past to investigate these areas of fear. He draws connections between the concept of nation and narration, thereby indicating that what is generally considered political, social or cultural, is also an aspect of the narrative and the text.[4]

Edward Said is, no doubt, one of the first to have raised the question of Orientalism as a problematic issue and to shake the confidence with which orientalistic themes were generally dealt with. Said shows how the construct Orient later becomes the basis for much of the ethnographic studies and political decisions. But Said does not try to perpetuate this concept of the Orient and the Occident. He would rather that such mutually opposed terms as Orient and Occident vanish altogether.[5] A number of critics who are interested in postcolonialism have certainly been inspired by Said's work, and are contributing to this "better understanding of the way cultural domination has operated."[6]

Even though I have tried to connect the three prominent post-colonial intellectuals, there is no clear-cut common theoretical model to which these critics adhere. Spivak has even expressed displeasure at the use of the word 'postcolonialism.'[7] The term 'postcolonial' itself has been used in so many different ways by so many writers. The discursive field that we now term postcolonial studies defies any attempt at systematizing it because it represents different voices and different theoretical positions. Yet these differences are to be taken as a distinctive feature of the discourse which in turn can be traced back to a dislike for anything that essentializes and universalises. This is where its inter-relatedness with postmodernism and poststructuralist modes of thinking comes into picture. In fact, the postcolonial discourse is more closely related to these two discursive areas than to the earlier prominent commonwealth studies because there is a vast difference between the conception of the ex-colony as represented in the commonwealth studies and the glimpse of postcoloniality that we get through the contemporary discourse on colonialism.

It is important to make this distinction between commonwealth and postcolonial studies because quite often the latter is considered a successor to the former and the two terms are used as though they are interchangeable. It is also possible that in the Indian academic set-up which has for a long time lived under the shadow of the tradition of Arnold, Eliot and Leavis, the interdisciplinary nature of postcolonial studies lends itself to suspicion.[8] If one were to approach the literary texts with postcolonial tools one might face resistance because there is always an assumption that such tools remove these texts from the realm of the literary to the realm of the sociological, cultural and the historical.

But connecting the literary with the sociological, the historical, the cultural, the political and the economic is what the postcolonial investigation actually does. To show how, for these critics, the literary texts are constituted by and constitute in turn these contexts we have to go back to their works. That is why this book has to have the theoretical part where these connections are clearly seen. However, this work hopes to use the postcolonial theories as tools in reading literary texts. I wish to bring the arguments of the post-colonial intellectuals 'to crisis' by way of problematizing the question of location, and by choosing a novelist for whom hybridity, nationalism, postcoloniality have never been obvious themes. I borrow the term 'bringing to crisis' from Gayatri Chakravorty Spivak, who views such an attempt positively:

> What I mean by crisis is the moment at which you feel that your presuppositions of an enterprise are disproved by the enterprise itself. These are not necessarily moments of weakness. It seems to me that this is the only serious way in which crisis can become productive, when one feels for example, that the women's movement challenges the project of feminism.[9]

I would like to use the theories of the postcolonial critics to point out that several of the presuppositions of this discourse are brought to crisis when the question of location is raised. Postcolonial discourse shares with other contemporary forms of theory, a dislike for essentialism and universalising tendencies. Yet often in terms of the theoretical tools that they use and the institutional sites from which they speak, they are still located in the West. The postcolonial intellectuals have had to learn to negotiate in their attempt to deconstruct the centre-periphery ideology. As Vivek Dhareshwar rightly points out, it is the accessibility of the Western discursive and institutional space which has enabled the voice of the postcolonial intellectuals to be heard:

> Having been subjected to the theories and narratives of the West, the postcolonial intellectuals' access—however limited—to the institutional and symbolic space of the metropolis has given them the means to deconstruct those theories and narratives.[10]

This accessibility does not mean that the 'asymmetries between the metropolis and the former colonies' has changed now. (150) Therefore the question raised by Dhareshwar bears great significance:

> What sort of knowledges are [the postcolonial intellectuals] aiming to produce? How is this production tied to their location—geographic and symbolic? (151)

These are the questions that justify my attempt to bring to crisis the postcolonial arguments by way of an encounter between them and literary texts of a particular kind.

But such a project is based on the assumption that postcolonial discourse offers us certain theoretical models which can be used in the discussion of literary texts which come either from the colonial period—written by the colonised as well as the coloniser—or from the contemporary world.[11] Edward Said has shown us how the canons of English literature can be read differently by using the perspectives of writers from the former colonies. There have also been attempts made to include the contemporary literary works in these discussions. However, we have to remember that this kind of literary criticism certainly makes no attempt to hide its political concern. It is possible that even when we apply postcolonial theoretical framework for the discussion of literary works, we look for works where these theories find an echo. It will not be surprising if in its attempt to destabilise the 'great tradition' of writing, the postcolonial world produces its own counter canon. If that happens then the very questions that postcolonial critics have been asking will have to be asked of the postcolonial arguments too. What happens when a postcolonial critic is confronted by a seemingly apolitical novel? This is one of the major concerns of this book.

Even though many critics are careful not to talk about the Postcolonial Literature but use its plural, a certain amount of generalization seems to be unavoidable.[12] How close are the postcolonial critics and the postcolonial novelists to the geographical space which can be termed a postcolonial nation? This question is of special interest because, there are many expatriate intellectuals and novelists who are identified with India, but whose location still needs to be specified. The context from which different postcolonial intellectuals speak are equally important for the present study. That is why the questions raised by Dhareshwar are so important: "What sort of knowledges are [the postcolonial intellectuals] aiming to produce? How is this production tied to their location—geographic and symbolic?"

Geographical location and the discursive terms are not so easily interchangeable anymore in the contemporary world where most of the postcolonial discussions seem to be originating outside the postcolonial nations. Very often postcolonialism is associated with such discursive terms as the 'margin,' the 'periphery,' the 'ex-centric' and there seems to be an assumption that these terms can be interchanged. A very interesting analysis of the use of such terms as 'Third World,' 'developing countries,' 'underdeveloped countries,' the 'East' and the 'Orient' is made by Fernando Coronil, who mentions the prevalence of an assumed relationship between such categories and some kind of an external reality.[13] According to him even though these terms seem to have fixity as geographical referents, historically they have possessed fluidity. Commenting on Noam Chomsky's use of Europe as a metaphor, he says

> [if], like Chomsky's 'Europe,' these terms are used as metaphors, what are their original referents? Were they ever not metaphor. . . . And if we managed to freeze history and replicate geography in a map, wouldn't this representation be ephemeral? Since space too is located in time and is changing constantly, how could a map represent geography without apprehending its movement? But perhaps this shows that maps do not mirror reality, but depict it from partial perspectives, figuring it in accordance with particular standpoints and specific aims.[14]

In trying to break the binary terms Orient-Occident, East-West, Self-Other from their metaphoricity, are the postcolonial critics, along with the poststructural, postmodern, deconstruction and feminist theoreticians, trying to depict the many 'partial perspectives' which a term like postcolonial can create, or be made to create?[15] Or is postcolonial only a metaphor for a certain condition of being at the margin in a society? What are the criteria for the making of a postcolonial critic as well as a postcolonial writer?

It will be seen that even the claims of various peoples to the term postcolonial is contested on various grounds. In the Latin American world, the question 'Who is postcolonial?' will have many answers depending on who is answering about which epoch of domination. Therefore it is essential to remember that the term postcolonial is indicative of many different historical contexts.

It is also necessary to acknowledge the presence of difference within a given postcolonial nation-state. Even when there is a recognition of the different, and at times contradicting identities of the subjects in a nation-state such as India, this recognition often overlooks the complexities of power structures among the marginalised in a society. It does not notice that there is also a repetition of the centre/margin scheme in many cases, in a manner of ripple, where the old margin becomes the new centre and the other becomes the self.[16]

We cannot ignore the fact that neither authors nor readers of such literatures as Dalit Literature[17] and the Protest Literatures in Indian languages will be happy if their interest in the questions of caste-struggle, class-struggle, or the gender-struggle is going to be given a unifying title. It has been already established that caste, class and gender equations were rewritten during the colonial regime as well as in the post-independence search for a national identity. These questions are as political and as existential as the questions dealing with the ambiguities of colonialism. These are the questions which demand a reconsideration of our own queries, and need to be dealt with as urgently as the colonial questions. Does postcolonialism take into account the existence of such questions and issues? The danger that power structures have strange ways of repeating themselves in different contexts with different co-ordinates is an important issue which cannot be overlooked. The danger of being the 'emerging dominant' at the cost of others with whom we claim similarity is a hazard to be reckoned with in all these ripple-like power relationships.

To show how the politics of nomenclature can also be generalizing, I wish to give here the example of the various terms used to describe the Dalits. In an excellent article, Simon Charsley deals with the inappropriate limitations of the term Untouchable in the context of the hierarchical caste system in the Indian society.[18] For many of the political leaders as well as social reformers in India, starting with Gandhi, the attempt to emancipate those people who were considered as belonging to the lowest level in the hierarchy of the caste system has been an important issue. Apart from the preferred name, the Dalits, these communities have been named differently by different agencies for different purposes. To be named in this manner did mean some positive changes in terms of job reservations, reservation in schools, and so on. However, Charsley traces how the negativity of characterization under never been properly paid attention to.[19] Charsley argues that the initial category of 'untouchables', while retaining its negative meaning, equated a variety of economically, socially, culturally and politically differently placed castes. Even here the numerically small, socially isolated poor sub-castes are the ones who are often denied attention.[20] Will postcolonial studies take into account these hierarchies among the oppressed?[21]

Postcolonial Studies: Some Important Issues

The above examples of the continued presence of power structures in what is commonsensically held as the 'colonial' and the 'subordinated' suggests that we can no more use these words in a reductionist manner. Yet some amount of generalizing does go on in postcolonial discourse. But this should not result in the continuation of the violent hierarchies that are as oppressive as the colonizer-colonized bind.

This shows clearly that postcolonial discourse has to constantly avoid the danger of being essentialist in nature. It has to continue the work of all those who have in various ways inspired the postcolonial intellectuals. Many of them depend on Frantz Fanon's anticolonialist texts for their theoretical formulations. The theoretical positions which are referred to by many of the postcolonial writers, are those of Jacques Derrida, Jacques Lacan and Michel Foucault. Foucault's ideas of History and of Discourse, Derrida's concepts of Textuality and Deconstruction have certainly influenced the works of these critics. This does not mean that these theoretical models are blindly adhered to. A critic like Gayatri Spivak seems to be wary of being called a deconstructionist, Marxist or feminist critic. Kwame Anthony Appiah, while critically commenting on the postmodern, points out to an uneasy relationship between this term and the term postcolonial. The word Postcolonialism as used by him seems to be conveying a different meaning altogether.[22] What do these different critics suggest, hint at, when they use the term Postcolonialism or, when they seem to be talking about something that was or is colonial? How does one differentiate amongst such terms as decolonization and recolonization or postcolonialism and neocolonialism?[23]

One of the early attempts to theorize postcoloniality is made by Bill Ashcroft, Gareth Griffiths and Helen Tiffin in their book, *The Empire Writes Back: Theory and Practice in Postcolonial Literatures*. This is a useful book for those who need introduction to the field of postcolonialism because it tries to give an answer to the question "What are Post-Colonial Literatures?," in addition to the historical and theoretical details that actually made the creation of the concept of postcolonial literatures necessary. It has been one of those first books which tried to provide a comprehensive reading list for those who wished to explore this field in greater detail. There is now a flourishing publishing industry in the name of postcolonial, cultural and theoretical studies. Quite a number of Readers and collections of essays have been produced and if the number of books being published in this area is any indication, postcolonial studies has become one of the most significant areas of all the contemporary theories.[24] One has to set clearly one's boundaries before beginning a study of the postcolonial themes for fear of repeating ideas and for fear of getting carried away by the flood of printed matter in this area. Although most of the works on postcolonialism have been produced in the English language, postcolonialism as a theme is not anymore an area associated only with the British Empire or pertinent only to the English language. The increased awareness about the persisting world economic structures which very often repeat the colonial power structures, has made postcolonialism a matter of interest for academics coming from different parts of the world. Talking about the relevance of the theories of postcolonialism in the German-speaking territories, Paul Michael Lützeler mentions the authors reporting on their visits to the so called Third World countries. In the contemporary world, marked by its movements across the boundaries in the name of tourism, of economic benefits, of cheap labour, no country can be free from getting contaminated by colonialistic tendencies.[25] Thus we see that there is even a blurring of distinctions between what was formerly identified as a colonial country and what is now seen as a powerful partner in the economic transactions of the world. Once again the presence of connections between the various contexts such as the cultural, the economic, the textual and the political becomes self-evident. The first step towards using the postcolonial theories as literary theories is then to acknowledge that a purely literary use of these theories is impossible. The interdisciplinary nature of theory itself forbids any such attempt. Thus even when texts are discussed along with theories they are not to be taken as texts that exist in a vacuum but as texts which are constituted by and are constituting the various terms of their existence.

Postcolonial Theories as Tools for Literary Interpretations

Even though there seems to be no specifically charted out area of literary theories called postcolonial criticism, its presence marks any attempt at presenting the contemporary scene in the field of literary theory. The editors Peter Collier and Helga Geyer-Ryan think that these developments in the field of literary and cultural studies is important enough to allot a part of their book *Literary Theory Today* to post-colonial criticism. In their "Introduction: Beyond Postmodernism," the editors say that Homi Bhabha and Gayatri Spivak "challenge the identities imposed by Western discourse in general on the third world, thus calling into question the limited horizons within which many critics tend to operate."[26] In their own books Homi Bhabha and Gayatri Chakravorty Spivak do not always talk directly or exclusively about post-colonialism. It has already been mentioned that in the book *Nation and Narration*, a collection of critical essays edited by Homi K. Bhabha, the possibility of offering the readers different readings and exposing the basic ambiguities involved in the concept of narration and through narration, the ambiguity of such a concept as nation, are the important issues that have been taken into consideration. Even Spivak's *In Other Worlds: Essays in Cultural Politics*, has no such direct theme as post-colonial literary theory.[27] In this collection of essays, there are not only interpretations of Wordsworth, Coleridge and Virginia Woolf, but also translations of two Bengali short stories written by a contemporary writer, Mahasweta Devi. Her analysis of Mahasweta Devi's "Breast-Giver," in fact, is an answer to one of the questions that post-colonial literary criticism raises: "What is post-colonial about the method adopted by these critics when they handle a postcolonial text?" Here, she tries to place the text about a subaltern in what she calls "alien arguments" and exposes some of the drawbacks of these theories and arguments.[28]

However, exposure of the inadequacy of many of the accepted theories is not a new phenomenon in the field of literary theories. Many of the other books on literary criticism, on historicism, on cultural criticism have also directly or indirectly spoken about the need for a rejection of old totalizing concepts.[29]

Many critics who have been inspired by such a concept as postcolonialism have turned once more to the canons of English Literature and analyse these canonical writings and their authors in such a way as to extract a reading that would reveal the compliance of literature, culture and history with that powerful organization called the Empire.[30] One interesting effort in this regard is that of Sara Mills, who, in her book *Discourses of Difference: An Analysis of Women's Travel Writing and Colonialism*, discusses the literary works of the women of the Empire—the neglected genre of travel writing and the significance of such writings in our understanding of colonialism.[31] As the work of Gauri Viswanathan shows us, there is a need to go back to the archives to read colonialism's methodologies and strategies from a postcolonial perspective.[32] She charts out in this work the politics behind the introduction of English as a part of the curriculum, the secularization of English literature and the affirmation of an ideal English 'self' projected through its literature. Thus "[t]he English literary text, functioning as a surrogate Englishman in his highest and most perfect state, becomes a mask for economic exploitation . . . "[33] Her conclusions are drawn from 'evidence' that she gets in the archival materials. Bhabha and Spivak also depend heavily on the written documents of the missionaries and the officers of the empire. Quite often these documents become the basis for their oppositional approaches to literary texts of the colonial era.

A general survey of the material available on postcolonialism and the literary texts that the recent critics of colonialism are engrossed in suggests that there is a very strong tendency to rework the texts belonging to the colonial period.[34] Kipling continues to be an author who inspires and challenges numerous critics.[35] E.M. Forster and Joseph Conrad have been analysed by Homi K. Bhabha as the writers who represent the uncanny nature of the imperial discourse which occupies the space between sense and non-sense.[36] It is interesting to observe that Bhabha puts together Forster and Conrad with Alexander Duff, a missionary in India, and with Sir Henry Maines, while contemplating the articulation of the archaic. If Jane Austen fans are shocked by Said's post-colonial reading of her works in *Culture and Imperialism*,[37] the admirers of the Bronte sisters must be equally bewildered by the many non-traditional and challenging modes of readings adopted by their recent interpreters.[38] A re-reading of the different texts from the colonial era not only explores the various modes of representation of the colonised subject but it challenges the tendency to project the coloniser as a unified subject without any self-knowledge. Laura Chrisman, for example, goes back to the texts and documents of the colonial period in order to counter the arguments of Gayatri Chakravorty Spivak.[39]

When these literary critics are not re-reading the texts of the colonial period, many of them have also shown an equal amount of interest in the postcolonial texts as such. By postcolonial texts, I mean here the texts written during the postcolonial period and texts written by the writers who have experienced the postcolonial situation. Much interest has already been shown in exile literature and the literature of the emigrants from the postcolonial situation. V.S. Naipaul and Salman Rushdie have been discussed and re-analysed by students and teachers of literature. In fact, Naipaul's *A House for Billy Biswas* has been taken as an example by Bhabha to prove his point that many of the generally accepted theories of interpretation fail in their readings of the colonial text.[40] If Spivak tries to suggest that a postcolonial text must be wrenched out of its context and put within the context of alien theories, Bhabha is of the opinion that articulation of the colonial fantasy results in a loss of narrative authority and control. Fredric Jameson and Stephen Slemon talk about Allegory as being the most important aspect of the third world and the Post-Colonial texts.[41] It is very tempting to consider the third world texts or the postcolonial texts as being allegories, yet, one cannot but question the argument of Fredric Jameson that all third world texts are allegorical. Although he himself acknowledges that he is making a sweeping hypothesis, one ought to remember that such a concept as a national allegory will be a forced concept in a context like that of India. Jameson says:

> All Third World texts are necessarily, I want to argue, allegorical—and this in a very specific way: they are to be read as what I will call national allegories, even when, or perhaps I should say, particularly when their forms develop out of essentially Western machineries of representation, such as the novel. (141)

If we hold on to the meaning of allegory as a trope that is basically disjunctive in nature, this statement of Jameson is acceptable to some extent. Yet there can be only a limited use for this. The most important aspect of allegory is its use of personification, especially in saying one thing to mean something else.[42] We could thus say that, in the words of Jameson, the novel personifies the nation. The novel form, then, resembles that of a parable.[43] Even when its parable-like nature resists direct interpretation, we have to reckon with the aspect that "in allegory, as a linguistic procedure used at any time or place, one shifting bar is the dividing line between the realistic story and the spiritual or moral meaning."[44] In the context of Jameson's argument, we could say that there is a dividing line between the story and its meaning in terms of nation. Now, even with regard to India, one can apply such a statement only to such authors as Salman Rushdie, Rohinton Mistry and others who are of Indian origin, and who consciously make nation a part of their narrations.[45] But do we have enough examples to justify the statement that all the writings produced in the third world are national allegories?

What is to be questioned in Fredric Jameson's interpretation of Third World Literature is not the term 'national allegory' but the generalized expectation that all Third World texts be read as national allegories.[46] It is true that the nation does get inscribed in many novels which by themselves are no national allegories. But is it not the case even in non-Third World novels? The complexities and the differences among Third World countries or the postcolonial societies are submerged in this kind of generalization.

This tendency to simplify is seen in many of the texts dealing with postcolonial discourse. The danger is that this tendency to simplify can easily get transformed into an expectation, which will in turn reject novels which do not fulfil the requirements of the expectation.

The participation of certain sections of the colonized world in furthering the interests of the colonial power is often suppressed. What needs to be stressed in any work dealing with colonization and decolonization is that the play of power in the colonized societies was very complex. In the same manner, it is wrong to assume that the colonizing structure was without ambiguities. Bhabha's works are partly aimed at achieving this end. He shows that the colonial power was not the superior authority it assumed to be because even at the moment of enunciation, this power was beset with fear which reveals itself in such things as uncanny repetitions of ideas and images and in the creation of stereotypes.

It needs to be mentioned here that the relationship between the colonizer and the colonized was never completely on the basis of the oppressor-victim opposition but required at times involvement of the colonized at different levels; without the possibility of grafting onto the 'hospitable traditional analogues' in the colonized society, colonization would not have been possible over such a long period of time.[47] This is sometimes forgotten in our attempts at overplaying the power of the empire. As Jan Pieterse and Bhikhu Parekh say, there are "as many different modes of decolonization as there are modes of colonization and ways of conceptualizing them." (4) Postcolonial studies must be seen as one method of decolonization. But it is an area which allows diverse modes of decolonization to be imagined and presented. This is one of my justifications for narrowing down my area of research to postcolonial writings and India. I quote once again from Pieterse and Parekh: "Engaging the collective record requires confronting both the universal and the particularist dimensions of empire." (3) One of the powerful agents of the British empire was its literature. And the novel genre has come to be peculiarly associated with the empire (see Chapter Four). Extending the statement of Pieterse and Parekh to the field of postcolonialism one could argue that if postcolonialism is concerned with the universal dimension of the empire, it should also be interested in the particular dimension of literature—in this case the novel, as the colonizer's genre, has been adopted by the authors living in the postcolonial societies. The relationships become more complex when we realise that some of these authors choose to write in English. How do postcolonial critics, apart from re-reading the canons of British literature or reading the archival materials that reveal an unsteady centre, react to postcolonial texts? Can one use postcolonial concepts as strategies for literary interpretation of the contemporary texts too?[48]

Bearing in mind that most of the critics mentioned in this work are not in favour of extracting an essence called post-colonialism, I would still like to take up a study which would try to analyse their writings. I am interested in the theories of literary criticism. However, it is also my view that the theories of literature must be used as techniques of reading texts. A research project which talks about literary theories ignoring altogether the literary context where they may be of help, does not appear complete to me. Therefore, I intend to take up a study which would include an analysis of such a concept as Postcolonialism in literature along with an analysis of the texts of a writer writing in postcolonial India. In doing so, I am orienting myself in this field according to the suggestions made by Wolfgang Iser: there should not be a '*Niemandsland*' separating the texts and the theory which prevents any contact between the two.[49]

It is not only to avoid the danger of this '*Niemandsland*,' but also to prevent another kind of canon formation that the novels of Shashi Deshpande are selected for a juxtaposition with the theoretical statements made by the postcolonial critics. Many of the postcolonial critics, who can also be termed cultural critics, are by profession teachers of literature, and they do make use of literary texts in their writings. However, there is a process of selective reading which is at work in this area. Writers like Salman Rushdie, Gabriel Garcia Marquez, Carlos Fuentes, Chinua Achebe, Wole Soyinka, Faiz Ahmad Faiz are all seen as representatives of a 'fairly novel emergent culture' of the postcolonial scene.[50] What makes authors eligible to be termed postcolonial? What is the principle by which these prominent postcolonial writers are recognized as being so?[51] Is there a danger that postcolonial criticism too becomes a literary ideology that "consecrates" and "excommunicates"?[52] If the postcolonial critics counter the canons of English literature coming from the colonial era, are they also in some manner creating some form of counter-canon, in which case, we will have to agree with Aijaz Ahmad when he says:

> The axiomatic fact about any canon formation, even when it initially takes shape as a counter-canon, is that when a period is defined and homogenized, or the desired literary typology is constructed, the canonizing agency selects certain kinds of authors, texts, styles, and criteria of classification and judgement, privileging them over others which may also belong in the same period, arising out of the same space of production, but which manifestly fall outside the principles of inclusion enunciated by that selfsame agency . . .[53]

Even though Ahmad is making these remarks to remind us that the project of modernism also involved questioning the canons of realistic literature, he has clearly in mind the postcolonial scene too. The doubt raised by Ahmad needs to be taken seriously so that postcolonial literary and cultural studies do not end up being one more dominating discourse which has forgotten its initial enthusiasm for raising questions about itself as well as questions about canonized texts. Just as the postcolonial critique of literary and cultural texts which dominated the respective fields needs the strategy of reading differently, so does the whole project of postcolonial theorization, demand to be read differently so that it avoids creating its own canons.

Ahmad's warning that postcolonial discussions could lead to counter-canon formation which in turn might suppress another set of texts is seriously taken up by Doris Bachmann-Medick who observes that this threat can only be answered from the side of the regional cultures and literatures.[54] But I do not fully agree with Doris Bachmann-Medick that the answer to counter-canon formation lies in projecting the regional culture and literature.

However, it could be the first step towards destabilizing the tendency to label certain novels as postcolonial on the mere basis of the contents of these novels. But her proposal that we should approach those texts which are not canonized is very helpful, especially if we choose to read Shashi Deshpande's novels from the postcolonial perspective. Nevertheless it must be stated here itself that in these novels 'difference' is not a theme. Even though the peripheral role of woman is represented, the figure of woman is overwhelmingly—and not marginally—present in her novels. Read differently, the protagonists and the other female characters in her novel could problematize the centre-margin binary and suggest that postcolonial arguments could be used as reading tools even when nation, narration, history, hybridity are not serious issues in the world of the novels.

The Enterprise of Reading Differently

This project of reading differently can be justified on two points: The first one is only an extension of what has been mentioned above. The fear that postcolonialism can create its own canons cannot be removed unless some of the neglected texts are taken into consideration. It has been my intention that one of the contemporary writers who does not seem to be overtly or allegorically speaking about the nation or its politics, should be read along with the many theories and the suggestions made by the different critics regarding post-colonialism. Many of the Indian women writers who write in English, have made themselves heard in the wider academic circles. If one takes a look at the critical material available on the different writers coming from the Indian background, one is surprised to see that very little attention has been paid so far to one of the contemporary writers, who is often considered a 'good' writer in her own province. The writer Shashi Deshpande, was considered good enough to be awarded the Sahitya Akademi award, which is a prestigious national award given to writers for outstanding literary achievement. Her novels show a preoccupation with women, a theme 'fashionable' enough to make the literary work significant. However, someone who has been reading postcolonial literary criticism, may ask the question, "What is postcolonial about Shashi Deshpande?" If we are trying to search for a specific model of writing called the 'postcolonial,' then Shashi Deshpande could not be considered a postcolonial writer. But if writing in post-independence India is enough qualification, she is a postcolonial novelist. There seems to be an unwritten assumption that postcolonial or third world literature must deal with the nation, with colonialism, with the trauma the colonial era has created in order to receive recognition in the international scene. As Aijaz Ahmad rightly points out:

> The range of questions that may be asked of the texts which are currently in the process of being canonized within this counter-canon must predominantly refer, then, in one way or another, to representations of colonialism, nationhood, postcoloniality, the typology of rulers, their powers, corruptions, and so forth. There is no gainsaying the fact that these are among the great questions of the age. What is disconcerting, nevertheless, is that a whole range of texts which do not ask those particular questions in any foregrounded manner would then have to be excluded from or pushed to the margins of the emerging counter-canon. Worse still, a whole range of other kinds of questionings—pertaining to other sorts of literary influences and experiential locations, the political affiliations of the author, representations of classes and genders within the text, and myriad such issues—would then have to be subordinated to the primacy of the authorized questions: about 'nation' and so on.[55]

Why has Shashi Deshpande not succeeded in attracting much critical attention? Is she too old-fashioned for the feminist critics? Is she unable to make an allegory of her writing and therefore does not qualify to be a postcolonial writer? Has she no views at all about the postcolonial aspect of her context? Is it just a matter of the international recognition that she does not possess? Has she proved herself to be no modern writer, with her not so experimental literary techniques? Her novels cannot be thrown into that ignominious category "Second Class Literature." But it is not pleasant to notice that she still has to be advertised as the daughter of "the renowned dramatist and Sanskrit scholar, Sriranga."[56] Her writings are not political in the traditional sense of the word; but they do expose the different politics of human sexuality as experienced by a woman, and also the politics of power among women, coming from a certain province with a certain class and caste background.

The second point of justification for this project of reading differently is that such a different reading calls for a different reading of postcolonial critics too. My arguments in the following pages are not aimed at rejecting postcolonial theories. On the other hand, it is an attempt at continuing the process of containment of differences within this area. One of the aims of the present project is to juxtapose the theories with the texts of Shashi Deshpande in such a way that we gain a different perspective to the critics as well as to the novelist.

The title of this book is derived from two texts: the first part is from Priyamvada Gopal's review of the two volumes entitled *Women Writing in India: 600 B.C. to the Present*, edited by Susi Tharu and K. Lalita.[57] Commenting on the wish of the authors that these writings of Indian women spanning over twenty five centuries will not be called upon to perform the same services to society and nation as the mainstream literature, Priyamvada Gopal observes that whether this is heeded "will depend on the collective efforts of all those engaged in the enterprise of reading differently for a different cause."[58] I have intentionally left out the "for a different cause" because "reading for a cause" distorts the idea of "reading differently." As far as I am concerned, postcolonial literary criticism has primarily suggested a way of reading differently the colonial/postcolonial texts. Reading differently and challenging any accepted mode of reading is thus a feature of postcolonial criticism and this has inspired me to attempt to present a different reading of some postcolonial critics also. In one of her articles Gayatri Chakravorty Spivak writes about the continued subalternization of the so-called third world literatures. However, the increased circulation of such terms as postcolonial discourse and postcolonial critic as well as the renown that some writers born in a third world country have received, have made quite a few works coming from the 'third world' escape this fate. But it is true that Shashi Deshpande's works have not gained much recognition from the postcolonial critics. Therefore I would like to 'place' Shashi Deshpande within the arguments of the postcolonial critics.[59] To read differently is what the postcolonial critics set out to do. If in the process of reading a different postcolonial book in a different manner, a different reading of postcolonial literary criticism emerges, that will be all the more meaningful for this study. This is important, because only such a project will help us understand the concept 'postcolonialism' in literature or help us answer the question, "What are the postcolonial theories of literary interpretation?"

If one could talk about the objectives of a novelist, then, Shashi Deshpande is preoccupied with the idea of representing a woman who comes from a particular social and class background. There are many things in the works of this novelist which surprise her reader. After reading two or three of her novels one can fairly well predict the plot in the next novel. With a few exceptions events are generally narrated by a woman whose special interest is writing. Quite often this woman is not too happy with the kind of writing that she produces, and knows very well that she is capable of writing better. She seems to be either disillusioned or uneasy about her husband who is generally incapable of appreciating the real value of her writing. But there is always this conscious choice of coming back to the husband, like a 'true' Indian wife. The writer appears to be insistent in her choice of the narrative context and consistent in her choice of the realistic mode of narration. In many novels there is a representation of the joint family which controls narration in spite of her attempts to release her protagonist from the clutches of this joint family. There is always a longing for, as well as a sense of repulsion towards, the huge house which has sheltered generations of children.

What is the author trying to say or what is she not able to say, and what does she say in spite of herself in these novels? The repetition of the same kind of characters and their similar nature, the circularity of structure which one often witnesses in her works reminds us once again of the concept of the time-wheel, or the *Kala Chakra*, which is a well-known concept in the traditional Hindu understanding of time. Since Postcolonialism, like other contemporary theories, does not believe in the linear movement of time it is also interesting to see how this understanding of circularity of time is used traditionally by the orientalists.[60]

An analysis of the different critical materials listed here have made it clear to us that such a work has not been done so far.

The above arguments justify that the choice of Shashi Deshpande is not rooted in a form of nativism but in a desire to provide some kind of oppositional reading to postcolonial concepts. Owing to the wide range of topics and the number of nations which can be considered postcolonial, selecting the different areas of importance to this study has not been easy. Since it is not possible to talk about postcolonialism without trying to answer the question "What does the term 'postcolonial' imply?" Chapter Two of this work tries to present the different meanings of this term as used by different critics and scholars. This chapter will, in addition, try to trace the basic differences between such terms as Commonwealth literatures and Postcolonial literatures and show how these two terms are supported by totally different ideologies. Postcolonialism has a postmodern interest in the question of difference and this goes against the generally perceived idea of commonness of experience that one expects from Commonwealth literatures. In this context, it is necessary to distinguish the various strands of influence and the various contexts which made it possible for the concept of postcolonial studies to make its presence felt in the contemporary literary and cultural areas. Chapter Three has been divided into two parts: in the first part the three important postcolonial theoreticians—Said, Bhabha and Spivak will be discussed in detail and an attempt will be made to see how they approach literary texts and to locate their strategies of reading. The second part of this chapter will present some of the other postcolonial critics, the principle of selection being the degree of difference between their understanding and articulation of postcoloniality from those of the three who appear in the first part.[61] Chapter Three will also try to show how important the process of migration and the condition of exile have been for many of these critics. There seems to be a growing irritation on the part of some 'native' critics at the visibility postcolonialism has given to those who are originally from the postcolonial societies but have pursued their career now in Western and North American universities. Much of the work on the postcolonial condition has also come from the Australian continent and without this there would not have been a widespread acceptance of this concept. Chapter Three will briefly touch upon some of these discussions too. Chapter Four takes up the works of Shashi Deshpande and tries to interpret her novels in the context of postcolonial arguments. It is possible to take into consideration only a few novels as it is not the aim of this project to present a monograph on Shashi Deshpande. Chapter Five provides the Conclusion where the different strands of arguments will be summarized and an attempt will be made to spell out my own position in the area of postcolonial studies—a position that is largely shaped by this project.

It is hoped that this study will help us realize that the term 'postcolonial' has to be used with caution. I am sure many of the critics themselves would not like such labels to be applied to them. However, the term 'postcolonial' appears in literary and cultural studies more often now than before. I am sympathetic to the works of these critics and acknowledge that they made the breakthrough in the field of theory by inserting the postcolonial into a discourse which pretended as though colonialism were a thing of the past. But I would also like to remind myself and the reader that there are many areas where even the term postcolonial would suggest unwanted generalization. Postcolonialism should not give rise to another kind of intellectual hierarchy that would undo the tenets of the concept itself. So far, the critics who have been talking about the inadequacy of the earlier theories, while dealing with the literatures coming from the former colonies, have also been self-critical in their approach. They are aware of the fact that the indigenous and the colonial are intermingled with other influences in such a way that there is no one national literature that we can speak of. By analysing the silences in the novels of Shashi Deshpande,[62] I hope to be able to investigate some of the gaps as well as the useful innovative strategies used by these critics.

NOTES

1. Gayatri Chakravorty Spivak, "Teaching for the Times," in *The Decolonization of Imagination: Culture, Knowledge and Power*, ed. Jan Nederveen Pieterse and Bhikhu Parekh (London: Zed Books, 1995), p. 179.

2. See Gayatri Chakravorty Spivak, "Questions of Multi-Culturalism," Interview with Sneja Gunew, *The Post-Colonial Critic: Interviews, Strategies, Dialogues*, ed. Sarah Harasym (New York: Routledge, 1990), pp. 60-61.
3. See Gayatri Chakravorty Spivak, "Postcoloniality and Value," *Literary Theory Today*, ed. Peter Collier and Helga Geyer-Ryan (Cambridge: Polity Press, 1990), p. 228.
4. See Homi K. Bhabha, "Introduction," *Nation and Narration*, ed. Homi K. Bhabha (London: Routledge, 1990).
5. Edward W. Said, "Introduction," *Orientalism* (New York: Pantheon Books, 1978), p. 28. "If this stimulates a new kind of dealing with the Orient, indeed if it eliminates the 'Orient' and 'Occident' altogether, then we shall have advanced a little in the process of what Raymond Williams has called the 'unlearning' of 'the inherent dominative mode.'" The reference here is to Raymond Williams, *Culture and Society*, 1780-1950 (London: Chatto & Windus, 1958), p. 376.
6. Edward Said, "Introduction," *Orientalism*, p. 28. Meyda Yegenoglu, in her *Colonial Fantasies: Towards a Feminist Reading of Orientalism* (Cambridge: Cambridge University Press, 1998), continues the work pioneered by Said by providing a feminist critique of orientalism.
7. Gayatri Chakravorty Spivak, for example, while accepting postcoloniality as a condition of neocolonialism, finds "the word postcolonialism just totally bogus." See Spivak, "Neocolonialism and the Secret Agent of Knowledge: An Interview," interviewed by Robert Young, *The Oxford Literary Review*, 13, 1-2 (1991): 224.
8. To understand how literary evaluation and the concept of culture, as understood by Arnold, Eliot and Leavis were important influences in shaping concept of modernity in Indian literatures, especially in Kannada Literature, see Tejaswini Niranjana, "Whose Culture is it? Contesting the Modern," *A Way of Leaving so as to Stay*, ed. Sudhakar Marathe et al (Madras: T.R., 1994), pp. 127-52.
9. Gayatri Chakravorty Spivak, "Negotiating the Structures of Violence," *The Post-Colonial Critic: Interviews, Strategies, Dialogues*, ed. Sarah Harasym (New York: Routledge, 1990), p. 139.
10. Vivek Dhareshwar, "Toward a Narrative Epistemology of the Postcolonial Predicament," *Inscriptions*, 5 (1989):149. Successive citations from the same article/book are indicated in the main text itself. This pattern is followed throughout this work.
11. One interesting effort towards making use of postcolonial theories in the interpretation of texts can be seen in the contribution by Harveen Sachdeva Mann, "'Cracking India': Minority Women Writ-

ers and the Contentious Margins of Indian Nationalist Discourse," *The Journal of Commonwealth Literature*, Vol. 29, 2 (1994): 71-94.

12. For example, *The Empire Writes Back: Theory and Practice in Post-colonial Literatures*, ed. Bill Ashcroft et al (London: Routledge, 1989).
13. Fernando Coronil, "Beyond Occidentalism: Toward Nonimperial Geohistorical Categories," *Cultural Anthropology*, 11, 1 (1996):52.
14. Fernando Coronil, "Beyond Occidentalism," p. 53. His reference is to Noam Chomsky, "The New World Order," *Agenda* 62, (1991):13-15.
15. It must be mentioned here that the idea of 'Europe' itself is being rewritten in many ways. One imporant work in this regard is that of Jacques Rossel, *The Roots of Western Civilization* (Basel: Basileia, 1995), where he uses the word 'interculturation' to indicate that what is often considered monolithic European civilization has been for centuries represented by 'intercultural encounters' which "initiate a long process of reciprocal cultural appropriations with overt and covert grievous conflicts." p. 9. Another example for such a reconsideration of the ideas of Europe can be found in Jacqueline Kaye, "Islamic Imperialism and the Creation of Some Ideas of 'Europe,'" *Europe and its Others*, ed. Francis Barker (Colcheseter· University of Essex, 1985), pp. 59-71.
16. A similar formulation about the other becoming the self has also been made by editors Jan Nederveen Pieterse and Bhikhu Parekh in "Shifting imaginaries: decolonization, internal decolonization, postcoloniality," *The Decolonization of Imagination: Culture, Knowledge and Power*, p. 9.
17. Dalit Literature is the name given to the literatures produced by the different Dalit communities of India. For detailed analysis of the Dalit issue, see James Massey, *Dalits in India: Religion as a Source of Bondage or Liberation with Special Reference to Christians* (Delhi: ISPCK, 1995).
18. Simon Charsely, "'Untouchable': What is in a Name?," *The Journal of the Royal Anthropological Institute*, 2, 1 (1996): 1-23. Although I indicate that I diverge from the topic, I should mention that the caste question in India is also linked with the question of colonialism. Nicholas B. Dirks mentions that even though the caste system is normally taken as a "timeless tradition," it is in fact, "the paradoxical effect of colonial rule." See Dirks, "Introduction: Colonialism and Culture," *Colonialism and Culture* (Ann Arbor: The University of Michigan Press, 1992), p. 8.
19. See Sathianathan Clarke, *Dalits and Christianity: Subaltern Religion*

and Liberation Theology in India (Delhi: Oxford University Press, 1998), for an attempt to retrieve and relocate the subjugated knowledge of the Paraiyar of South India.

20. Charsley, "'Untouchable': What is in a Name?," p. 19. It should be remembered that Charsley is not referring to the minor castes within the four castes of the *Varna* system but to the minor castes among the former category of the so-called Untouchables. Since it justifies my point that power relationships are repeated in different configurations I would like to quote here Charsley's observations about these minor castes: "little seems to be said about them. Like the acutely poor anywhere, their deprivation consists in a lack of resources to do much about their circumstances beyond seeking to survive. It is not, at any rate, these poorest and the most deprived who have attracted attention but, paradoxically, the better-placed groups within the category. They are better placed by being more numerous, needing to be courted by others for their labour and their votes, and increasingly by having, at least collectively, resources with which initiatives are possible. It is these who have sometimes been seen as 'replicating the caste system,' setting up service relationships and treating others as polluting." p. 19. See also S. George Vincentnathan's "Caste Politics, Violence, and the Panchayat in a South Indian Community," *Comparative Studies in Society and History*, 38, 3 (July 1996): 484-509, for an interesting analysis of the conflicts between a lower caste group and the Dalits in a village. He points out how the horizontal hierarchy of the caste system does not always function as simply as it has been generally projected. Those who receive the fruits of affirmative discriminatory system are not always united; the language of hierarchy and the language of equality are used simultaneously by the powerful among the oppressed groups to subjugate those who are denied power for various reasons.
21. For a vivid account as to how the idea of caste, or that of belonging to the oppressed caste, can be associated with political power, and also to understand how hierarchy and structures of power operate within the boundaries of caste, see William Dalrymple, "Caste Wars," in *Granta*, 57 (Spring 1997):173-84.
22. Kwame Anthony Appiah, "Is the Post- in Postmodernism the Post- in Postcolonial?," *Critical Inquiry*, 17, 2 (Winter 1991): 336-57. Appiah makes use of the term 'otherness machine' which was first employed by the author Sara Suleri in her *Meatless Days* (Chicago, 1989), p. 105. Appiah seems to be suggesting that the postmodern world expects certain things from the otherness machines. "Perhaps

the predicament of the postcolonial intellectual is simply that as intellectuals—a category instituted in black Africa by colonialism—we are, indeed, always at the risk of becoming otherness machines, with the manufacture of alterity as our principal role. Our only distinction in the world of texts to which we are latecomers is that we can mediate it to our fellows. This is especially true when postcolonial meets postmodern; for what the postmodern reader seems to demand of Africa is all too close to what modernism—in the form of postimpressionists—demanded of it. The rôle that Africa, like the rest of the Third World, plays for Euro-American postmodernism—like its better-documented significance for modernist art—must be distinguished from the rôle postmodernism might play in the Third World; what that might be it is, I think, too early to tell." p. 356.

23. For one version of differentiation between postcoloniality and neocolonialism see "Neocolonialism and the Secret Agent of Knowledge: Interview," interviewed by Robert Young, *The Oxford Literary Review*, 13, 1-2 (1991): 220-51.

24. To name a few:

—*Past the Last Post: Theorizing Postcolonialism and Postmodernism* ed. Ian Adam and Helen Tiffin (1991; New York: Harvester Wheatsheaf, 1993).

—*From Commonwealth to Postcolonial* ed. Anna Rutherford (Sydney: Dangaroo Press, 1992).

—*Colonial Discourse and Post-colonial Theory: A Reader*, ed. Patrick Williams and Laura Chrisman (New York: Harvester Wheatsheaf, 1993).

—*Colonial Discourse Postcolonial Theory*, ed. Francis Barker, et al (Manchester: Manchester University Press, 1994).

—*De-scribing Empire: Post-colonialism and Textuality*, ed. Chris Tiffin and Alan Lawson (London: Routledge, 1994).

—*The Post-colonial Studies Reader*, ed. Bill Ashcroft et al. (London: Routledge, 1995).

—*After Colonialism: Imperial Histories and Postcolonial Displacements*, ed. Gyan Prakash (Princeton: Princeton University Press, 1995).

25. Paul Michael Luetzeler, "Der postkoloniale Blick: Deutschsprachige Autoren berichten aus der Dritten Welt," *Neue Rundschau*, Heft 1/1996, 107. Jahrgang, p. 56.

26. *Literary Theory Today*, p. 7. The editors say that the inspiration for the book came from the critical and self-critical inquiry engaged in by the authors of the different essays published here: "We find that the sophisticated voices of the new feminist consciousness and the

post-colonial third-world intelligentsia are not to be contained by traditional ideologies, even those speaking in their favour. They will use the terminology of Marx and Freud, but they will constantly question the ideological schemata which these systems also presuppose. However, they do not contradict the new political conscience of deconstruction or the heightened social awareness of post-Freudian psychoanalysis."

27. Gayatri Chakravorty Spivak, *In Other Worlds: Essays in Cultural Politics* (1987; New York and London: Routledge, 1988). In the "Foreword" to the book, Colin MacCabe says, "Spivak's theme here is large: the micro-politics of the academy and its relation to the macro-narrative of imperialism. But this is a theme without a subject: one that lacks reading lists, introductory guides, and employment opportunities. It is not easily located in relation to the established subject divisions (what is a literary critic doing discussing economic theory?) nor vis-a-vis what are becoming the relatively well-mapped fields of Marxist, feminist, and deconstructionist criticism." p. x.
28. Gayatri Chakravorty Spivak, "A Literary Representation of the Subaltern: A Woman's Text from the Third World," *In Other Worlds*, p. 241. Spivak acknowledges her much-favoured subject-position of the teacher of literature and proposes the following things:

    a. The performance of these tasks, of the historian and the teacher of literature, must critically "interrupt" each other, bring each other to crisis, in order to serve their constituencies; especially when each seems to claim all for its own.
    b. The teacher of literature, because of her institutional subject-position, can and must "re-constellate" the text to draw out its use. She can and must wrench it out of its proper context and put it within alien arguments.
    c. If thus placed in arguments from Western Marxist-Feminism, Western Liberal Feminism, and French high theory of the Female Body, "Stanadayini" can show us some of their limits and limitations.
    d. This might have implications for the current and continued subalternization of so-called "third world" literatures.

    These arguments are used in Chapter Four for my reading of the novels of Shashi Deshpande. "Stanadayini" is the original Bengali name of the short story "Breast-Giver."
29. For example, New Historicism, another term much in circulation in the academic circles now, seems to be a collaborator of Postcolonialism. One does not find the arguments of the contributors to *The*

New Historicism, H. Aram Veeser, ed. (London: Routledge, 1989), contradictory to that of the postcolonial discourse. In fact, this book also includes an interview with Gayatri Chakravorty Spivak. See pp. 277-92. In his "Introduction," the editor gives the following explanation to the term New Historicism: "By discarding what they view as monologic and myopic historiography, by demonstrating that social and cultural events commingle messily, by rigorously exposing the innumerable trade-offs, the competing bids and exchanges of culture, New Historicists can make a valid claim to have established new ways of studying history and a new awareness of how history and culture define each other." (xiii)

30. One important work which traces the changing attitudes of the English society towards the colonies by way of readings of novels and tales, written before, during and immediately after the Victorian period, is Patrick Brantlinger's *Rule of Darkness: British Literature and Imperialism, 1830-1914* (Ithaca: Cornell University Press, 1988).
31. Sara Mills, *Discourses of Difference: An Analysis of Women's Travel Writing and Colonialism* (1991; London: Routledge, 1993)
32. Gauri Viswanathan, *Masks of Conquest: Literary Study and British Rule in India* (New York: Columbia University Press, 1989).
33. "Introduction," *Ibid.*, p. 20.
34. Perhaps one of the earliest cases of re-reading is Achebe's essay on Conrad, where he shows how *Heart of Darkness* presents an image of Africa as the antithesis of Europe and of civilization. See Achebe, "An Image of Africa," *Massachusetts Review*, 18 (Winter 1977): 782-94.
35. Gayatri Chakravorty Spivak, "Imperialism and Sexual Difference," *The Current in Criticism: Essays on the Present and Future of Literary Theory*, ed. Clayton Koelb and Virgil Lokke (West Lafayette, Indiana: 1987), pp. 319-337. Spivak's critique of the concept of global sisterhood is based on her analysis of three masculist texts which also contain imperialistic views: a poem by Baudelaire, Kipling's "William the Conqueror" and a document of the East India Company.

    Another interesting essay on Kipling is by Satya P. Mohanty, "Drawing the Color Line: Kipling and the Culture of Colonial Rule," *The Bounds of Race: Perspectives on Hegemony and Resistance*, ed. Dominick LaCapra (Ithaca: Cornell University Press, 1991), pp. 311-43.
36. According to Bhabha, "The articulation of nonsense is the recognition of an anxious contradictory place between the human and the not-human, between sense and non-sense, which no dialectic can de-

liver." (p. 205), in Homi K. Bhabha, "Articulating the Archaic," *Literary Theory Today*, pp. 203-18.

37. Edward Said, *Culture and Imperialism* (New York: Alfred Knopf, 1993).

38. Sandra Gilbert and Susan Gubar, *The Madwoman in the Attic: The Woman Writer and the Nineteenth-Century Imagination* (New Haven: Yale University Press, 1984). I am not claiming that Gilbert and Gubar are postcolonial critics, but merely pointing to the different readings done by these authors.
Gayatri Spivak, "Three Women's Texts and a Critique of Imperialism," *Critical Inquiry*, 12 (1985): 243-61. See also, Laura E. Donaldson, "The Miranda Complex: Colonialism and the Question of Feminist Reading," *Diacritics*, 18, 3 (Fall 1988): 65-77. Another essay which is equally exciting and which offers a slightly different perspective is that of Elsie Michie, "From Simianized Irish to Oriental Despots: Heathcliff, Rochester and Racial Difference," in *Novel*, 25, 2 (Winter 1992):125-40.

39. Laura Chrisman, who in her contribution "The Imperial Unconscious? Representations of Imperial Discourse," *Critical Quarterly*, 32, 3 (Autumn 1990): 38-48, writes about Spivak's reference to India as the subject of Colonization, to the extent of the exclusion of other colonies in Africa and Caribbean. In her reaction to Spivak's essay on the three women's texts and also to the interpretation of imperialism given by Gilbert and Gubar in *No Man's Land: The Place of the Woman Writer in the Twentieth Century*, Vol. 2, *Sexchanges* (New Haven: Yale University Press, 1989), she takes up Rider Haggard's novels *She* and *King Solomon's Mines*. It is her view that "imperialism even at its most basic is capable of constructing itself as a contradictory process, of commenting upon its own self-mythologising, and economic, imperatives, while in the course of pursuing them; is able, in sum, to reveal a great deal of self-knowledge but doesn't know what to do with this knowledge." p. 41. Chrisman's essay also appears in *Colonial Discourse and Postcolonial Theory: A Reader*, pp. 498-516.
David Trotter looks at the words of the journalist and Liberal politician, C.F.G. Masterman, of British India's one-time Governor General Lord Curzon, Wells's *The New Machiaveli* and some of the other popular novels which, according to him, "portrayed Imperialists of every conceivable variety, at home and abroad." "Colonial Subjects," p. 13.

40. See Homi K. Bhabha, "Representation and the Colonial Text: A Critical Exploration of Some Forms of Mimeticism," *The Theory*

of Reading, ed. Frank Gloversmith (Brighton: Harvester Press, 1984), pp. 93-122.

41. Fredric Jameson, "World Literature in an Age of Multinational Capitalism," *The Current in Criticism*, pp. 138-58 and "Post-Colonial Allegory and the Transformation of History," Stephen Slemon, "Post-Colonial Allegory and the Transformation of History," *The Journal of Commonwealth Literature*, XXIII, 1 (1988):157-68. Fredric Jameson's comments have been attacked by many critics. See for example, Ketu H. Katrak, "Decolonizing Culture: Toward a Theory for Postcolonial Women's Texts," *Modern Fiction Studies*, 35, 1 (Spring 1989): 159-60.
42. I have depended on the explanations given by Samuel R. Levin for this argument. See Samuel R. Levin, "Allegorical Language," Allegory, *Myth and Symbol*, ed. Morton W. Bloomfield (Cambridge: Harvard University Press, 1981), pp. 23-38.
43. Hillis Miller compares allegory to a parable. See Miller, "The Two Allegories," also in *Allegory, Myth, and Symbol*, pp. 355-70. There is an explication of Walter Benjamin's concept of allegory: "Allegorien sind im reiche der Gedanken was Ruinen im reiche der Dinge." Miller is quoting from *Ursprung des deutschen Trauerspiels* (Frankfurt: Suhrkamp Verlag, 1969), p. 197.
44. *Ibid.*, p. 358.
45. In addition to Rushdie's *Midnight's Children* and *Shame*, I have in mind Rohinton Mistry's *Such a Long Journey* (London: Faber and Faber, 1991).
46. Stephen Slemon, even when he is being sympathetic towards Jameson's 'interventionary project' of reading, thinks that "Jameson's argument overprivileges a culturally expressive reading of 'ex-centric' allegorical practice at the expense of a much more immediate energetics of dialects and relationality." See Slemon, "Monuments of Empire: Allegory/Counter-Discourse/Post-ColonialWriting," *Kunapipi*, 9, 3 (1987): 9. Slemon, on the other hand, suggests that instead of considering the Third World texts as allegories, it is more productive to concentrate on certain allegorical texts coming from the post-colonial context as a form of reading.
47. Jan Nederveen Pieterse and Bhikhu Parekh, "Shifting Imaginaries: decolonization, internal decolonization, postcoloniality," *The Decolonization of Imagination: Culture, Knowledge and Power*, p. 2.
48. We see Helen Tiffin striving to arrive at some kind of theoretical formulation about the 'postcolonial text' based on the texts which are available. According to her the counter-discourse provided by the postcolonial literary discussions can be put under 'sub-groupings'

such as 'magic realism,' 'allegory'—as a site of post-colonial discourse (as suggested by Stephen Slemon) and 'canonical counter-discourse.' The last sub-grouping, according to Tiffin is exemplified by Jean Rhys' *Wide Sargasso Sea*, which is a kind of 'writing back' to Charlotte Bronte's *Jane Eyre*. Though interesting, this kind of classification might once again result in counter-canon building, which, in my opinion, goes against the prevalent understanding of the term 'postcolonial.' See Tiffin, "Post-Colonial Literatures and Counter-Discourse," *Kunapipi*, 9, 3 (1987):17-34, esp. 22.

49. Wolfgang Iser, "Vorwort," *Der Implizite Leser* (1972; München: Wilhelm Fink Verlag, 1979), p. 7. A fine example for the bringing together of theories and texts can be found in Helga Schwalm, *Dekonstruktion im Roman: Ezähltechnische Verfahren und Selbstreflexion in den Romanen von Vladimir Nabdkov und Samuel Beckett* (Heidelberg: Carl Winter Universitätsverlag, 1991).
50. Edward Said, "The Voyage in and the Emergence of Opposition," *Culture and Imperialism* (New York: Alfred A. Knopf, 1993), p. 243. Perhaps we could add Michael Ondaatje to this list. If 'postcolonial' refers to a blurring of boundaries, of nationalities, of identities, then his *The English Patient* (London: Bloomsbury, 1992) is a fine example of this.
51. Gayatri Chakravorty Spivak voices uneasiness at the growing tendency to identify 'magic realism' with the so-called Third World. The questions that she asks in this context are significant: "Why is 'magical realism' paradigmatic of Third World literary production? . . . What are the implications of pedagogic gestures that monumentalize this style as the right Third World style?" See Spivak, "Poststructuralism, Marginality, Postcoloniality and Value," *Literary Theory Today*, p. 223.
52. I have borrowed these terms from Wole Soyinka. See Soyinka, *Myth, Literature and the African World* (1976; Cambridge: Cambridge University Press, 1992), p. 61.
53. Aijaz Ahmad, "Salman Rushdie's *Shame*: Postmodern Migrancy and Representation of Women," *In Theory* (1992; London: Verso, 1994), p. 123.
54. Doris Bachmann-Medick, "Multikultur oder kulturelle Differenzen? Neue Konzepte von Weltliteratur und Übersetzung in postkolonialer Perspektive," in Bachmann-Medick (Hrsg). *Kultur als Text: Die Anthropologische Wende in der Literaturwissenschaft* (Frankfurt a. Main: Fischer Taschenbuch Verlag, 1996), p. 268.
55. Aijaz Ahmad, "Salman Rushdie's *Shame*," *In Theory*, p. 124.
56. See the details regarding the author, in Shashi Deshpande, *The Bind-*

ing Vine (London: Virago, 1993).

57. Susi Tharu and K. Lalitha, ed., *Women Writing in India, Volume 1: 600 B. C. to the Early Twentieth Century* (New York: Feminist Press, 1991). *Volume 2: The Twentieth Century* (New York: Feminist Press, 1993).
58. Priyamvada Gopal, "Review: Women Writing in India: 600 B.C. to the Present." *The Oxford Literary Review: On India: Writing History, Culture, Post-Coloniality*, 16, 1-2 (1994): 294.
59. The reference here is once again to Spivak's position that the texts have to be wrenched out of their context and placed in 'alien' arguments.
60. An elaboration of the concept of circular time and the importance given to this understanding of time at the cost of other measures of time by those who were interested in the construction of 'otherness' is given by the noted Indian historian Romila Thapar in her *Time as the Metaphor of History* (Delhi: Oxford University Press, 1996). In Chapter Four this association between time and repeatability in the context of Shashi Deshpande's novels will be taken up in a more detailed manner.
61. This is an attempt to give fair representation to the various critics located in India as well as outside India. It is possible that while attempting to react to the various arguments coming from the field of postcolonial criticism, one is ignorant of the critical material which comes from the local or national context. It is necessary to be careful because very often this ignorance is rooted in a habit—the habit of respecting only that which comes from the metropolitan academic centres. It is necessary to be careful because what Roberto Fernández Retamor said already in the 70s could be true even now. According to him some of us are ignorant of the critical material available in our own context because "we have been so thoroughly steeped in colonialism that we read with real respect only those anti-colonialist authors *disseminated from the metropolis.*" In "Caliban: Notes Towards a Discussion of Culture in Our America," *The Massachusetts Review*, 15 (Winter-Spring 1974): 31.
62. Including *If I Die Today* (Sahibabad: Vikas, 1982); *Roots and Shadows* (1983) (Hyderabad: Disha Books, 1992); *That Long Silence* (London: Virago, 1988) and *A Matter of Time* (New Delhi: Penguin India, 1996).

Chapter Two

From Commonwealth Literature to Postcolonial Literatures

English literature has continued to provide an impetus and an inspiration to Commonwealth writers, whether their medium is English or one of the indigenous languages. There is hence no gainsaying the fact that Commonwealth literature today is spearheaded by literature in English, or literature that has been influenced by English literature.

K.R. Srinivasa Iyengar,
Two Cheers for the Commonwealth

We colonised form a community, with a common heritage of oppression and a common cause of working toward positive social change. To recognise what we hold in common is not to underestimate our differences, but to provide us with a context for understanding them more clearly.

Diana Brydon,
"Commonwealth or Common Poverty?" in *After Europe*

Commonwealth Literature: A Search for a Common Poetic?

In *The Commonwealth Pen: An Introduction to the Literature of the British Commonwealth*[1] published in 1961, A.L. McLeod, expresses optimism that the new subject matter introduced by the Commonwealth literature will be of special interest to scholars of English literature. However, in the wake of serious interest in postcolonial discourse, the term commonwealth literature seems to have been pushed into oblivion.[2]

This chapter will try to analyse the difference between the two terms and show how, conceptually, they are two disparate terms even though they share some common concerns. The first part of this chapter will show how central the issue of common experience is to the conception of the Commonwealth Literature. In India, this also resulted in the search for common poetics, which in turn reflected the nationalist desire for the creation of an overarching Indian sensibility. The second part of this chapter will specifically deal with the term 'postcolonial' and the various ways in which it is used. In the context of the present study, the prefix 'post' does not simply mean 'after'; the complexity of the issues related to colonialism as well as the other structures of power in post-independence India make it impossible to restrict it to a simple matter of chronology. Therefore it will also be shown in the last part of this chapter that postcolonial discourse has lot of affinity towards the postmodern rather than the commonwealth concerns. It is important to chart out these affinities because this makes way for a reading of the text that does not simply deal with its purely 'literary' aspects. Moreover, the strong link between the postcolonial discourse and the other anti-foundationalist discourses show us that unless the glorification of Literature stops, unless there is an acknowledgement of different literatures and cultural activities that are shaped by and shaping in turn, their contexts, discussions that explore the 'common heritage of oppression' will not lead us anywhere. Also, the contemporary response to the project of colonialism can afford to be so varied and multi-voiced because of its links with postmodern thinking.

One striking difference between the idea of commonwealth literature and the postcolonial approaches to various literary works is that there were only very few attempts made in the former case to make use of methodological and theoretical models. Dieter Riemenschneider, in his Introduction to the collection *The History and Historiography of Commonwealth Literature*, does express the view that there should have been an attempt made to probe into 'the methodological problems' involved in the arguments regarding commonwealth literature.[3] He lays importance on attempts at developing models of literary history because "inquiries into the methodology of Commonwealth literary history are altogether rare while histories of individual Commonwealth literatures, more often than not, bypass theoretical comments or considerations."[4] In the same collection, Helen Tiffin, too, points out that to a large extent, there is a dearth of theoretical and methodological studies of Commonwealth literature.[5] Her article suggests that comparison was the decisive factor for the setting up of such an area as Commonwealth Literature. What distinguishes this contribution of Tiffin from the other articles in the collection is her uneasiness with the term 'Commonwealth Literature':

> . . . most of us . . . have been for a number of reasons uncomfortable with the term "Commonwealth Literature." Firstly, there are the political overtones; secondly and more importantly, the problems of scope. . . . The term itself, "Commonwealth Literature" should mean the literatures of all Commonwealth or former Commonwealth countries including Britain and excluding the United States. But the practice of our discipline has not generally been along these lines. The creation of a new word like "terranglia" would seem an ideal solution—but then which word? ("Terranglia" itself connotes an English proprietorship over land and would make all post-colonial Commonwealth nations a little uncomfortable). "The new literatures in English" is a laudable compromise, and in its plural it avoids the problem often offensive to writers, of apparent claim to collective psyche, is disturbingly vague and relative, and unlike the term "post-colonial" it does not imply anything shared except recent arrival on the scene. (23)

At this stage, the term 'post-colonial' is not yet the preferred term. It is still the prefix which determines the meaning of the word and that is the reason why Helen Tiffin is unhappy about the implications of the term 'post-colonial':

> "Post-colonial" has the obvious difficulty of needing political explanation: one needs to explain that this does not refer to particular dates of achievement of independence from Britain or to a mood of political embitterment, but to a set of shared

> circumstances that have a fundamental effect on the literature produced in those areas, and are likely to continue to do so. The unfortunate political connotations aside, this term has the advantage of allowing comparisons with British literature where these might be applicable, as in the case of Ireland; of including the literature of the United States; and of suggesting in colonialism itself the basic genesis of these shared concerns not just in their political aspects, but in their social, metaphysical, moral, metaphorical and linguistic ones. If we added "Comparative post-colonial literatures in English" we would, I think, have an appropriate title, but alas, a cumbersome one. (23-24)

Interestingly, Helen Tiffin does not look for easy alternatives to the term 'commonwealth.' She is not very comfortable with the term 'Post-colonial' and its 'unfortunate political connotations,' either. What is clear from the above passage is that even though a comparative approach supports the formation of 'Commonwealth Literature,' a forced projection of a 'collective psyche' is not one of its objectives.[5] However, comparison and the acknowledgement of the 'shared concerns' of the peoples of the formerly colonised nations are revealed as the major issues for scholars in this field. The need to talk about the continuation of colonialism in the form of neo-colonial structures does not appear here, even when there is a plea for the inclusion of the literature of the United States of America in this comparative practice.

This confusion regarding nomenclature seems to have vanished in the later book co-authored by Helen Tiffin, *The Empire Writes Back: Theory and Practice in Post-colonial Literatures*, which does not really mark the continuation of the commonwealth tradition. It reveals a preference for the term 'post-colonial' over the other terms considered by her earlier, and it offers one of the earliest theoretical explanations for the term 'postcolonial.' The discussions regarding the nature, scope, and the validity of such a term as 'post-colonial' have not yet stopped. The fact that the term lends itself to more than one interpretation, and the fact that these different interpretations allow its use in different contexts make it more interesting as well as visible than 'commonwealth literature' or 'New

Literatures in English.' The need for comparative studies has not lost its importance in *The Empire Writes Back*. Nor is the argument for including literature of the United States under this category given up.[7] Yet, there seems to be a major shift in the approach of the authors. The question, 'What can be considered postcolonial?' rather than identification of 'commonwealth countries' becomes the crucial step in a search for theoretical models in this work.

The question 'What can be considered postcolonial?' does not offer any simplistic answer, but rather leads to, as we shall see later on, questions regarding 'neo-colonialism' in postcolonial discourse. The absence of such a concept in commonwealth literary studies is perhaps due to the overemphasis placed on the so-called political independence of the ex-colonies and also due to the eagerness to include settler countries like the United States of America, Canada, New Zealand and Australia. It is true that comparison was of primary importance to the practice of Commonwealth literary studies but the intention was not always to point out the commonality of the literatures of the Commonwealth countries. Even English language which gave rise to this element of commonness is seen as a superficial element rather than something which forms an intrinsic binding unit.[8] The natural alternative to the element of commonality, in terms of language and the common experience of being the colonised seems to be the plurality of the distinct cultures of the independent nations. One of the few articles which point to culture as a determining force in the creation of Commonwealth Literature is that by G.N. Devy in *The History and Historiography of Commonwealth Literature*. His argument for locating differences under the category Commonwealth Literature is based on his recognition of dialectics between the 'wind' of Westernization and the 'roots' of the native sensibility.[9] Once again, the response to culture in the field of commonwealth literary studies has more to do with a depiction of the distinctive nature of the countries rather than in an interest in the complicated relationship between the cultures of a country and the literatures produced in it.[10] The desire to show one's own culture as a very distinctive culture overshadows the concern for raising questions regarding the impact of colonialism on these cultures.

Therefore, any discussion of the literatures of India, especially of the creative writing in English in India feels obliged to make a reference to the 'Indianness' of the experience that is presented through such literary works. The need for a very close involvement with the regional or the culturally familiar is often evoked. Even when the diversity that exists in terms of language is acknowledged there always seems to be a desire to look for something that is also common to all these diverse languages and literatures. This should not be seen apart from the same nationalist spirit which aspired to forge common identity for the Indian citizen. Different prominent Commonwealth scholars seem to have taken up different strategies in order to set up a plea for seeing India as an organic whole. K.R. Srinivasa Iyengar sees a uniting function performed by the literature written in English. Indo-Anglian writers, according to him, will project 'a total view of India'—not only to the outside world but also to the 'diverse linguistic groups within the country.'[11] However, even when he recognizes the influence of Sanskrit on all the modern literatures in India, he also mentions the presence of Arabic and Persian influences after the medieval period.[12]

The importance of the influence of Sanskrit on Indian literatures cannot be denied, not only because it is the mother language for most of the modern Indian languages, but also because of its literature and because of the many treatises on criticism and appreciation of art written in Sanskrit language. The next step after assuming a common identity which is 'Indian' seems to be the revoking of the culturally distinctive features of the Sanskrit poetic tradition. Such an attempt to bring out the distinctive elements of the poetics of Sanskrit literature and to use it in the contemporary scene, formed by literatures written in English as well as in regional languages, was made in 1984 in Dhvanyaloka, Mysore, in South India at a seminar "Towards the Formulation of a Common Poetic for Indian Literatures Today," organized by the noted Commonwealth scholar C.D. Narasimhaiah. Once again, the inherent cohesiveness of the Indian society is being evoked as an important factor to be reckoned with. The obvious preference for Leavis and Eliot seems to be based on the appropriateness of the views of these critics in the Indian context:

> It will be seen the discriminating Indian writer finds affinities with Leavis more than with most other critics, Eliot excepting, as when he appeals to the 'organic society' which is still available to the Indian for all the modernization that is in his own society. Consider his concept of collaborative approach or seeking collaboration from one's fellows in the business of criticism. One would have thought the Indian concept of *Sahrdaya* (the responsive reader) was the closest to it.[13]

The goal of the seminar is apparently the formulation of some kind of common poetic for the Indian literatures, which is not completely 'western,' which borrows from the classical Sanskrit poetics and proves itself rational and binding in the criticism of modern literatures in India.[14] What is significant in the formulation of such a poetic is the understanding that there have been certain dominant, unifying elements in Indian society and in the Indian literary scenes all the while:

> What applies to the poet or novelist applies with greater force to the critic, or the reader as well. But what does one do with personal tastes of the reader? His maturity and training in reading or lack of these? We have to ascertain, in addition, in the Indian context, not only the writer's but the reader's religion, philosophy, caste, language and literature, the last two today seen at different stages of development. Add to these the local traditions pertinent to each language area variously co-existing, superseding, subsuming the national tradition.[15]

This raises the important question of difference in the religious, philosophical, linguistic backgrounds of the reader and acknowledges the presence of different traditions. This recognition of differences is, however, submerged under claims of unity and a common heritage. Is it once again a case of a 'desire to elide differences' which looks for a 'mythic organicist view of cultural history'?[16] For, there is a curious twist in the last sentence when 'the national tradition' is spoken of and when this assumption regarding the national tradition is justified by assertions about 'mainstream of Indian thought' and the 'mainstream of literary sensibility':

> It is a piece of good luck that although Buddhism and Jainism are major religions they are offshoots of Hinduism and have much in common with it. Islam and Christianity flourished on converts from Hinduism notwithstanding which Hinduism has shown a surprising degree of tolerance towards them. As with religion so with language: Sanskrit. . . . The fact that a large number of Hindus wrote in Urdu and the Tamils participated in the Sanskrit tradition, has given them all a cohesiveness. And a common poetic shouldn't sound unworkable. And it will not therefore be wrong to posit that the mainstream of Indian thought is Hindu and the mainstream of literary sensibility is Sanskrit as the back-bone of the country's cultural unity.[17]

Such a claim for cohesiveness and for the presence of cultural unity ignores many of the counter-claims regarding oppression and cultural apartness made by the Dalit and protest writers who also come under the broad heading Indian Literature.[18] The weakness of such a move 'towards a common poetic' is not its search for an indigenous theory which would be more suitable than a western theory, but its inability to locate literary criticism in a context. Mere talk about a nationally specific entity called Indian Literature or even about Common Poetics for Indian Literatures, places undue priority on some forms of writing and ignores all the other literatures which might seem threatening to the cultural unity referred to in the above passage. Aijaz Ahmad rightly points out that such privileging of the mainstream culture is caused by its preoccupation with a kind of literary history which is viewed in separation from other kinds of history:

> The difficulty in thinking of an 'Indian' literature, therefore, is not that it is spread over many languages, with histories of uneven development, nor that the state boundaries which have historically contained these literary productions have been shifting through all the centuries we know of. The dif-

> ficulty lies, rather, in the very premises that have often governed the narrativization of that history, which has (1) privileged High Textuality of a Brahminical kind to posit the unification of this literary history; or (2) assembled the history of the main texts of particular languages (in a very uneven way) to obtain this unity through the aggregative principle; or (3) attempted to reconstruct the cross-fertilization of genres and themes in several languages, but with highly idealistic emphases and with the canonizing procedures of the 'great books' variety, with scant attempt to locate literary history within other sorts of histories in any consistent fashion.[19]

But with this criticism of the manner of looking at the history of Indian Literature, we are already in the realm of postcolonial arguments. Ahmad's reaction is not only restricted to our understanding of a unifying-yet-distinguishing area called Commonwealth Literature but also to the academic subject called literary theory.

The coming into existence of Commonwealth literature and more specially, the search for common poetics for literature in India, denotes a wish to locate a common, undivided heritage for India. Taken to its extreme, it could lead to a kind of essentialism which would once again exclude oral and literary traditions which obviously do not belong to what is recognised as the 'mainstream.' We could thus draw similarities between this search for a common tradition and the search of the early nationalistic historiographers for an 'authentic India.'[20] It is here that we see a difference in the approach of postcolonial critics towards literature and nation. The next section of this work will, therefore, consider the different nuances of the term 'postcolonial' as it is used in the present theoretical discussions because these are the nuances which distinguish the 'postcolonial' from the Commonwealth.

Post-Colonial and Postcolonial: In Pursuit of a Meaningful Term

In the context of post-modernism and post-structuralism, it is difficult to accept any 'post-something' as 'that which comes after something.' That means the beginning of the post-independence phase in a country need not mean the beginning of the postcolonial period. Nor does the term postcolonial have a strictly spacial connotation. In fact one could be called a postcolonial writer or postcolonial critic even when one does not actually inhabit the post-independence space, even when one does not work for a postcolonial institution. Terms like 'commonwealth,' 'postcolonial,' 'Third World' are not identical so that we could replace one with the other. Not all the Commonwealth countries are Third World countries; not all the Third World countries are *post*colonial, and not all of them really produce New Literatures in English. Yet when one uses all these terms, there seems to be a certain consensus as to what these terms mean. If postcolonial does not simply mean 'after colonialism,' what then are its implications?

The many discussions regarding the term 'postcolonial' make it clear to us that in the field of literary theories, this term is very rarely being used to denote something that comes after colonialism. *The Empire Writes Back* uses it for the first time as a concept, or rather as a term which is far more inclusive and politically acceptable than the other previously mentioned terms. Even though their choice of the term appears to have opened up a whole new area of conceptualizing, theorizing and marketing possibilities, the authors of *The Empire Writes Back* come under attack for their tone of 'tolerant pluralism of liberal humanism,' which recognizes difference but contains it within a single pattern.[21] What emerges from this critique of Vijay Mishra and Bob Hodge is that the term postcolonial refers to ideological orientations instead of a historical stage:

> When we drop the hyphen, and effectively use 'postcolonialism' as an always present tendency in any literature of subjugation marked by a systematic process of cultural domination through the imposition of power, we can begin to see those aspects of the argument of *EWB* which could be profitably extended. This form of 'postcolonialism' is not 'post-' something or other but is already implicit in the discourses of colonialism themselves. (284)

This leads the authors to distinguish between two meanings of post-colonialism which are perceived as ideological orientations:

> The first, and more readily recognizable, is what we call oppositional postcolonialism, which is found in its most overt form in post-independent colonies at the historical phase of 'post-colonial.' The second form, equally a product of the processes that constituted colonialism but with a different inflection, is a 'complicit postcolonialism,' which has much in common with Lyotard's unhyphenated postmodernism: an always present 'underside' within colonization itself. (284)

We do not come across many texts where this kind of a differentiation between a hyphenated post-colonialism and a non-hyphenated postcolonialism is clearly used for defining the term 'postcolonial.'[22] Although Vijay Mishra and Bob Hodge make the point that there is a connection between postmodernism and post-colonialism, they are careful not to make postcolonialism a kind of successor to postmodernism. Theoretically, they see in postcolonialism an ally of postmodernism. They try to define a form of postcolonialism that is unhyphenated, which goes beyond the point of independence in the non-settler colonies, and which makes it possible to recognise differences. Such a version of the term 'post-colonial' does not deal with mere chronology. It in fact defies linearity of history and it takes into consideration the complex histories of the colonized and accepts the notion of opposition as well as complicity among the colonised. By defying the commonsensical notions of time and space, the term 'postcolonial' makes room for various interpretations and acts as a reminder of the fact that colonialism is not a thing of the past and that colonising tendencies are not restricted to certain groups of people.

Whether one agrees with the claim that 'the postcolonial as a category subsumes the postmodern'[23] or not, without postmodernism, postcolonialism would not really have been conceived as a critical concept.[24] Is it postmodernism which makes the prefix "post-" gain greater currency in the contemporary world?[25] Anne McClintock sees this fondness for the prefix post-as signalling "a widespread, epochal crisis in the idea of linear, historical 'progress.'"[26] Contrary to her stand that 'post-colonial' borrows from the marketability of the term 'post-modern,' Francis Barker, Peter Hulme and Margaret Iversen are of the opinion that the term which has been used in titles at least from 1970s, got sucked by the vortex of such terms 'post-structuralism' and 'post-modernism.'[27] Aijaz Ahmad makes a similar complaint that there is a 'suppression of memory' with regard to the use of the term post-colonial. It is his contention that the theoreticians of postcolonialism often forget its existence in the 1970s in political debates where it had been used 'in relation not to literary production but to the class character and social projects of states and regimes that had arisen in Asia and Africa in the wake of decolonization.'[28] Ahmad not only alleges that postmodernism and poststructuralism are responsible for the loss of memory regarding this earlier use of the term postcolonial in the strictly political context, but also holds some key figures in the present postcolonial discussion as being the creators of an aggrandized sense of the term. He is very critical of some of the prominent postcolonialists who, he says, enabled the term 'post-colonial' to gather force 'through a system of mutual citations and cross-referencing':

> As the terms 'postcolonial' and 'postcolonialism' resurfaced during the 1980s, this time in literary and cultural theories and in deconstructive forms of history writing, and as these terms were then conjoined with a newly coined 'postcoloniality,' this resurfacing was combined with a very modern kind of erasure: the lapsing from memory of the history of the term's own origin. One no longer needed to know about or engage with that earlier debate. This erasure involved a characteristically postmodernist indeterminacy of meaning as well, not in the philosophical sense of indeterminacy but in the more mundane sense of unclarity as to what words signify in simple lexical ways. In some usages, the word 'postcolonial' still attempted a periodization, so as to refer to that which came after colonialism—though this sense of periodization was itself used differently by different critics. But the word 'postcolonial' was to be used increasingly not so much for periodization as for designating some kinds of literary and

> literary-critical writings, and eventually some history writing, as *generically* postcolonial, while other writings in those same domains of literature, literary criticism and history writing presumably were not. (28)

What is important here is this critique of the term 'postcolonial' which is quite different from the earlier mentioned discussions of the term. Ahmad tries to deflate the force gained by this term by taking us back to the political debate where it first made its appearance and shows the implications of the term 'postcolonial' as a political paradigm also. Ahmad expresses a certain degree of cynicism about the work done by other contemporary postcolonial critics. His distrust is directed against the indeterminacy of the meaning as well as the globalization of the term postcoloniality, and this distrust becomes more pronounced when countries like the United States are considered postcolonial.

The above controversies that surround the term 'postcolonial' reveal a fear that the term could easily be used as a label that once again categorises without bearing in mind the different versions of colonialisms. These controversies also remind us that unless the specificities of a particular postcolonial context are mentioned the use of the term 'postcolonial' could be misleading and as Ahmed warns us it could just reflect the 'mundane sense of unclarity.' This would mean that any consideration of the postcolonial issue must also specify and frame the location that is being spoken of lest the researcher falls into the pit of essentialism and generalisation.

The question of location is gaining significance in contemporary discourse on postcolonialism. It is interesting to note that most of the critics who initiated discussions in this area are originally from postcolonial nations, but most of them are working in the context of the European or the American institutions. Especially in the light of the fact that our age is an age of migration, of dislocation, the question of the location has to be considered as an essential aspect of any inquiry into the postcolonial project. The postcolonial intellectuals working in the western universities almost equate the postcolonial experience with the experience of migration, of a life in exile.[29] This preoccupation with the migratory experience can also problematize the postcolonial theories and the postcolonial critic as we see in the editorial of the special issue of *The Oxford Literary Review* entitled *On India: Writing History, Culture, Post-coloniality*. This issue is, in a way, a response to the abundance of the publications available in the area of postcolonialism and other related areas. The editors try to map "a familiar territory differently" obviously because the representation of what is postcolonial cannot be compared with what in their part of the world can be termed postcolonial.[30] They are concerned about the fact that even the many discussions that deal with postcoloniality can inadvertently give rise to generalisations. The location that they talk of does not have the ambiguous nature of an exile's or a migrant's location. Even though they are against any kind of naive distinction, they also indicate the existence of a divide between the Anglo-American Academy and the "scholars who, for the most part, live and work in India." (3) Their talk about dialogue with the Anglo-American Academy or the mention of overlapping and mutual help does not stop them from clearly pointing out what they see as the pitfalls in postcolonial studies. If, in the case of Homi K. Bhabha, his use of the terms 'ambiguity' and 'hybridity' obviously comes from his personal experience of migration, the critique of location of the postcolonials by these other scholars also originates from a similar subjective experience of living and working in India. This kind of distinction cannot be rejected as a simple difference of opinions, or difference between internationalism and nationalism, or even between the geographical locations of the debating scholars. The distinction is being sought at a more fundamental level—at the level of the nomenclature itself. It once again tries to answer the question, "What is postcolonial?" or rather "What is not postcolonial?" Pointing to the imbalance which exists in academic circles, the editors Ania Loomba and Suvir Kaul state that the

> institutional and political frameworks which foster the study of non-western societies today partially account for this situation, which applies not just to 'history' but also to literary and cultural studies, or to that overarching rubric 'postcolonial studies,' a term that inevitably carries the following under-

> pinnings: (a) that all postcolonial societies are more similar than dissimilar, (b) that the study of these societies requires little training and is more or less a matter of affiliation and identity (and thus that all post-colonial individuals should 'do' post-colonial studies), (c) that the issues of minority politics in the first world will more or less reflect the concerns of the 'third world' societies and (d) that post-coloniality is more or less the experience of 'hyphenated,' fractured, doubled identities. While these assumptions may not be true of all individuals or even institutions, they are part of institutional structures, the organization of teaching, hiring, publication, of the circulation of materials, fellowship funding and certainly of conference agendas. These imperatives also dictate which work produced in the 'third world will become visible and where, which will be seen as part of 'area studies' or 'post-colonial studies,' which regarded as revisionist within a wider sphere, and which never considered worthy of circulation. (15)

Loomba and Kaul are obviously trying to warn us against a kind of intellectual Orientalism. Just as a critique of Enlightenment exposed the complicity between knowledge and power, so does this kind of postcolonialism, they seem to be saying, has become an agent of power. They resent the fact that postcolonialism has increasingly turned into an exclusive field that is represented by a certain kind of intellectuals who forget the innumerable specificities of the postcolonial nations.

Criticism of another sort is hurled at these expatriate Indian critics by Bharati Mukherjee, an expatriate Indian novelist, because she feels that they have exchanged the language of fiction with a political theory:

> I have referred to them [Gayatri Spivak, Homi Bhabha, Edward Said] elsewhere as 'assassins of the imagination'—people who desperately need a political theory to which they reduce the quirkiness and interrogativeness of fiction. Aijaz Ahmad has questioned the right of people like Edward Said and his chelas to speak for critics here when they are per-

> manently located in their privatised worlds of lucrative Chairs. They've refashioned themselves, given themselves false biographies of marginalised peoples. They are enemies of the literary critics living in India.[31]

Even though Mukherjee points out to the difference in location, her speaking for the 'literary critics living in India' does not arise from the same ideological concern as those of Ania Loomba and Suvir Kaul.[32] Mukherjee finds the reduction of fiction to political theories problematic. I do not think that the critics she mentions and the literary critics living in India such as Loomba and Kaul would ever have any misgivings about the close association between literature and the politics of interpretation. However, these comments show us that location and the choice of location is no more a neutral question.

Location and exclusivity become major concerns for Arif Dirlik in "The Postcolonial Aura: Third World Criticism in the Age of Global Capitalism," when he attacks the prominent postcolonial critics for making India more visible because they happen to be of Indian origin.[33] Dirlik comments that the postcolonial intellectuals can be identified only when the postcolonial discourse is delineated. In his view, at least in the fields of cultural and literary studies, the term postcolonial is the domain of a few important postcolonial critics whose epistemologies dominate the present discussions on postcolonialism:

> What then may be the value of a term that includes so much beyond and excludes so much of its own postulated premise, the colonial? What it leaves us with is what I have already hinted at: postcolonial, rather than a description of any thing, is a discourse that seeks to constitute the world in the self-image of intellectuals who view themselves (or have come to view themselves) as postcolonial intellectuals. That is, to recall my initial statement concerning *Third World intellectuals who have arrived in First World academe*, postcolonial discourse is an expression not so much of agony over identity, as it often appears, but of newfound power. (338; emphasis added)

The politics of location takes strange turns in all these arguments. The use of the term postcolonial seems to create resentment because it has become a highly visible term, and more so because of the "newfound power" which is associated with it. Whether the prominent postcolonial critics would have succeeded in getting themselves heard if they had not arrived in First World academe, is another important question which has to be raised here.

The question of location becomes a central issue because of diverse reasons. The positions of the postcolonial critics conflict with one another because of the indeterminacy of the term and because of the difficulties involved in finding out the parameters of such a concept.[34] Since the term 'postcolonial' has given rise to such contradictory views, especially in relation to the question of location, a scholar needs to spell out her own position before embarking on a study that makes use of the postcolonial critical arguments. It makes us ask: "What would it mean to make it work for us as something other than a threatening chaos?"[35]

What makes one happy is, however, that it is exactly because of this multiplicity of connotations that postcolonialism becomes a very fertile area for research and literary analyses. As Stephen Slemon correctly points out, the different methodologies of the postcolonial critics are responsible for the discordant notes that are being heard in the field of postcolonialism.[36] In this "pattern of accusation and counter-accusation," it is easy to see "neo-colonialism in disguise" in the different anti-colonial discourses. Going along his argument, conflicts arising due to methodological differences are peculiar to postcolonialism. However, the question as to whose anti-colonialism will return as neo-colonialism remains an open question:

> This means that the question of anti-colonial work returning in the ghostly mask of neo-colonialist discursive practice remains also an abiding and lurking threat for future researchers, and for all those new students who might be turning to postcolonial studies precisely because of its political grounding in anti-colonial work. (29)

It is in this connection that Slemon uses the word tolerance. Taken together, perhaps, the word tolerance and the statement quoted above, lead us to acknowledge not only that postcolonialism is peculiar but also that it is desirable. The different methodologies used to critique colonialism, imperialism, neo-colonialism, late imperialism, all add to the multi-faceted existence of the term postcolonial and allows for such an expression as 'postcoloniality.' What is important is to retain this kind of tension among the different voices claiming to be postcolonial and to accept being partners in dialogue.

It has already been pointed out that while some critics accuse postcolonialism of being an exclusive field, some criticise it for its tendency to include anything and everything. Both these extremes can lead to a silencing of the arguing voices and that will be a pity for postcolonialism. In the same way, arguing about a hyphenated and a non-hyphenated form of the term postcolonial seems unimportant here. However, for the sake of convenience and in order to retain some form of uniformity, the term postcolonial will be used in this study without the hyphen. The different voices of postcolonial critics will be studied at length, when some of the important postcolonial critics and their positions will be individually discussed later on. The discordant notes should be welcomed rather than resented, as Stephen Slemon points out:

> [i]f the field of postcolonial studies resembles a geographical terrain upon which discordant methodologies scramble agonistically for purchase, it also remains the one institutional location upon which the ideal of anti-colonialist human agency can trouble the monologic droning of Western self-reference, and can insert within that drone-note the babble of cultural alterity. (32)

Postcolonialism: The Ex-centric of Postmodernism?

In the light of the many controversial discussions on the nature and the meaning of the word postcolonialism, it is necessary to analyse the relationship between postmodernism and postcolonialism in detail because postcolonialism is accused of having been made fashionable through postmodernism. I am using Linda Hutcheon's term 'ex-centric,' from her *A Poetics of Postmodernism*, because she lists many challenging counter-cultures that have made multiplicity and difference possible and have revealed the centre as being a fiction, a construct.[37] Hutcheon's ex-centric could also be a postcolonial intellectual because this discourse too tries to destabilise the centre. What is important to her discussion of postcolonialism is her refusal to ascribe monolithic existences to even the ex-centrics. The doubts regarding the question of location mentioned in the earlier sections of this discussion only supplement the postmodern phenomenon of decentering. We can say that if there is a reaction to the theory of hybridity, of migration, of multiculturalism, it is a postmodern reaction to postcolonialism, for, according to Hutcheon,

> [w]hat is always important to recall, however, is that difference operates within each of these challenging cultures, as well as against the dominant. Blacks and feminists, ethnics and gays, native and "Third World" cultures, do not form monolithic movements, but constitute a multiplicity of responses to a commonly perceived situation of marginality and ex-centricity. (62)

The opposition to postcolonialism and the criticism which the postcolonialist theorists sling at each other are the manifestations of these differences which operate 'within the challenging cultures.' The presentation of the differences in order to decentre any privileged position is necessary if one does not wish to succumb to the various kinds of totalizing tendencies. Thus in Linda Hutcheon's arguments we can also see that both postmodern and postcolonial arguements take into consideration the presence of differences even when these different voices try to demolish the idea of the centre. In order to analyse the common factors which appear in the fields of postmodernism and postcolonialism, Lyotard's own explanations of the postmodern condition can be used. The 'post' of postmodernism has given rise to as much discussion, confusion and ambiguity as the 'post' of postcolonialism. In his observations regarding the meaning of the term 'post,' he provides us with three aspects of postmodernism.[38] The first meaning attributed by him to this prefix goes against the linear chronology accepted by modernism. If modernism found it necessary to break with tradition and to establish "new ways of living and thinking," this 'post' indicates a conversion, in Lyotard's words, "a new direction from the previous one." (76) The second point that he makes is to dissociate developments made in the fields of "arts, technology, knowledge and freedoms" from the idea of progress that benefits all the human beings. The failure of the project of modernity which had the emancipation of the whole of humanity as its objective, is visible in the fact that humanity is divided into two disparate groups: "One faces the challenge of complexity, the other that ancient and terrible challenge of its own survival." (77) The most complex aspect of postmodernity, ultimately, is the "question of expressions of thought" (77) in art, literature, philosophy and politics.

I have deliberately paraphrased his discussion of the term 'post' here in order to support my own arguments and also to suggest that postmodernism cleared the way for a highly visible postcolonialism. The three points made by Lyotard can be matched with three of the observations made in this chapter. As the title of this chapter suggests, postcolonialism, though very different from what was once known as the Commonwealth literature, cannot deny its relationship to this term. What has happened is exactly what Lyotard means by 'conversion'—it is a new direction from the previous one. Discussions of the literatures of the Commonwealth countries reveal a very strong idea of progress and development, which makes us suspect that Commonwealth literature is one more manifestation of modernity's eagerness to emancipate the whole of humanity. In contrast, the postcolonial critics have been able to opt not for a movement of repetition, but for "a procedure in 'ana-': a procedure of analysis, anamnesis, anagogy, and anamorphosis that elaborates an 'initial forgetting.'"[39]

But the danger which Lyotard observed in modernity is a constant threat in the field of postcolonialism also. The part of humanity which faces the "challenge of complexity" also faces the danger of trivializing the other part of humanity which has to deal with "that ancient and terrible challenge of its own survival." The cynicism of the native intellectuals towards the strategies of the diasporic intellectuals in euro-american academic circles have to be seen in this light. To take sides would amount to simplification of a very complex phenomenon called postcolonialism. Should we then, consider this cynicism, too, as a feature of postcolonialism? Should we attribute this to the postmodernist nature of postcolonialism and agree with Ihab Hassan that it is a question of beliefs which has been exacerbated by the postmodern condition itself?[40]

Yet it would be incorrect to say that there are no significant differences between postcolonialism and postmodernism. Resistance to colonialism is not new either in literature or in literary criticism. It has already been shown how postmodernism made such a concept as postcolonialism easily acceptable in cultural as well as literary criticism circles. But as Ian Adams says, postmodernism and postcolonialism converge as well as diverge.[41] However, the patterns formed in the contemporary discourse on postcolonialism because of this convergence and divergence of postcolonialism are interesting as well as intriguing. Once again these patterns point out the problem of location. Edward Said, in his Afterword to the 1994 Edition of *Orientalism*, takes stock of the different kinds of arguments that dominated the literary scene after the first appearance of his book till the beginning of the nineties.[42] In his view postmodernism and postcolonialism are two separate currents, because the urgent historical and political imperatives of postcolonialism make it different from the relative detachment of postmodernism. Lyotard's critique of the grand narrative is rejected by Said's version of postcolonialism:

> [w]hereas post-modernism in one of its most famous programmatic statements (Jean-Franois Lyotard's) stresses the disappearance of the grand narratives of emancipation and enlightenment, the emphasis behind much of the first generation of postcolonial artists and scholars is exactly opposite: the grand narratives remain, even though their implementation and realization are at present in abeyance, deferred, or circumvented. (349)

With this kind of a general statement about the work of the first generation of postcolonial artists and scholars, Said is taking us back to the centre of the controversy among the postcolonial critics themselves. Said does not ignore the emphasis on 'the local, regional and contingent' but for him postcolonialism is

> most interestingly connected in its general approach to a universal set of concerns, all of them having to do with emancipation, revisionist attitudes toward history and culture, and a widespread use of recurring theoretical models and styles. (350)

This is clearly not the view of many other postcolonial critics who are opposed to any kind of homogenization in the name of postcolonialism. There is an uneasiness among critics, who favour more of culture-specific postcoloniality, and such a statement as the one quoted above will lead to a suppression of differences among the many postcolonial cultures and this suppression will enable the continuation of imperial power in a different form. Thus within postcolonialism itself, one could talk about the existence of two currents: one that privileges trans-cultural approaches and the other which foregrounds culturally specific approaches.[43]

The term postcolonial will be used in the following pages for a critical concept that recovers resistance of various kinds to the colonial project, as an explanatory term that tries to explain the presence of the silenced voice in any dominant discourse, as a tool to tease out the various readings that could be used for the analysis of a textual narrative and as a response to the politics of creating canons and counter canons.

NOTES

1. A.L. McLeod, *The Commonwealth Pen: An Introduction to the Literature of the British Commonwealth* (Ithaca, New York: Cornell University Press, 1961). This optimism that Commonwealth Literature will come to stay is expressed in the Introduction to the book by McLeod: "Commonwealth literature is new and engaging; it has gained a remarkable following and a rapid preferment in academic circles. It is experimental. It has new subject matter. It offers novel

approaches and unconventional forms. Whereas seventeenth-century literature was the especial interest of the first fifty years of the present century, it appears that Commonwealth literature will be the particular interest of English scholars in the next fifty." (p. 10)

2. There are however some interesting attempts made to positively evaluate Commonwealth Literature as in Diana Brydon, "Commonwealth or Common Poverty?," *After Europe: Critical Theory and postcolonial Writing*, eds. Stephen Slemon and Helen Tiffin (Sydney: Dangaroo Press, 1989), pp. 1-16. In this article which asks whether there is a kind of "new form of cultural imperialism that now appropriates instead of silencing postcolonial literary productions," the author questions the validity of a downright rejection of the term Commonwealth Literature by many prominent postcolonial critics and observes that "[c]olonial and postcolonial writers have tended to ignore the 'wealth' hidden in 'Commonwealth' to focus on the poverty the imperialist would like us to see: the poverty of indigenous cultures as well as the poverty resulting from imperialist thefts." (p. 6) I do not think that the postcolonial critics are interested in the 'poverty of indigenous cultures' and Brydon's objections to postcolonial criticism expressed in this manner appear rather simplistic.

3. Dieter Riemenschneider, "Introduction," *The History and Historiography of Commonwealth Literature*, ed. D. Riemenschneider (Tubingen: Gunter Narr Verlag, 1983), p. vi.

4. *Ibid.*, n. 5. Even *The Commonwealth Pen* is a collection of essays which give an overview of the literary works written mainly in English in the countries belonging to the British Commonwealth. There is absolutely no attempt, as well as desire, to formulate any theory regarding the literatures of these countries. The other histories and introductions include

   —John Press, ed., *Commonwealth Literature* (London, 1965).

   —K.R. Srinivasa Iyengar, *Two Cheers for the Commonwealth* (London, 1970).

   —K. L. Goodwin, ed., *National Identity* (London, 1970).

   —William Walsh, *Commonwealth Literature* (London, 1973).

   —Bruce King, ed., *Literatures of the World in English* (London, 1974).

   —Bruce King, *New English Literatures: Cultural Nationalism in a Changing World* (London, 1980).

5. Helen Tiffin, "Commonwealth Literature: Comparison and Judgement," *The History and Historiography of Commonwealth Literature*, pp. 18-34.

6. This kind of forced projection is already there in *The Commonwealth Pen* whose subtitle is *An Introduction to the Literature of the British Commonwealth*.
7. See *Empire Writes Back*, p. 2. Though there is a mention of the neo-colonizing role played by the United States, its common experience of colonization, according to the authors, requires its literature to be considered under this heading: "So the literatures of African countries, Australia, Bangladesh, Canada, Caribbean countries, India, Malaysia, Malta, New Zealand, Pakistan, Singapore, South Pacific Island countries, and Sri Lanka are all postcolonial literatures. The literature of the USA should also be placed in this category. Perhaps because of its current position of power, and the neo-colonizing role it has played, its postcolonial nature has not been generally recognized. But its relationship with the metropolitan centre as it evolved over the last two centuries has been paradigmatic for postcolonial literatures everywhere. What each of these literatures has in common beyond their special and distinctive regional characteristics is that they emerged in their present form out of the experience of colonization and asserted themselves by foregrounding the tension with the imperial power, and by emphasizing their differences from the assumptions of the imperial centre. It is this which makes them distinctively postcolonial."

   That the authors should be talking about a monolithic literature of the USA, even after recognising the influence of post-structuralism and post-modernism on theories of postcolonialism, is unfortunate here. If we were to take the literature of the USA as an organic structure then, there are more differences than shared concerns between it and the literature written in English in a country like India, so much so, that they cannot be clubbed together under any heading.
8. G.N. Devy, "The Wind and the Roots: The Problem of Historiography of Commonwealth Literature," *The History and Historiography of Commonwealth Literature*, p. 79.
9. *Ibid*., p. 80. In the light of the contemporary arguments about 'hybridity' and 'ambiguity' even this kind of differentiation seems to be very simplistic. In this easy opposition between the alien and the native, in the first group it is self-evident that the native is acted upon by the wind of westernization to produce commonwealth literature and in the second case it is the interaction between the inherited culture of the settler in a new landscape that gives rise to Commonwealth Literature. There is no mention of the culture of the native in the second case.
10. Arthur Ravenscroft, for example, definitely writes against a mono-

lithic conception of Commonwealth literature and gives more importance to the "differences and divergences" within this field. The positive aspect of this category is that it has brought the work of "non-metropolitan writers which deserves more than a merely national scholarship" to the attention of more readers than before. See Ravenscroft, "Foreword," *Commonwealth Literature Periodicals: A Bibliography, including Periodicals of former Commonwealth Countries, with Locations in the United Kingdom*, compiled and ed. Ronald Warwick (London: Mansell Publishing, 1979), pp. vii-xiii.

11. K.R. Srinivasa Iyengar, "The Literature of India," *The Commonwealth Pen*, pp. 115-41. Srinivasa Iyengar insists that there prevail "forces of unity and harmony," in modern Indian literature which is an "outcome of a long, long process of evolution and growth." pp. 116-17. Even his concluding remarks repeat this wish for bringing about unity through literature written in English: "It may, therefore, be confidently hoped that, as in the past, in the future also, the Indo-Anglian writer will primarily aim at projecting a total view of India—interpreting her aspirations and hopes and recording her ardour and achievements—not only before the outside world, but also before the diverse linguistic groups within the country. There is no reason why Indo-Anglian literature should not, in the fullness of time, grow with the growth of the various regional literatures, giving and taking freely, and so achieve a position comparable to the distinctive national literatures like modern American literature and become an expression of the Indian genius and a means to national unity and international understanding." p. 141.

12. It is interesting to note here that Iyengar uses a similar explanation for his justification of Commonwealth Literature, as well as for the prominence of English as the language of Commonwealth, in his *Two Cheers for the Commonwealth: Talks on Literature and Education* (New York: Asia, 1970).

13. C.D. Narasimhaiah, "Foreword," *A Common Poetic for Indian Literature*, ed. C.D. Narasimhaiah and C.N. Srinath (Mysore: Dhvanyaloka, 1984), p. vi.

14. Viney Kirpal identifies this kind of advocating of the Sanskrit Poetics as being an attempt to rectify the uncritical attachment to the Eurocentric norms while discussing literary works created in India. She sees limitations in the arguments which propose Sanskrit Poetics as an alternative. One of the most important limitations is that this kind of Sanskrit aesthetics was not written for prose writing, especially not for something like the novel genre. See Kirpal, "Has the Indian Novel Been Understood?" *From Commonwealth to Post-*

colonial, pp. 303-15.

15. C.D. Narasimhaiah, "Towards the Formulation of a Common Poetic for Indian Literatures," in *Ibid.*, p. 2.
16. I have borrowed these terms from Christopher Norris, who writes the Editor's Foreword to Michael Bell's *F.R. Leavis* (London: Routledge, 1988), p. xiv. Even though Norris does not hide his critical stance towards Leavis, Bell's study itself is more sympathetic and is interested in giving a more positive evaluation of Leavis as a critic.
17. C.D. Narasimhaiah, "Towards the Formulation of a Common Poetic for Indian Literatures," p. 2.
18. The literature of the Dalits (the oppressed, the so-called Untouchables) is one such body of writing that refuses to accept any such idea of cultural unity in the Indian literary set-up. For some more infomation on this theme, see my unpublished M.Phil. dissertation with the title *Outsiders and Insiders: Differing Perspectives on Bondage—A Comparative Study of Black-American Literature and Modern Kannada Literature*, with Particular Reference to Harriet Beecher Stowe's *Uncle Tom's Cabin*, Shivaram Karanth's *Chomana Dudi,* Ralph Ellison's *Invisible Man* and Devanoor Mahadeva's *Odalala*, submitted to Mangalore University in April 1988.
19. Aijaz Ahmad, *In Theory: Classes, Nations, Literatures* (1992; London: Verso, 1994), pp. 244-45.
20. See Gyan Prakash, "Writing Post-Orientalist Histories of the Third World: Indian Historiography Is Good to Think," in *Colonialism and Culture*, ed. Nicholas B. Dirks (Ann Arbor: The University of Michigan Press, 1992), p. 362. Gyan Prakash traces very carefully the various stages in the historiographical efforts in India and shows how the nationalistic historiographers shared many of the views of the Orientalists which had earlier constructed India as an object of knowledge, as the Other. The difference between them and the nationalists was that the latter tried to break completely from the West and tried to recover an ontological tradition for India, its authentic culture and its authentic history. Since I find this also in the desire to create and promote a common tradition for Indian literary productions, I have tried to draw similarities between those who plead for a common tradition of literary criticism and those who valorize the long singular authentic Indian tradition.
21. Vijay Mishra and Bob Hodge, "What is Post(-)colonialism ?," *Colonial Discourse and postcolonial Theory: A Reader*, ed. Patrick Williams and Laura Chrisman (New York: Harvester Wheatsheaf, 1993), p. 278. The article is also in *Textual Practice*, 5, 3 (1991): 399-414. Suggesting that the authors of *The Empire Writes Back* could have,

through their homogenizing tendency, produced unconsciously an unproblematic theory of the 'other,' Mishra and Hodge, point out to a basic paradox in the text itself. "The paradox that surfaces—a paradox that we would call post-orientalism—is part of an historical process that grew out of Europe's reading of the Other. Orientalism's heavily skewed and ideologically marked discourses—haunt the post-colonial in ways that make, in places, the postcolonial itself post-oriental." p. 279.

22. One more author to make a similar distinction is Elleke Boehmer, in *Colonial and Postcolonial Literature: Migrant Metaphors* (Oxford: Oxford University Press, 1995), p. 3. The author uses the hyphenated form as a period term—to designate the post-Second World War era.
23. Vijay Mishra and Bob Hodge, "What is Post(-)colonialism?," p. 288.
24. I would like to mention here an interesting observation made by Dirk Hohnsträter connecting postcolonialism and poststructuralism in an article which not only presents Homi K. Bhabha's arguments in favour of the in-between space and moments of hybridity, but also raises questions about their use in a concretised manner in intercultural debates. See Hohnsträter, "Homi K. Bhabhas Semiotik der Zwischenräume—Eine, überzeugende Konzeptualisierung interkultureller Konflikte?" in *Arcadia*, Band 31 Heft 1/2 (1996): 62-68.
25. Ella Shohat is of the opinion that the prefix 'post-' aligns this term with a series of other post-words. For an interesting interrogation of the term 'postcolonial' see her "Notes on the 'postcolonial,'" which has become one of the most important contributions to the postcolonial discourse. Shohat, "Notes on the 'postcolonial,'" *Contemporary Postcolonial Theory: A Reader*, ed. Padmini Mongia (London: Arnold, 1996), pp.321-34. This essay also appears in *Social Text*, 31/32 (1992):99-113.
26. Anne McClintock, "The Angel of Progress," *Colonial Discourse and postcolonial Theory: A Reader*, p. 292. This essay also appears in *Social Text*, Spring 1992, pp. 1-15. While criticising the use of a universal term 'the postcolonial' which seems to lack the element of multiplicity in its usage, Anne McClintock makes an interesting observation about the marketability of the term: "How, then, does one account for the curious ubiquity of the preposition 'post' in contemporary intellectual life, not only in the universities, but in newspaper columns and on the lips of media moguls? In the case of 'postcolonialism,' at least, part of the reason is its academic marketability. While admittedly another p-c word, 'postcolonialism' is

arguably more palatable and less foreign-sounding to sceptical deans than 'Third World Studies.' It also has a less accusatory ring than 'Studies In Neo-colonialism,' say, or 'Fighting Two Colonialisms.' It is more global, and less fuddy-duddy, than 'Commonwealth Studies.' The term borrows, moreover, on the dazzling marketing success of the term 'post-modernism.' As the organizing rubric of an emerging field of disciplinary studies and an archive of knowledge, the term 'postcolonialism' makes possible the marketing of a whole new generation of panels, articles, books and courses." (p. 299)
Whether the term 'postcolonial' has borrowed from the marketing success of 'post-modernism' or whether it has a marketing success by itself, what McClintock says about the 'whole new generation of panels, articles, books and courses,' is a fact. The term could have been used by many critics as a strategy to get attention. The number of readers, volumes and encyclopaedia in the related area which have been published in the past few years is astounding.

27. Francis Barker, Peter Hulme and Margaret Iversen, "Introduction," *Colonial Discourse/Postcolonial Theory* (Manchester: Manchester University Press, 1993), p. 5.
28. See Aijaz Ahmad, "Postcolonialism: What's in a Name?," *Late Imperial Culture*, eds. Roman De la Campa et al (London: Verso, 1995), p.12. Here Aijaz Ahmad mentions an article written by Hamza Alavi in *New Left Review* 74 (July-August, 1972) entitled "The State in Postcolonial Societies: Pakistan and Bangladesh," and the ensuing debate on the nature of postcolonial state, which he says, assumed international dimensions.
29. See Homi K. Bhabha, "DissemiNation: Time, Narrative, and the Margins of the Modern Nation," *Nation and Narration*, ed. Homi K. Bhabha (1990; London: Routledge, 1993). What strikes us here, as well as in the arguments of the critics who question the locality of the postcolonial critics, is the subjective element which lurks behind them. Bhabha connects the title of his essay to his experience of migration: "I have lived that moment of the scattering of the people that in other times and other places, in the nation of others, becomes a time of gathering. Gatherings of exiles and emigrès and refugees, gathering on the edge of 'foreign' cultures; gathering at the frontiers; gatherings in the ghettos or cafès of city centres; gathering in the half-life, half-light of foreign tongues, or in the uncanny fluency of another's language; gathering the signs of approval and acceptance, degrees, discourses, disciplines; gathering the memories of underdevelopment, of other worlds lived retroactively; gathering the past in a ritual of revival, gathering the present. Also the gath-

ering of the people in the diaspora: indentured, migrant, interned; the gathering of incriminatory statistics, educational performance, legal statutes, immigration status . . . " (p. 291).

Even though Bhabha speaks of the modern western nation in the next paragraph, and refers to the periods of mass migration within the west, the essay later on talks about nation in a vaguely non-specific manner. The above-mentioned article establishes the nation space as a space that is internally marked by cultural difference and heterogeneous histories. According to Bhabha this could be a strategy for the minority communities and they "no longer need to address their strategies of opposition to a horizon of 'hegemony' that is envisaged as horizontal and homogeneous." (p. 301)

30. Ania Loomba and Suvir Kaul, "Introduction: Location, Culture, post-coloniality," *The Oxford Literary Review: On India: Writing History, Culture, postcoloniality*, Vol. 16, Nos. 1-2, p. 3.
31. Bharati Mukherjee in an interview with Vrinda Nabar in *The Sunday Times of India Review*, December 31, 1995, p. 2.
32. Bharati Mukherjee's anger at the postcolonial critics seems to be shared by Makarand Paranjape too. But this time his anger is against postmodernists. In a denunciation of postmodernism he announces that it is one more case of the West wielding power over the rest. See Paranjape, "Postmodernism and India: Some Preliminary Animadversions," *A Way of Leaving so as to Stay*, pp. 89-109. In India the abuse of power represented by postmodernism is reproduced "under the peculiar logic of postcolonialism. Here those who are closest to the West, those with Western degrees, with books and articles published in the West, and whose work has been recognized in the West are in control." (pp. 93-94) Unfortunately, his sweeping arguments against postmodernism and, by extension, against postcolonialism, are not convincing enough. Even though Ania Loomba and Suvir Kaul raise the problem of location and point out to the divide between those postcolonial critics working in the Anglo-American academies and those working in India, they do so bearing in mind the peculiar problems facing the contemporary Indian society, not by romanticizing its nationalist struggle, or traditional heritage as Paranjape seems to be doing here.
33. Arif Dirlik, "The Postcolonial Aura; Third World Criticism in the Age of Global Capitalism," *Critical Inquiry*, 20 (Winter 1994): 328-56.
34. It is interesting to see how the term postcolonial is on the one hand accused of being exclusivistic, as by Arif Dirlik, on the other hand, it is seen as a term which can be used to refer to anything in any

period. See Michael Sprinker, "Introduction," *Late Imperial Culture*, pp. 4-5. Frustrated by this kind of indeterminacy of meaning Sprinkler suggests another term 'late imperialism,' to indicate the ongoing process of imperialism.

35. I am borrowing this question from Wayne C. Booth raised in a different context. Pointing out that the politics of interpretation is often associated with questions of power rather than the idea of freedom of interpretation, he suggests that freedom is not always attained by casting off, but also by taking in the many voices which we have inherited. See his "Freedom of Interpretation: Bakhtin and the Challenge of Feminist Criticism," in *The Politics of Interpretation*, ed. W.J.T. Mitchell (Chicago: The University of Chicago Press, 1983), p. 82.
36. Stephen Slemon, "The Scramble for postcolonialism," *De-Scribing Empire: postcolonialism and Textuality*, ed. Chris Tiffin and Alan Lawson (London: Routledge, 1994), pp. 15-32.
37. Linda Hutcheon, *The Poetics of Postmodernism: History, Theory Fiction* (New York: Routledge, 1988), p. 62.
38. Jean-Francois Lyotard, "Note on the Meaning of 'Post-,'" *The Postmodern Explained: Correspondence 1982-1985*, trans. ed. Julian Pefanis and Morgan Thomas (1992; Minneapolis/London: University of Minnesota Press, 1993), pp. 75-80.
39 *Ibid.*, p. 80.
40. "Beliefs, . . . are crux to the postmodern condition precisely because that condition is pluralist, conflictual, indetermanent, consciously or unconsciously, they inform all our labors of legitimation, let alone our fanaticisms." Ihab Hassan, *The Postmodern Turn* (Ohio State University Press, 1987), p. 226. Ihab Hassan's own belief in the pluralism of postmodern condition takes him back to the pragmatic pluralism of William James.
41. Ian Adam, "Breaking the Chain: Anti-Saussurean Resistance in Birney, Carey and C.S. Peirce," *Past the Last Post* (1991), ed. Ian Adam and Helen Tiffin (New York: Harvester Wheatsheaf, 1993), p. 79. According to Adam, postmodernism and postcolonialism converge in that they have become prominent literary practices in postcolonial cultures and are committed to "a subversion of authoritative and monocultural forms of genre, history and discourse." In addition to this concern, they also share some formal practices which makes it possible for us to discuss writers like Rushdie and Kroetsch under either label. According to Adam, they diverge in their historical reach: postmodernism is contemporary while postmodernism can be detected "in the heyday of colonialism and in works of its most

articulate defenders (e.g. Kipling)"; in their sites of production and in theoretical base also.

42. Edward Said, "Afterword," *Orientalism* (1978; New York: Vintage Books, 1994), pp. 329-52.

43. See John Thieme, "Editorial," *Journal of Commonwealth Literature*, 30, 1 (1995):3-4.

Reading Postcolonial Critics

> What [the genealogical project] really does is to entertain the claims to attention of local, discontinuous, disqualified, illegitimate knowledges against the claims of a unitary body of theory which would filter, hierarchize, and order them in the name of some true knowledge and some arbitrary idea of what constitutes a science and its objects. Genealogies are therefore not positivistic returns to a more careful or exact form of science. They are precisely anti-sciences. Not that they vindicate a lyrical right to ignorance or non-knowledge: it is not that they are concerned to deny knowledge or that they esteem the virtues of direct cognition and base their practice upon an immediate experience that escapes encapsulation in knowledge.
>
> Michel Foucault,
> "Two Lectures," *Power /Knowledge*

The previous chapter has shown us that the term postcolonial does not lend itself to any fixed definition. If one tries to broadly explain the project of postcolonial critique, it will have to include something of Foucault's description of genealogies as well. Postcolonial discourse offers a different perspective in the field of theory, by way of bringing in different voices from the ex-colonies. Even though the discourse is interdisciplinary in nature, the literary canon provided one of the earliest evidences for the postcolonial critics to show that the colonial enterprise manipulated and shaped the various cultural productions of the colonies. Thus what most of the postcolonial critics have articulated is a counter-claim to the canons of English literature and to the models of Euro-American literary theory by way of entertaining the "claims to attention of local, discontinuous, disqualified, illegitimate knowledges."[1]

Critics Against Unitary Discourses

This chapter will make a selective reading and analysis of the works of some of the well-known and not so well-known postcolonial critics. Most of the critics chosen here are of Indian origin not because I wish to uphold the virtues of 'direct cognition' or 'immediate experience' but because I wish to show how the question of location alters one's understanding of the postcolonial situation. At times seemingly provincial, at times ideologically divergent, the differences among these intellectuals seem to translate into oppositional tones. For many of these critics, the condition of being in exile, of being a minority, shapes the nature of theorization. But there are also others who feel that this previous group unnecessarily privileges the exilic condition without paying attention to the contemporary political and cultural aspects of the former colonies. There is thus a kind of tension between the articulations of different critics—most of them associated with the postcolonial societies. I propose to present the arguments of some of these critics in order to show the presence of such a tension.

This kind of tension can be located in the fear of many academics who are cautious not to set up another canon-forming discourse and who are worried that postcolonial critique too would be taken over by the western academic institutions. We find here echoes of the same question that Michel Foucault asked many years ago:

> is it not perhaps the case that these fragments of genealogies are no sooner brought to light, that the particular elements of the knowledge that one seeks to disinter are no sooner accredited and put into circulation, than they run the risk of re-codification, re-colonization? In fact, those unitary discourses, which first disqualified and then ignored them when they made their appearance, are, it seems, quite ready now to annex them, to take them back within the fold of their own discourse and to invest them with everything this implies

> in terms of their effects of knowledge and power. (86)

Is it possible that postcolonialism, which provides a different reading of imperialism and colonialism, is letting itself get annexed by "those unitary discourses"? Instead of searching for an immediate answer to this question, we could look at the works of various postcolonial critics who actually brought prominence to the word 'postcolonial' and at the works of those who appear to be simply dissatisfied with some of the things which pass as postcolonial. Since the scope of this study is limited, I shall be concentrating mainly on Said, Bhabha and Spivak, who are considered the pioneers of postcolonial critique and on a body of selected works which give another variety of response to the postcolonial question.

Although culture studies, politics, ethnology, archival researches and literary criticism cannot be separated from one another anymore in all these works, the focus of the following study will be overwhelmingly on the use of the strategies and methods adopted by these critics for reading and interpreting texts. The arguments presented here are not exhaustive because that has never been the objective of this work. This book tries to show how a theoretical field called postcolonial discourse can be used to give rise to different readings. This is an attempt to present examples rather than justify or 'make clear' any mode of writing or reading. In a different way, this work puts into practice what Michael B. Naas suggests while introducing Derrida's *The Other Heading*:

> whether one speaks for the prosecution or the defence, whether one sees in this work the same old heading, be it impotent or threatening, or a new direction, be it a radical departure from the past or the cautious unfolding of it, one will at a certain point have to present one's case. And if the argument is to be more than mere accusation or intuition, more than personal feeling or sentiment, one will have to provide a few examples.[2]

What follows is an attempt at providing a few examples for postcolonial arguments.

Said, Imperialism and Culture: Orientalism and the Beginnings

Though highly controversial, Said's *Orientalism* gets the credit for having opened the floodgate of postcolonial criticism.[3] What Said establishes in his book *Orientalism* and continues to explore in *Culture and Imperialism* is that in a society, culture, literary creations, and literary criticism, cannot be separated from the various actualities which give shape to an epoch. To put it rather crudely, his objects of investigation in both these books are the role of culture in the colonial enterprise and the representation of the colonial subjects in various cultural productions such as literature and music. The Orient that Said finds in the various documents is the Orient that is knowledgeably identified by the West: "Knowledge of the Orient, because generated out of strength, in a sense creates the Orient, the Oriental, and his world."[4] And it is the creator of this knowledge—the Orientalist—who is revealed as an accomplice along with the colonialists. Thus Orientalism itself is a creation which need not bear any relationship to the 'subject' who is known as the Orient.[5] Said questions many of the assumptions behind a field which was considered the domain of the experts in Orientalism for a long time. The oriental subject who emerges through these representations is rather passive. However, in his *Culture and Imperialism*, Said also makes it a point to stress the importance of resistance in the native. Said has been accused of a strong anti-West leaning in his *Orientalism* and is said to have done exactly what he condemns in the Orientalists, namely, representing peoples as being monolithic and uniform. According to many critics Said is not consistent in his use of theoretical positions and his statements contradict and cancel each other.[6] Said is also aware of the criticism that in spite of all his arguments about Orientalism, he does not suggest an alternative way of conceiving the orient.[7] But there is little doubt in the fact that Said has been successful in reviving interest in representations of the orient—both in scholarly fields such as orientalism, ethnography as well as in the creative field of literature. In fact, few would disagree with Aijaz Ahmad, one of the strongest critics of Said, when he says

> [it] has been Edward Said's achievement to have brought this question of cultural imperialism to the very centre of the on-going literary debates in the metropolitan university by posing it in terms that were acceptable to that university.[8]

Ahmad's recognition that Said has succeeded in bringing the debate on cultural imperialism to the foreground is tinged with an inherent criticism that it had to be done in terms that were acceptable to the metropolitan university. If Said had not used "terms that were acceptable" would he not have been heard? The question must caution all the postcolonial intellectuals against the danger of turning postcolonial discourse into another dominant discourse that functions the way orientalism functioned for many decades.

Some of the criticism which his *Orientalism* precipitated has been taken into consideration by Said in his article, "Orientalism Reconsidered," as well as in his "Afterword" to the 1994 Vintage edition of *Orientalism.*[9] There is no doubt that Said is one of the earliest scholars to show us that even an academic subject like Orientalism, taken to be 'objective,' is, at a later phase, deeply involved in the project of colonialism. This observation gains added significance in the contemporary period, especially when we realise that orientalist studies very often influenced many of the later areas of interest such as world history, ethnology, anthropology, and even literary criticism. Said himself keeps crossing over boundaries and by moving across various disciplines, he provides us a model for navigating between different fields such as literature, philosophy, history and anthropology.[10] In this work, I am primarily interested in Said's exposure of the prejudices that operated in the field of literature and 'literary criticism.'

To understand Said's approach to the literary text, we must also know how, according to Said, the text is connected to the context. His repeated use of such a term as 'actuality' indicates the possibility of representing this actuality and the belief that this actuality about the Orient was distorted in the many images that the orientalists have given us. We also notice that this fondness for the word 'actuality' or even for 'worldliness'[11] exists in opposition to his dislike for the word 'textuality.' It must be added here that this criticism of textuality is also an inherent criticism of "American literary theory"[12] as well as the Derridean understanding of the textuality. In fact, his use of the term 'textuality'—whereby he seems to have in mind only the written text taken in isolation—clashes with his idea of the text as being located in actuality:

> My position is that the texts are worldly, to some degree they are events, and, even when they appear to deny it, they are nevertheless a part of the social world, human life, and of course the historical moments in which they are located and interpreted. (4)

Locating the text in the social, historical, cultural, temporal context is pivotal to his other observation regarding the role of the novel in an imperial society. This leads him on to the conclusion that the authors of these novels are inevitably associated with the empire.

Said thus draws connections between the genre of novel writing and the empire. Yet his research is useful for us not only on this count. Even though he does not name it as postcolonial discourse, his preoccupation with the cultural manipulations of the colonial period does not stop with this kind of linking. He also sees a continuation of this imperialistic attitude in the contemporary world too. For him, a reconsideration of Orientalism becomes necessary today because in our world it stands for all that which has been misrepresented or silenced:

> we can now see that Orientalism is a praxis of the same sort, albeit in different territories, as male gender dominance or patriarchy, in metropolitan societies: the Orient was routinely described as feminine, its riches as fertile, its main symbols the sensual woman, the harem, and the despotic—but curiously attractive—ruler. Moreover Orientals, like Victorian housewives, were confined to silence and to unlimited enriching production. Now much of this material is manifestly connected to the configurations of sexual, racial and political asymmetry underlying mainstream modern western culture, as adumbrated and illuminated respectively by feminists, by black studies critics and by anti-imperialist activists.[13]

Thus we see that Said tries constantly to connect, to contextualize. This need for connecting things can be seen even in his suggestion for contrapuntal reading of literary works. This is a need which in turn stems from his understanding of the interdependent, interconnected nature of the world. The first move in using Said for our reading of the novels of Shashi Deshpande, is to see how he relates some of the well-known realist novelists belonging to the nineteenth century with the expanding enterprise of Imperialism.

Novelist and the Consolidation of Authority

If in his *Orientalism*, Said expresses the idea that an author is involved "as a human subject in his own circumstances," (11) he reinstates the idea in *Culture and Imperialism too*:

> I do not believe that authors are mechanically determined by ideology, class, or economic history, but authors are, I also believe, very much in the history of their societies, shaping and shaped by that history and their social experience in different measure. (xxii)

This idea that an author is shaping and is shaped by the history of his/her society is crucial to all areas of postcolonial discourse. However, one could ask Said whether it is really possible or necessary to disassociate history and social experience from ideology, class or economic history.[14] This view contradicts his own argument that novel is a cultural form whose connection to the "expanding societies of Britain and France is particularly interesting to study."[15] In a way, *Culture and Imperialism* does two things which Orientalism does not do. It tries to connect the critique of colonialism more clearly with literature produced in the heyday of colonialism and it acknowledges the presence of resistance among the colonized. In addition, we also notice Said's eagerness to prove that he is not really anti-West, nor a provincialist who tries to homogenize the West as the evil counterpart of the East. It is in this connection that he talks of an approach to the well-known novelists of the empire—an approach, which "actually and truly enhances our reading and understanding of them." (xiv) There is no hasty rejection of Jane Austen here. The tone is more cosmopolitan in nature, and is more in accordance with his upholding of the exilic condition later in the book.

Thus we could say that it is in *Culture and Imperialism* that we find a methodology for reading differently the classics of English literature.[16] Said does not really question the validity of the canons of European Literature. According to him traditional literary criticism has not taken into consideration the fact of imperialism and it has not paid attention to the authors' comments and silences regarding the 'actuality' of colonialism. It is especially here that we get some kind of a suggestion for using postcolonialism as an interpretative method because there is an extensive report on the nature of the novel as a cultural artefact:

> Of all the major literary forms, the novel is the most recent, its emergence the most durable, its occurrence the most Western, its normative pattern of social authority the most structured; imperialism and the novel fortified each other to such a degree that it is impossible, I would argue, to read one without in some way dealing with the other. (71)

We realise soon that Said's terms for the novelistic form actually apply to novels of the realistic mode. Just as the Empire grew in strength, so did the novel become steadily popular. As he points out, Britain did not really have any rival in this field for a long time:

> By the 1840s the English Novel had achieved eminence as the aesthetic form and as a major intellectual voice, so to speak, in English society. Because the novel gained so important a place in "the condition of England" question, for example, we can see it also as participating in England's overseas empire. (71-72)

In this regard, the novel form has had a unique existence. Novels, so goes his argument, are events and not the products of "lonely genius." (73)

Imperialism was an event of such global proportions that it

is difficult to say that it did not leave its mark on the cultural productions of the imperial societies. Although he agrees that novels and other media as ethnography and travel writing did not have it as their overt political agenda, they reinforced the idea of the empire and were thus the conforming collaborators in this enterprise. The authority of the empire was consolidated especially by the vision created by the realistic novels. Perhaps one of the most provocative conclusions which Said has drawn from such an observation is that in their attitudes towards the empire, Kipling and Conrad are already anticipated by other novelists like Austen, Thackeray, Scott and Dickens and are also connected with their own contemporaries like Hardy and James, the differences between them being only those of "inflection, emphasis, stress." (75)

Yet, very few readers would associate Jane Austen with imperialism even though she does make occasional references to the plantations abroad. However, reading novels by authors like Austen and Dickens, paying attention to what has been said or not been said about the different activities of the empire, could add another perspective to our interpretations. In addition, it will be clear to us, as Said correctly points out, that in these writers we could already identify "the quest for, the concern about, and consciousness of overseas dominion." (68) What intrigues Said in the case of Jane Austen's *Mansfield Park* is that by an "odd combination of casualness and stress, Austen reveals herself to be *assuming* (. . .) the importance of an empire to the situation at home." (89) By locating a direct relationship between works of the famous novelists of nineteenth-century England and the British Empire and by claiming that the European novel was consolidating, refining and articulating "the authority of the *status quo*,'" (77) he is questioning many of the assumptions in the field of literary criticism. Said charges that all these writers whom he mentions as predecessors of Kipling and Conrad were accomplices in the 'consolidation of power.'

Thus, according to him the preoccupation of late-nineteenth-century novels with issues related to the Empire are only an extension of the consolidation of power found in earlier historical and realistic novels. (78) The spatial differentiations which make the reader recognise the 'here' and the 'there' are also indicative of the discriminations which were authorized by these novels. Novels by Jane Austen and Dickens, according to Said, uphold a spatial moral order and "[a]s the conclusions of the novel confirm and highlight an underlying hierarchy of family, property, nation, there is also a very strong spatial hereness imparted to the hierarchy." (79) The one who imparts such a hierarchy is ultimately the novelist and, one feels, that it is here that Said finds fault with these novelists. They were legitimizing the role of the empire by not questioning it. Such narrative events as fiction and history "premised on the recording, ordering, observing powers of the central authorizing subject, or ego." (79) However, the authority of the author is also, in a way, regulated by the society. In Jane Austen's society, the authority of readers supported the authority of the author and the authority of the narrator.

Connecting the 'here' and the 'there'

In all these discussions Said is not questioning the greatness of Jane Austen or of Dickens as writers. He is simply pointing out that it was impossible for them not to be contaminated by the Empire and also not to believe in the natural right of the English people to be dominating over geographical space abroad. Said seems to believe in the duty of the writer to be a critical observer of her or his society and in this aspect, and by failing to be critical of the desire for acquiring space 'there,' they become involved in colonialism. At the same time, he points to the glaring absence of any significant comment in the field of literary criticism on the representation of the 'there' in these novels. It was in the days of modernism that the European cultures learnt to look at the encounter between the empire and the domains situated 'there' with scepticism. When these cultures began to take due account of the myths of the empire, they did so, "not oppositionally but ironically, and with a desperate attempt at a new inclusiveness." (189) Said feels that, during this period of modernism, the 'there' was imported to 'here.' (188)

I have dwelt upon these terms 'there' and 'here' because in Said's articulations such boundaries are very significantly present. They are associated with 'they' and 'us' which in turn refer to a hierarchy of accepted values and also to social discriminations. Boundary itself is a very important concept in Said because it defines his own position as a critic in exile. Paradoxically however, he is also interested in connecting over the boundaries. For him, the later migration of people, especially writers and artists in the other direction or "*the voyage in*"—as he calls it—is an important event to be reckoned with because, on the one hand, this could be taken as "an alternative way of conceiving history" which involves "[t]he conscious effort to enter into the discourse of Europe and the West, to mix with it, transform it, to make it acknowledge marginalized or suppressed or forgotten histories," (216) and, on the other hand, it is also a "sign of adversarial internationalization in an age of continued imperial success." (244)[17]

It is not unusual to get the feeling, while reading Said, that he does this kind of adversarial internationalization, rather in a traditional manner. He does not call for a rejection of the novels which he takes up for analyses. Said is actually suggesting a way of reading these canons of British Literature without losing sight of the historical set-up which, in his view, cannot be detached from the authors.[18] But, sometimes, Said creates a sense of *déjà vu*, especially when he says, "[w]hen we read the novels attentively, we get a far more discriminating and subtle view than the baldly 'global' and imperial vision I have described thus far," or "[i]n insisting on the integrity of an artistic work, as we must, and refusing to collapse the various contributions of individual authors into a general schema," or even when he says, "[t]his obliges critics to read and analyze rather than only to summarize and judge, works whose paraphrasable content they might regard as politically and morally objectionable."[19] The plea for a discerning reader, for attentive reading and analytical skills is not new in the field of literary criticism.[20] Said too seems to be giving greater responsibility to the literary critic. While declining to attribute greater responsibility to a literary critic, I choose to concentrate on his other suggestion that novels should be read contrapuntally. Deriving basically from the principles of comparative literary criticism, his method of contrapuntal reading could be described as a means of juxtaposing, of reading simultaneously from a different area or from a different period to throw more light on the interconnectedness of literature and history, of the centre and the margin.[21]

Reading Contrapuntally

To explain what he means by reading contrapuntally the texts of the centre and of the peripheries, he suggests that such a work as Jane Austen's *Mansfield Park* should be read along with the works of Eric Williams and of C.L.R. James.[22] In a way, this kind of reading, as Said envisions it, is much more inclusive than what it initially seems to suggest:

> We must therefore read the great canonical texts, and perhaps also the entire archive of modern and pre-modern European and American culture, with an effort to draw out, extend, give emphasis and voice to what is silent or marginally present or ideologically represented (. . .) in such works. (66)

It is Said's way of formulating an "alternative to the politics of blame and to the even more destructive politics of confrontation and hostility," (18) his intention being one of "moving beyond insularity and provincialism" and of providing an "antidote to reductive nationalism and uncritical dogma." (43) The references to this kind of reading are scattered through the text; we often get the impression that this contrapuntal reading is not only a tactic in the practice of comparative literary criticism but also a tool for recovering and establishing the note of resistance against the project of colonization. Writing about Kipling's *Kim* and of Kipling's India he says:

> In reading a text, one must open it out both to what went into it and to what its author excluded. Each cultural work is a vision of a moment, and we must juxtapose that vision with the various revisions it later provoked—in this case, the nationalist experiences of post-independence India. (67)

If on the one hand, this kind of contrapuntal reading is retrospective, in the sense that it suggests 'revisions,' on the other, it is also a juxtaposition of the political and the creative fields, which opens up the discrepancies between the two. Once again, referring to *Kim* and to the Indian independence movement, he says:

> Either the novel or the political movement represented or interpreted without the other misses the crucial discrepancy between the two given to them by the actual experience of the empire. (32)

Going by this explanation of contrapuntal analysis, we could say that in addition to being retrospective or revisionary, the method of reading contrapuntally also involves juxtaposing things which were contemporary, such as *Kim* and the growing Indian independence movement. Said himself does not stick to a particular period or a particular type of text. In fact, he suggests that we learn from the comparative methodology of seeing "several cultures and literatures, together, contrapuntally." (43) Taking our cue from all these arguments for contrapuntal reading, one could say that the novels of Shashi Deshpande too could be read contrapuntally. It is possible to consider her novels as a revision of the story of colonization because, as Said maintains, the influence of imperialism can be felt in our postcolonial societies even now. It is possible to read her contrapuntally in the context of postcolonial discussions, and in the context where nation and narration have become important themes for critical discourse. This kind of contrapuntal reading could be, in turn, juxtaposed with the current arguments and essays which have been written about her novels and about the women characters created by her. This is the manner in which Said will be used in the following pages.

Even when he writes at length about the interdependence of cultures—which is in itself rather idealistic—he ultimately seems to value the experience of exile more than anything else. (317) Or perhaps, it is because of the experience of exile that this kind of interdependence of cultures appear significant for him. The exile, the migrant, and those who occupy the space in-between are themes which appear frequently in Homi Bhabha. With Bhabha, postcolonial discourses show their interdependence on areas in poststructuralism and in psychoanalysis.

Bhabha and Ambivalence in Postcolonial Discourse: The Third Space of Enunciation

Said concludes his *Culture and Imperialism* by mentioning the 'hybrid counter-energies' which are at work in many fields to provide a 'community or culture made up of numerous anti-systemic hints and practices for collective human existence.' (335) This optimistic view in Said is inspired by his opinion that the empire has also given rise to different communities which have shared histories. Unlike Said, Bhabha does not look at shared histories as something that has given rise to common reactions.

The event of colonization is described differently by Bhabha. For Bhabha too, the cultural implications of the period of colonization on the postcolonial world is important, but if Said ultimately lays importance on the borrowings, appropriations, common experiences of all cultures, Bhabha shows us how difficult it is for communities to have a common response to their shared histories:

> How do strategies of representation or empowerment come to be formulated in the competing claims of communities where, despite shared histories of deprivations and discrimination, the exchange of values, meanings and priorities may not always be collaborative and dialogical, but may be profoundly antagonistic, conflictual and even incommensurable?[23]

"Strategies of representation or empowerment" or, better still, 'strategies of representation **as** empowerment' are what intrigue Bhabha. Both Bhabha and Said are interested in the strategies of representation used by the colonials. However, we see that Bhabha's approach is completely different from that of Said. It is his recognition of the fact that even shared histories can give rise to "antagonistic, conflictual and even incommensurable" reactions within the postcolonial communities, that prevents him from giving us any kind of ideal picture. He does not entertain the notion of 'transforming the present by trying rationally and analytically to lift some of its burdens.' (*Culture and Imperialism* 319)

Thus we see that Bhabha deviates from Said in his understanding of the shared histories of the colonised. Another major area of difference is the authority that has been accorded to the centre by these two. Bhabha questions the accepted unified version of the colonizer and the absolute power attributed to the colonial institution. He deconstructs this authority given to the centre by exposing its basically ambivalent nature. The absolute entities like the colonized and the colonizer, the 'self' and the 'other' become blurred in the world of Bhabha's arguments because according to him, such an ambivalence lies in the very practice of representation.

Recharting words and signs, relocating desire and fantasy, redefining identities and nationalities—these are the methods adopted by Bhabha to show how complex the act of representation is.[24] Poststructuralism[25] and psychoanalysis, Foucault and Derrida, Freud and Lacan, Fanon[26] and Toni Morrison have all had important roles in shaping his arguments. While deconstructing the assumed authority of the colonial world, he questions all binaries, and looks for a "third space of enunciation." In this regard, the structure of language is an important tool which helps him understand how cultures represent themselves. Any act of cultural enunciation is similar to the enunciation of a statement: There is disjuncture between "the subject of a proposition (*énoncé*) and the subject of enunciation, which is not represented in the statement."[27] This makes it difficult for us to take interpretation as simply being an act of communication between 'I and You':

> The production of meaning requires that these two places be mobilized in the passage through a Third Space, which represents both the general conditions of language and the specific implication of the utterance in a performative and institutional strategy of which it cannot 'in itself' be conscious. What this unconscious relation introduces is an ambivalence in the act of interpretation. The pronominal I of the proposition cannot be made to address—in its own words—the subject of enunciation, for this is not personable, but remains a spatial relation within the schemata and strategies of discourse. The meaning of the utterance is quite literally neither the one nor the other. This ambivalence is

> emphasized when we realize that there is no way that the content of the proposition will reveal the structure of its positionality; no way that context can be mimetically read off from the content.[28]

The ambivalent nature of the utterance makes it impossible to read the context mimetically. The example of the structure of enunciation serves in Bhabha as a metaphor to describe cultural enunciation too. He tackles the problem of mimesis at the point of enunciation itself. If his proposal that no context can be mimetically read off from the content is acceptable to us, many other lines of argument in his writings become clearer. An extension of this argument about the ambivalent nature of enunciation is that any claim for originality or purity of culture is "untenable."[29]

Locating the Problem of Culture as the Problem of Enunciation

Bhabha's proposal to locate the problem of culture as the problem of enunciation of culture is important for the postcolonial studies especially as it counters any attempt at appropriation and vulgarization. This problem of difference, as seen in the resistance of the colonised people to the language and the religion of the colonisers, questions the colonial cultural authority, or we could even say, it already questioned the colonial authority in those days.

An extension of this argument can be seen in Bhabha's proposal to distinguish between the concepts of 'cultural diversity' and 'cultural difference.' The idea of cultural diversity, which has been an important issue for the contemporary theory sees culture as an "empirical object," it is a "category of comparative ethics, aesthetics, ethnology," it is the "recognition of a pre-given cultural contents and customs," and it entertains such ideas as "cultural exchange" or the "culture of humanity"; it believes in the existence of separate "totalized cultures that live unsullied by the intertextuality of their historical locations, safe in the Utopianism of a mythic memory of a unique collective identity." (34) Refusing to accept this idea of different cultures, Bhabha defines cultural difference as "the process of the *enunciation* of culture as 'knowledge*able*,' authoritative, adequate to the constructions of systems of cultural identification." (34) It is the moment of enunciation which is important here, and which problematizes any easy understanding of culture. Bhabha talks about the limit-text of culture, and of the "need to think the limit of culture as a problem of the enunciation of cultural difference." (34) He thus problematizes easy comparison of cultures yet does not reject transactions over the cultural borders. Hence the use of the metaphor of enunciation. The meaning is determined not just by what is stated but also by the context in which the statement is made:

> The analytic of cultural difference intervenes to transform the scenario of articulation—not simply to disclose the rationale of political discrimination. It changes the position of enunciation and the relations of address within it; not only what is said but where it is said; not simply the logic of articulation but the *topos* of enunciation. The aim of cultural difference is to rearticulate the sum of knowledge from the perspective of the signifying position of the minority that resists totalization—the repetition that will not return as the same, the minus-in-origin that results in political and discursive strategies where adding to does not add up but serves to disturb the calculation of power and knowledge producing other spaces of subaltern signification.[30]

Thus in the analytic of cultural difference, "not only what is said but where it is said" is of great significance, and presumably this is what makes the location of culture important for Bhabha's arguments. The calculation of power and knowledge is disturbed by the 'other spaces of subaltern signification.'

Thus for Bhabha, the methods of signification used by the colonial enterprise as well as the resistant notes raised by the other subaltern spaces are equally important to show us that power does not always operate the way it is supposed to. To make this clear he uses an array of concepts which are inspired by the psychoanalytical discourse.

It is among these spaces of subaltern culture that we come across the presence of hybridity. Hybridity is not a negative term in Bhabha. It is that which gives him a glimpse of the communities that live together in a manner quite different from the modern idea of community, such as the nation. It is something that operates between the accepted binaries such as the centre and the periphery. It is a 'cultural construction' of nationness that he is interested in. This cultural construction is 'more hybrid in the articulation of cultural differences and identifications—gender, race or class—than can be represented in any hierarchical or binary structuring of social antagonism.'[31]

Bhabha shows, thus, that the presence of hybridity[32] and the enunciatory nature of culture make it impossible to talk about culture without ambivalence. Even when the other cultures were presented without ambivalence it is still possible to notice the presence of ambivalence, of despotic fear in the construction of images and the stereotype which the colonial literature has produced.

For Bhabha then, these three issues are central especially when he approaches the various kinds of narrations: the impossibility of reading the cultural scene mimetically from forms of cultural representation, the ambivalent nature of images constructed through narrations and the fear lurking behind the construction of the stereotypes of the other. The first issue has been discussed already in the earlier paragraphs. If in dealing with cultural representations we are looking for the correct image of identity, we are going to be disillusioned because Bhabha sees an act of 'doubling' at the moment of identification.[33] It is the doubling of identity in the form of personal identity and the psychoanalytical concept of identification. For Bhabha, the image of identity marks the point of identification, and it is ambivalent in nature:

> The access to the image of identity is only ever possible in the *negation* of any sense of originality or plenitude; the process of displacement and differentiation (absence/presence, representation/repetition) renders it a liminal reality. The image is at once a metaphoric substitution, an illusion of presence, and by that same token a metonym, a sign of its absence and loss. (51)

This construction of the image as being at once an illusion of presence and a sign of its absence and loss reminds us how difficult it is to talk in terms of identity politics. Even his construction of the stereotype is based on this concept of the ambivalent image.

Ambivalence and Stereotypes

Much of the effectiveness of the colonial discourse has depended on the use of the stereotypical images to describe the 'other.' Stereotypes are the figures which fix the image of a subject in terms of categorizations that do not entertain variations. A stereotype is also something that is known for its repeatability. Since the possibility of re-presenting an image of the 'real' in a mimetic manner is questioned, the question of comparing the stereotype with the original is not raised by Bhabha. The ambivalent nature of the strategies used by the colonial power is revealed in its construction of the stereotypical images of the 'other.' The fear of the other inspires the negation of the other by way of such stereotypes. This is discussed by Bhabha in "The Other Question: Stereotype, Discrimination, and the Discourse of Colonialism."[34] This ambivalence of the stereotype is located, according to him, in the process of anxious repetition which the stereotype, as a strategy of representation, calls forth. It is

> as if the essential duplicity of the Asiatic or the bestial sexual licence of the African that needs no proof, can never really, in discourse, be proved. . . . It is the force of ambivalence that gives the colonial stereotype its currency: ensures its repeatability in changing historical and discursive conjunctures; informs its strategies of individuation and marginalization; produces that effect of probabilistic truth and predictability which, for the stereotype, must always be in *excess* of what can be empirically proved or logically construed. (66)

Yet this tendency to create stereotypes can be seen even among those who have been colonised. The strategies of marginalization are used even in other power structures and the dominant even in the postcolonial context make the strategic use of the stereotypes in order to control and subjugate the other gender, class and caste. That is why the stereotype of traditional Indian woman and especially the stereotype of Brahmin widow are often used as prescriptive images that gloss over the pain of complying with the demands of a certain version of tradition or religion. Repetition can also be used as a technique to re-write the image that is generally created by a stereotype. And this is what happens to the image of a Brahmin widow in one of the novels written by Shashi Deshpande.

On Incorporating 'Third World Literature' into the Tradition of the Great English Books

The above discussions have made it clear to us why the contents of cultural enunciation cannot be mimetically read off and why an image cannot be considered as something which nonambivalently denotes a point of identification and how the repetition of the stereotypes only stems from the desire to give rise to a form of probabilistic truth. With these two strands of explanation, we can now go back to one of the early essays of Bhabha, where he makes similar observations in the context of literary criticism. This is one of the few places, where we can definitely notice Bhabha the literary critic at work, rather than Bhabha, the culture critic. This is also one of those essays which is directly associated with the question of incorporating the so-called 'Third-World Literature' into the Great Tradition of English literature.

The essay I have in mind is "Representation and the Colonial Text: A Critical Exploration of Some Forms of Mimeticism."[35] Bhabha identifies here three schools of criticism: Leavisian Universalist criticism, Nationalist criticism and the Althusserian ideological analysis. His conclusion in each case is that they are basically essentialist in nature, although he makes some kind of concession to the Althusserian ideological analysis which, according to him, does take into consideration a 'de-centred totality.' Bhabha finds that Universalist criticism tries to appropriate and relativize every other form of literature from the colonial (and postcolonial) society in terms of one particular tradition of literature, and then, elevates these literatures to the status of Literature. Yet, in the context of colonial literature, Bhabha finds that even the Nationalist critics share the same critical stance as the universalists because both these forms of criticism are basically tied to the question of representation and that of the image analysis. If the universalist critic searches for the original authentic vision, that reflects reality, by overcoming differences of race, class, gender and other contradictions, the particular form of nationalist criticism expects representation to be true to the particular reality. In other words, universalist criticism believes in the mimetic re-presentation of the reality in an objective manner while the nationalist criticism is overwhelmingly concerned about the idea of the correctness or the inappropriateness of an image in colonial literature. He finds both forms of criticism prescriptive in nature.[36] Even Althusser's concept of ideology is ultimately linked to a monolithic idea of Literature. This in spite of the fact that ideological criticism recognises the 'autonomy and materiality' of representation.[37]

Colonial Contramodernity and the Postcolonial Critic

It is clear from the above discussion that Bhabha has primarily used the postmodern, poststructural theoretical tools to discuss issues that could be termed postcolonial in nature. How does he connect himself to the postcolonial discourse if the tools are borrowed entirely from the field of contemporary western theory? By breaking the myth of the unity and the authority of the colonial text he has shown that the seeds of instability were already there in the project of colonialism. He wishes that the postmodernist theorists take this into account because without this knowledge, their own methods of questioning modernity will be incomplete:

> the encounters and negotiations of differential meanings and values within 'colonial' textuality, its governmental discourses and cultural practices, have anticipated, *avant la lettre*, many of the problematics of signification and judgement that have become current in contemporary theory—aporia, ambivalence, indeterminacy, the question of discursive closure, the threat to agency, the status of intentionality, the challenge to 'totalizing' concepts, to name but a few.[38]

This is a different way of connecting the postmodern with the postcolonial where the former is not seen as the precursor of the latter. There is a need to take the postcolonial arguments seriously because they offer different perspectives on the issue of assumed power relationships. To those who ask 'What is postcolonial about a critic like Bhabha? Is it not a rehash of poststructuralism, deconstruction or psychoanalytical register?' his answer is quite clear[39]:

> My use of poststructuralist theory emerges from this post-colonial contramodernity. I attempt to represent a certain defeat, or even an impossibility, of the 'West' in its authorization of the 'idea' of colonization. Driven by the subaltern history of the margins of modernity—rather than by the failures of logocentricism—I have tried, in some small measure, to revise the known, to rename the postmodern from the position of the postcolonial.[40]

Yet migration, diaspora, displacement, relocation are the important attributes of this subaltern history that Bhabha asks us to be conscious of, while studying the construction of culture and the invention of tradition. The transnational dimension of cultural transformation makes it difficult to accept easily the myth of such unifying discourses as the nation, peoples, authentic folk tradition but is he privileging migration over geographical rootedness? In other words, is it necessary to be a migrant to understand the post-colonial situation?

On Mimicry and Repetition

While accepting that most of the hybrid manifestation of the subaltern cultures are to be seen in the interstices of the metropolitan centres, one has to remember that the condition of being marginalised does not exclude accessibility to different versions of power. Bhabha rightly points out the differences and antagonisms that exist in the space occupied by those who share the history of domination. However, he does not seem to remember that even among the postcolonial subjects power structures operate in different ways in different contexts. Bhabha pays lot of attention to the condition of those who occupy the margins of the metropolitan centres but often forgets the contemporary contexts of the various postcolonial societies.

He indicates that repetition is the language of colonial fantasy. Stereotypes are repeated. Mimic men such as Anund Messeh in "Signs taken for Wonders" repeat the words of the European missionaries in a context that makes repetition become ambivalent in nature. It is my argument that repetition is not only the language of colonial fantasy. Repetition is also the language of domination which tries to create a ripple-like pattern. It is possible that the dominated in different configurations become the dominant agents and that the sly civility of the people gathered under a tree in Delhi questioning the English Book can very well be repeated after many years in a postcolonial context in order to subalternise the minority communities of the nation.[41] While claiming sympathy for the subaltern history of the margin, Bhabha must remind himself that margins too are protean in nature.

It is in "Signs taken for Wonders," that we come across the use of the terms hybrid and mimicry in connection with colonial authority. This is one more occasion where Bhabha shows that the demand of the colonial power to be shown as 'unitary' and 'nondialogic' in nature is unsettled by the reaction of the natives even when the reaction appears to be in the form of mimicry. The unsettling of the authority occurs when the natives question another native—a mimic missionary?—Anund Messeh, "one of the earliest Indian catechists." They are shown the 'English Book,' which is the translated version of the Bible, and the natives cannot comprehend the existence of such a book:

> The native questions quite literally turn the origin of the book into an enigma. First: *how can the word of God come from the flesh-eating mouths of the English*?—a question that faces the unitary and universalist assumption of authority with the cultural difference of its historical moment of enunciation. And later: *how can it be the European Book, when we believe that it is God's gift to us? He sent it to us at Hurdwar.* (116)

Anund Messeh and the people collected under a tree outside Delhi, are an example for the historical instance that questions the originality of the English book (for Bhabha, the Bible which is translated into the native language is an English book), and the purity of its culture. In his endeavour to deconstruct the idea of inherent originality of the colonial power, he puts forth the hypothesis that all cultural statements are constructed in contradictory and ambivalent space of enunciation.

I would like to extend this assumption to the scene of fundamentalism in India, where once again cultural purity is stressed and the minority communities are seen as the mimic foreigners following a foreign religion. In such a situation, the very questions that Bhabha is raising here can be transported from the colonial scene to a postcolonial scene and the subversive questions of the natives become the discriminatory questions coming from a dominant culture. The crux of the matter, if we take a look at Bhabha's quotation from the Missionary Register is not the "tasteless fact that most Hindus were vegetarians" (which is a bit of an exaggeration) but that the Europeans ate "cow's flesh."

The questions asked by the natives can be subverted by the native fundamentalist to ridicule the minority figure in contemporary India: How can you belong to India if you believe in a European religion or if you eat "flesh" like a European? In destroying the myth of the originality and the unitary nature of the colonial power, Bhabha seems to have paid less attention to the danger of presenting a unified native culture and also to have overlooked the implications these questions will have in the field of social discourse in the contemporary scene.[42] The hybrid in this scene is the minority figure who is a *native-and-yet-not-a-native.*[43] As both Robert Young and Benita Parry have argued, at times it is assumed by Bhabha that there was no recording of resistance either to the imposition of the colonialism or to that of the evangelising mission among the natives.[44] The fact that there are only 2.43% Christians in India today is a strong evidence to prove that the evangelising mission was not really successful.[45]

It is not my intention to suggest that the minority does not figure in Bhabha's theorizing. The marginalized minority appears repeatedly in all his arguments and it is in fact, the experience of being a minority which is very important in Bhabha's articulations. It is not even my intention to suggest that Bhabha is not aware of the tensions in many of the postcolonial societies. I would like to make use of Benita Parry's comments about the problems in the current theories of colonial discourse in the form of a question. Don't these articulations about colonization extend the phenomenon of colonization "as an explanatory notion applicable to all situations of structural domination, [and] are directed at formulating a grand theory valid for each and every discursive system of discrimination and oppression"?[46] It is indeed my argument that different situations of structural domination do exist. There is always the possibility of the victim of one kind of exploitation acting as the agent of oppression in another system of discrimination. More precisely these power structures are so linked with one another that mentioning the 'subaltern history of the margins of modernity' without bearing in mind the complex structures of the postcolonial societies in the contemporary world, will not be very helpful. However, Bhabha seems to have noticed that a privileging of the subaltern without differentiation leads to another form of essentialism, because, in one of his recent essays he mentions that oppressive control 'may be exerted by state institutions against minority groups, or by patriarchal and class structures within minority communities themselves.'[47] Problematizing the concept of subaltern is one of the interests of another postcolonial critic, Gayatri Chakravorty Spivak, too. It is with the 'subaltern' as a bridge word that we move on to an analysis and interpretation of her writings.

Gayatri Chakravorty Spivak and the Teacher of Literature
Spivak and the Concept-Metaphor Margin

Like Said and Bhabha, Gayatri Chakravorty Spivak too is involved in the project of deconstructing the centre-margin binary. It is not easy to categorise Spivak as representing any branch of the contemporary theory exclusively. As the editors of *The Spivak Reader* correctly point out, her competence in different areas of philosophical, cultural and political thinking have created an international audience which is heterogeneous in nature:

> During the past fifteen years, her career has followed a complex intellectual trajectory through a deeply feminist perspec-

> tive on deconstruction, the Marxist critique of imperialism and colonial discourse, and the critique of race in relation to nationality, ethnicity, the status of the migrant, and what it might mean to identify a nation or a cultural form as post-colonial in a neocolonial' world.[48]

Even though Spivak resists 'critical taxonomies,'[49] one could argue that her early career is marked by her interest in feminist issues, and these issues are confronted by her with the tools of deconstruction and Marxist theories.[50] A combined use of these two theoretical formulations can be seen in her construction of the term 'woman.'[51] She shows, for example, how a feminist approach to the traditional Marxist terms 'use, exchange and surplus values,' can deconstruct the meaning of production itself because, "[t]he possession of a tangible place of production in the womb situates the woman as an agent in any theory of production."[52] This kind of radical approach to theories, in fact, shapes her interpretation of the short story "Stanadayini" by Mahasweta Devi, which has been mentioned in Chapter One and which will be discussed in one of the following sections.[53]

The concept-metaphor of margin has intrigued her from the beginning of her career. At different stages of her academic career she problematizes the concept of 'margin' in many different ways. One of the early essays, where we see her using arguments from Marxist, feminist, deconstructivistic theoretical contexts, is her "Explanation and Culture: Marginalia."[54] Written in 1979, it already indicates the future directions Spivak is going to take. While mentioning the generally assumed hierarchy between the private (feminine) and the public (masculine) spheres, she indicates how a feminist handling of this dichotomy would require a deconstructive reading which would in turn show the interweaving of the private and the public. However, in deconstructive practice itself, displacing existing hierarchies does not necessarily mean a reversal of the hierarchy. She maintains that both deconstruction and feminism have the common cause of 'paying attention to marginality' because of 'a suspicion that what is at the center often hides a repression.' (104) This is not yet a rejection of the centre-margin binary.

In fact, the expectation that she use the 'marginal' card is met with resistance.[55] In the next phase of critical attitude towards this binary too, instead of either reversing or rejecting the dichotomy between center and margin completely, she problematizes these two terms by pointing out that the center at times invites selected members from the margin to be its inhabitants so that the rest of the margin can be marginalised:

> the only way I can hope to suggest how the center itself is marginal is by not remaining outside in the margin and pointing my accusing finger at the center. I might do it rather by implicating myself in that center and sensing what politics make it marginal. . . . a deconstructivist can use herself (assuming one is at one's own disposal) as a shuttle between the center (inside) and the margin (outside) and thus narrate a displacement.[56]

Ten years later, however, she seems to be taking stock of her position on the issue of margin, and decides that even this kind of stand is one which accords more importance to the center. In an interview, she indicates once again her disagreement with those who wish to locate her as part of the margin and suggests that the concept-metaphor margin could be used in a different way—"as not simply opposed to the center but as an accomplice of the centre."[57] She deflates the tendency to romanticize marginalization by reminding us of its functional aspect in a text:

> I am beginning to think of the concept-metaphor of margins more and more in terms of the history of margins: the place for the argument, the place for the critical moment, the place of interests for assertions rather than a shifting of the center as I suggested in that earlier essay.[58]

This combination of meanings for the term margin—as being an accomplice as well as the 'place for critical moment'—can be well used for my own argument that the centre-margin binary loses its sense if we remind ourselves that what is marginal in one context can occupy the position of the 'center' in a different context.[59]

This will threaten the uniform use of this binary and demand for other explanations. This also supports my later discussions of Deshpande, which are meant to show how even the broad distinguishing mark 'marginalized woman,' in the particular closed-world created by the novelist gets differentiated into 'different women,' thereby defying any attempt at introducing such binaries into the world of her novels.

If we extend this argument further, it would mean that in the context of postcolonial arguments, due to this suspicion of the binaries, simple divisions such as bad colonizers and good natives have no place. Just as Bhabha shows that the so-called authoritarian presence of the British and the discourse of power the empire employed were already flawed and divided, so does Gayatri Chakravorty Spivak point out that the elite natives found the structure of the colonial institution useful to strengthen their own positions.[60] There has already been a lot of research done to indicate how the elite of the country had a definite role to play in strengthening the hands of the colonisers especially in matters such as gender, class and caste constructions. Spivak's unique contribution in this field is the introduction of the concept of the gendered subaltern. In view of the novels that will be discussed in Chapter 4, it is the nature of the gendered subaltern, her silence and the way in which she has been silenced are the important issues that are going to be discussed in this section on Spivak.

Deconstructing Subaltern Historiography

It may not be wrong to say that the work of a group of Indian historians forming the Subaltern Studies Group has been instrumental in giving currency to the term 'subaltern' in contemporary theoretical discussions.[61] In his Preface to the first volume of Subaltern Studies, Ranajit Guha, the editor, indicates that this series of historiographical writings concentrates on the subordinate groups; it is in a way an acknowledgement of their claims for making history as opposed to the elite representation of history. In this context he uses the word 'subaltern' as

> a name for the general attribute of subordination in South Asian society whether this is expressed in terms of class, caste, age, gender and office or in any other way.[62]

Thus the term 'subaltern' indicates a heterogeneous group. Spivak, who upholds the project on the one hand, critiques it on the other because she finds that the gendered subaltern as a subject does not find any place in the construction of the agency of the other subaltern groups. In her "Subaltern Studies: Deconstructing Historiography," she discloses the discrepancies in the work when one reads against the grain.[63]

Spivak's arguments can be explained at two levels. First of all she feels that the Subaltern Studies Group has been inspired by the theoretical formulations of poststructuralists like Foucault and Barthes. Even though the historiographic practice of re-writing history from the perspective of the marginalised is in principle a poststructuralist practice, the unwitting engagement of the group with ideas such as 'consciousness' and 'subjectivity' reveals discrepancy in the project.[64]

The discrepancy lies in the fact that the idea of 'subaltern consciousness' is essentialist in nature and such an essentialist stance is against the anti-humanist critique of the poststructuralist collaborators of this kind of historiographical work. Spivak's own critique is aimed at both the Subaltern Group as well as the contemporary Western anti-humanist theory. With regard to the Subaltern Group, the critique is that they do not take into consideration the subjectivity of the female insurgent and with regard to the larger theoretical works it is that they show a 'symptomatic blank' when it comes to the question of the colonial enterprise. Spivak points out that the interest of the radical intellectual in the West in subaltern issues either renders the oppressed that same subjectivity that she/he criticizes or removes any possibility of representability; and this contradiction can only be explained by the fact that these intellectuals are not well-versed in the history of imperialism.[65] When we remember that humanism was an integral part of the European Enlightenment philosophy, and when we think of the connection between this Enlightenment and imperialism, then we realize that an anti-humanist critique cannot ignore colonialism.[66] It is for this reason that there is a necessity for recognising postcolonialism as an essential part of any contemporary literary theory.

The history of imperialism, as interpreted by Spivak, manifests itself as the "epistemic violence that constituted/effaced a subject that was obliged to cathect (occupy in response to a desire) the space of the Imperialists' self-consolidating other."[67] A corollary, in a way, of Said's explanation for the concept of the Orient, this presence of the constituted/effaced 'subject' makes the question of representation highly complicated in postcolonial discussions. Should one try to retrieve this subjectivity? Is it possible to make a strategic use of an essential idea of the 'subject'?

These questions can help us grasp Spivak's dissatisfaction with the work of the Subaltern Studies Group. It is her fear that while trying to restore consciousness to the subordinate, they have overlooked the subjectivity of the woman.[68] Woman, who is so carefully included in the works of the group, also comes under a sort of subject-effacing discourse. In her argument, even though the instrumentality of the woman is mentioned, these historians of the subaltern do not pause to reflect upon the many moments where 'woman' can be seen as the one with an effaced identity. In other words, they do not stop to think of the subalternity of women. While constructing a discourse for the subalternity of the insurgent movements, these historians of the Subaltern Studies group forget to take into consideration the female subaltern consciousness: "Male subaltern and historian are here united in the common assumption that the procreative sex is a species apart, scarcely if at all to be considered a part of civil society." ("Subaltern Studies: Deconstructing Historiography" 217) It is this concern that makes her ask the now famous question "Can the Subaltern Speak?"[69] Even though the context is that of a young woman who has committed suicide, the question still echoes the anguish that the subaltern woman is not able to make herself heard, that she is not able to take part in the speech act.[70]

Who is the Gendered Subaltern?

Her critique of the contemporary theory is also aimed at their use of the concept of representation. She points out to the Marxian use of the terms *vertreten* and *darstellen*. Spivak suggests that these poststructuralists have overlooked the category of representation in its two senses, *Vertretung* and *Darstellung*.[71] In her view, to account for the micrological texture of power one has to "note how the staging of the world in representation—its scene of writing, its *Darstellung*—dissimulates the choice of and need for 'heroes,' paternal proxies, agents of power—*Vertretung*."[72] This essay has to be seen as a reaction to the claim that the oppressed can speak and know their condition. She points out that there is a difference between the idea of substituting (Vertretung) and that of representing (Darstellung). Who represents the subaltern—a group comprising of 'subsistence farmers, unorganized peasant labor, the tribals and the communities of zero workers on the street or in the country side'?(84) How can the gendered subaltern be represented?

It is in this context that she brings out the issue of the female subaltern because, under patriarchal social structures, any form of exploitation is doubly complicated. In such a context, learning to represent the subaltern involves the process of learning to speak to them which in turn demands that we unlearn many things:

> In seeking to learn to speak to (rather than listen to or speak for) the historically muted subject of the subaltern woman, the postcolonial intellectual *systematically* 'unlearns' female privilege. This systematic unlearning involves learning to critique postcolonial discourse with the best tools it can provide and not simply substituting the lost figure of the colonized. (91)

It is then as a process of unlearning that she critiques postcolonial discourse even though she sees herself involved in such a discourse.

Yet, Spivak does not make it clear to us who the gendered subaltern is. Is it the urban sub-proletarian female who is caught between 'pre-existing structures of patriarchy and transnational capitalism'?[73] Is it the prostitute, who is also a 'bonded labourer' and is forced to sell her body so that the master who owns her gets money?[74] Is it the Brahmin woman who becomes a breast-feeding machine to the landlord's household so that the women of the family retain their 'figure'? Or is it constituted by the tribal communities spread in different parts of the country who have not really been able to feel the difference between imperialism and nationalism? Although her different essays make it clear that all these categories could be described as subaltern, in some places she is more specific as to what, for her, constitutes the subaltern. To make things clearer, perhaps, it would be better that we ask "What space does the subaltern occupy?" instead of "Who is the subaltern?" This question is linked with the question of both colonization and independence:

> the event of political independence can be automatically assumed to stand between colony and decolonization as an unexamined good that operates a reversal . . . it must be admitted that there is always a space in the new nation that cannot share in the energy of this reversal. This space had no established agency of traffic with the culture of imperialism. Paradoxically, this space is also outside of organized labor, below the attempted reversals of capital logic. Conventionally, this space is described as the habitat of the *subproletariat* or the *subaltern*.[75]

As we have already seen, Spivak differentiates even in this space, the space occupied by the subaltern woman. This space, according to the discussions charted out above, can mean a space of silence, of an incomplete speech act.

Alien Arguments and a Woman's Text about the Subaltern

It is in her "A Representation of the Subaltern: A Woman's Text from the Third World,"[76] that she shows one literary instance of the silence as well as the loneliness of the subaltern woman. This is actually one of the earliest instances where she shows how a text from the 'Third World' can bring the elite methodologies to a crisis. As in many of her articles, she clears out a space for herself before she starts the process of 'wrenching out' a 'sympathetic text' and putting it within 'alien arguments.'[77] She differentiates the teacher of literature from the historian. It is from this subject-position as the teacher of literature that she operates here. Even though "A Literary Representation of the Subaltern" is written two years after "Deconstructing Historiography," it shows both continuity with the previously written essay as well as suggests new approaches.[78] The historian in the subaltern historiography creates a place for the subaltern in historiography, thereby going against the norm of traditional history writing. The feminist literary critic, however, focuses her attention on the subaltern of the subaltern who has been denied subjectivity, even the strategic use of the subjectivity by the historian. Spivak does not say that the two positions annul each other. The historian and the teacher of literature can, through their different attitudes to history and literature, bring one another to crisis.[79] Bringing one another to crisis can mean a productive enterprise in the case of Spivak.

Her reading of the subaltern in literature must interrupt the construction of the subaltern in historiography. When the author of fiction claims historic accuracy—in terms of research supporting the historical moment of the fiction's world, and when a historian 'imagines a historical moment, within which shadowy named characters, backed up by some counter-insurgent or dominant-gender textual material, have their plausible being,'[80] the difference between the two writers is not very great. "A Literary Representation of the Subaltern" is a reminder to the author of subaltern historiography that history is also fictive. To interrupt this world of 'fact' which is also a narrative world, she picks up a woman from the world of fiction. Once again, there is a demand on the reader to be more vigilant as she/he reads.

To my mind, Spivak's method of putting the literary representation of the subaltern amidst the elite theories is slightly at variance with the first statements on the difference between the historian and the author. However, these statements accompany one as Spivak reads Mahasweta Devi's reading of her own work. In that specific style of connecting transnationally, Spivak is drawing lines between subaltern historiography, elite theories and the story of a gendered subject. One can once again hear the anguished cry "Can the subaltern speak?" written into the text of the essay as she makes Jashoda the breast-giver, the professional mother confront the many prominent contemporary theories. Since it will not suit the purposes of the present analysis to mention all the cases of 'theory-testing' by Spivak, I would only mention how she moves in this direction.

In the beginning of her analysis, she acknowledges that 'the authority of the author's reading still holds a certain glamor in the 'orthodox literary circles.' (246) She classifies her readers as follows: there is the reader from the orthodox literary circles elsewhere, who along with the dominant Indian reader will be in favour of the authority of the author and would uphold the 'original vision.' There is then the second group of readers: 'the dominant radical reader in the Anglo-U.S. [who] reactively homogenizes the Third World and sees it only in the context of nationalism and ethnicity.' (246) In Spivak's view, these readers, who are students learning theory in the elite Indian institutions, are influenced by a kind of radical literary pedagogy found in the United States and to an extent in Britain. That is why in her own readings she takes up the subject-position of the teacher. A literary representation of the subaltern can become a tool in the hands of this teacher.

However, it must be said that such appellations as the 'teacher' are also vague and the use of such a term by a prominent critic could lead to an uncritical repetition of the term in other cases, making us forget that there are different kinds of teachers and that the teaching conditions vary in different situations and locations. Keeping in mind these reservations, we may still assert that Gayatri Chakravorty Spivak's gesture of placing a literary text in different theoretical contexts is a very complex as well as necessary step in shaping our 'attitude' towards literatures coming from the post-colonial world.

By way of this example Spivak shows that the usual theoretical models are inadequate when used in the context of the 'Third World' literary text. It can be asked how one specific story written by a Bengali writer testifies to the inadequacies of the elite theories while responding to the subaltern representation?[81] It appears as though this is one more instance that proves to us that '[a]lthough a single example does not prove a case, a single counter-example makes human generalizations imperfect.'[82]

The short story taken up here is that of Mahasweta Devi. Devi's "Breast-Giver" is about a poor Brahmin woman who is employed by the landlord and his wife to be the wet-nurse for their grandchildren. For Jashoda, nursing other's children is a profession. Spivak, to start with, takes into consideration the author's own reading of this story. Even though in Spivak's reading Jashoda is the subaltern woman, her subjectivity is not taken into consideration by Mahasweta Devi. Mahasweta Devi considers this story to be a parable of India.[83] Spivak, the teacher, rejects this reading of "Breast-Giver" because it is not 'useful from the perspective of a study of the subaltern.' (244) For the author however, Jashoda, the subaltern, the professional mother stands for India. But we remember, the narrative of nationalism is an off-shoot of the narrative of imperialism and it has existed by excluding the resistance of the subaltern.[84] To make Mahasweta Devi's reading acceptable one has to overlook the story of the subaltern woman because she can function only as a part of the parable.

If the author's reading fails to give voice to the subaltern woman, a certain version of Marxist feminism becomes equally inadequate when confronted by a poor Brahmin woman. The traditional hierarchy of the caste and class structures are called into question by Jashoda. Spivak's warning to those who try to globalize Marxism is that in the world of Jashoda,

> when the economic as such (here shown in terms of the woman's body) enters in, mothers are divided, women can exploit, not merely dominate. Ideology sustains and interpenetrates this operation of exploitation. (252)

This is something applicable not only to Marxist analyses but also to different forms of feminist interpretation, because very often feminism, even though conscious of culture specificities, even though cautious not to generalize all women, tends, nevertheless, to see the women from the same class and cultural background as forming a homogenous group. The figure of Jashoda defies such a categorisation.

From a Marxist-feminist perspective, Spivak moves on to testing a liberal-feminist position, a position which many of Shashi Deshpande's novels appear to endorse. This kind of feminism seems to operate across national boundaries and, according to Spivak, can be detected in the tendency to appropriate Third World texts in translation in the curricula. In contrast to the faction of feminists which tries to homogenize, this other section of feminists is aware of differences and tries to make coalitions. But this again gives rise to questions: Who can theorize about the subaltern? Can an elite historian theorize about the subaltern?

It is important to note here that she refers to the oppositions women/black/subaltern vs. men/white/elite. These opposites are used in order to suggest that vigilance, rather than identity claim, is very essential because claims such as "only the subaltern can know the subaltern, only women can know women and so on, cannot be held as a theoretical presupposition either, for it predicates the possibility of knowledge on identity." (253-54) At the same time vigilance is necessary because very often those who can be denoted by the first group of terms mentioned above, also share the privileges of those in the second group What has to be made clear here is that Spivak is not making her arguments on the basis of identity. Once again she points out that there is a need for interruption: identity and knowledge should bring each other to crisis.

It is in this connection that she takes up the liberal feminist ideal of the development of female subjectivity. The story of Jashoda, the wet-nurse, belies the expectations of a feminist who awaits liberation in terms of 'growth in consciousness.' (257) Jashoda has to work as a professional mother so that the daughters-in-law fulfil a certain idea of liberation, so that they go out of the boundaries of the house. It is due to their love of their bodies—they feared that breast-feeding would spoil their 'figure'—that they accepted the services of this other woman. Liberation in terms of the growth of consciousness does not form a part of the story of the subaltern in this case.

In fact, in Spivak's view, Jashoda herself is presented as 'constituted by patriarchal ideology.' This issue seems to be important not only for Mahasweta Devi, the author of this story, but also for Spivak herself. Looking at the past from the perspective of the present, we tend to forget many of the elements which shaped the dominant narrative of a certain epoch or of a certain society.[85] Spivak points out how Mahasweta Devi's position on feminism which is also influenced by Western branches of feminism can be differentiated from the ideology of her protagonist, who does not question the internalized elements of a patriarchal society.

I have tried to analyse as well as to react to Spivak's use of the many elite theories because, in my opinion, of all the critics mentioned here, she seems to be the only one giving us an instance of postcolonial 'practical'. criticism. Her interpretation can thus be used as a methodology for employing postcolonial theories in reading the novels of Shashi Deshpande. However, reading Spivak reading Mahasweta Devi, going with her in her journey that takes her to many areas of literary criticism, one is always struck by her constant attempt at as well as appeal for vigilance.

The Decolonizing Feminist

Her appeal for vigilance mainly comes through in many of her articles because she thinks of herself not just as a postcolonial critic but as the decolonizing feminist. Another role that she often takes up is that of the teacher. Her institutional location compels her to specify the nature of this location. She talks of herself as the teacher of the multicultural course. In a re-reading of the myths of Narcissus and Echo and their use by Ovid, she points out the difference between the postcolonial feminist and the cultural difference which marks her apart from her subaltern friends whom she is expected to represent. It is the figure of Echo that helps her articulate the relationship between the feminist and the subaltern woman. The Ovidian Echo was cursed and could only repeat only the last part of another individual's statement. In the end she turns into stone out of grief when Narcissus spurns her and falls into the pond to join his own image. This image of Echo is a neglected image unlike Narcissism which is an important concept in fields like psychoanalysis. Echo inspires Spivak's statement that the subaltern women cannot take part in the speech act whereby speech act is a 'transaction between the speaker and the listener.'[86] According to Spivak, the contemporary debates based on national identity exhibit a form of narcissism. She would rather that the decolonising feminist 'imitate' Echo: Echo had no alternative than to repeat. The feminist with the decolonizing mission has to recognise this fact and try to complete her speech act by repeating the subaltern's words and by not showing her own narcissism to the subaltern. Spivak lifts the story of Echo from the contemporary scene of oblivion and finds in her an ethical response to the question of the subaltern woman.

This is a way of telling the postcolonial feminists that unless they are careful. their representation of the subaltern will remain their own stories without bearing any element of the lives of the subaltern. This note of caution can be seen in her questions: 'Who decolonises? and how?'[87] These questions remind her of the involvement of the critic with the object of her investigation. However, as mentioned earlier, she prefers to be known as a teacher than as a critic. It is in her role of the teacher who teaches a multiculturalist course that she sensitively analyses the reception and the construction of a novel such as *Guide*. Methodologically her approach could be termed as a practical instance of the contrapuntal reading practice advocated by Said. To show how the student can be cautious, she juxtaposes the text with two kinds of non-literary investigations done among the 'temple dancers.' In contrast to the version of the ethnographer who at times generalises. the actual interviews of the *devadasis* shows that in the contemporary context too the academics' words about decolonizing the mind can be utterly meaningless. That is why she puts obstacles in the path of the too eager multiculturalist students.

Even though I have not made use of all her articles here, one could try to give a name to the kind of theorizing that Spivak has undertaken in the project of postcolonialism. Her representations do not take her to one single place; her constant referring to various sources leaves her divided—but in a very productive manner. Perhaps one could best explain her work by using the words of Derrida:

> Everything begins by referring back (*par le renvoi*), that is to say, does not begin; and once this breaking open or this partition divides, from the very start, every *renvoi*, there is not a single *renvoi* but from then on, always, a multiplicity of *renvois*, so many different traces referring back to other traces and to traces of others. This divisibility of the *envoi* has nothing negative about it, it is not a lack,. . . . This di-

> visibility or this difference is the condition for there being an *envoi*, possibly an *envoi* of being, a dispensation or a gift of being and time, of the present and of representation.[88]

The idea of movement can also be attached to the idea of travelling as many in the field of postcolonial studies seem to have done. What happens to the question of location, if one sees this process of 'referring back to other traces and to traces of others' as something that makes theories travel?[89] The question of location, and its effect on the theoretical positions of the critics have been issues which have attracted many postcolonial critics. Can the possibility of travelling, of choosing to be away from the location which was once colonial and which may still be experiencing the authority of neocolonialism, be a privilege?

The Question of Location and Other Perspectives Travelling Theories and Portable Oppressions[90]

A section of Said's *Culture and Imperialism* has the heading "The Voyage In and the Emergence of Opposition." (261) It is the 'voyage in' that has created an ethos for the presence of the postcolonial voices in the western academic sites. The earlier 'voyage out' of the colonials justifies the present 'voyage in.' The question though remains: Is it a privilege to take part in this 'voyage in'? Can the 'emergence of power' be still located in those postcolonial sites where the postcolonial intellect cannot talk in terms of the privilege of 'voyage in'? The many voices that are claimed to be postcolonial are often divided on the issue of difference in terms of location. Even when we reject any essentialist notion of identity, the geographical and institutional axes that influence the theoretical stances of an intellectual cannot be overlooked. The discordant voices of postcolonial discourse must be used to bring each other to crisis.

This does not mean that I am going to privilege a kind of 'native intellectualism.' I just want to point out that even when the postcolonial critics like Spivak ask 'Who speaks?,' the site from which she asks this question is marked as being privileged. It is true that a 'native' intellectual asking the same question is not much different from her. The question cannot but haunt all those who are involved in this kind of discourse. Yet this kind of questioning is not without an inherent sense of hierarchy. To use Rey Chow's words:

> the posing of the question ["Who speaks?"] itself is already a form of privilege, mostly affordable for those who can stand apart and view the world with altruistic concern. The question that this question cannot ask, since it is the condition of its own possibility, is the more fundamental one of the inequality between theory—the most sophisticated *speaking* instance, one might say—and the oppressed.[91]

I do not share Chow's view that the postcolonial critics that I have discussed 'view the world with altruistic concern.' However, one has to take into consideration the differences in the context of the speaker, even when the concern is the same. This is perfectly in tune with Bhabha's own comments about the nature of 'cultural enunciation.'

Even the migratory experience, the experience of living in the margins of the metropolitan centres may not be something that either appeals to or refers to the many subordinate cultures that exist in a postcolonial nation-state. Spivak's own role as the teacher or the teacher of multiculturalist course can be deconstructed in a situation where the students live in a multicultural context that is riven by communal disharmony. To have the privilege of teaching a multicultural syllabus is still a dream for many of the teachers. The assurance of the tenured professorship needs only to be contrasted with the 'reality' of teaching 'English' literature as a part-time lecturer on an ad-hoc basis in a postcolonial India.

The priorities seem different in these different cases. This calls forth a revisioning of the positions held by many of these critics if only to suit the context in which they are being used. It is necessary to use theories in changed forms; it is necessary to see their use in decolonizing the mind but then this process of decolonizing has to follow its own course.

Postcolonial Conjuncturalism

Just as Spivak makes us aware of the inadequacy of various elite theories when they come in contact with the literary representation of a subaltern woman, so are the various strands of postcolonial theories inadequate if the discordant notes as well as the differences in locations are overlooked. Even though the postcolonial critics whom I have mentioned do not generalise, their prominence in the western academic field might give rise to a kind of 'synecdochization' of the postcolonial situation. The answer for this sort of dilemma lies in reemphasising the ambiguity of the 'post' in the postcolonial as done by Ruth Frankenberg and Latha Mani.[92] Based on Lawrence Grossberg's use of the term 'postmodern conjuncturalism,' they wish to use the expression 'postcolonial conjuncturalism.'[93] I agree that the concept 'postcolonial' needs to be

> carefully specified, used to describe moments, social formations, subject positions and practices which arise out of an unfolding axis of colonization/decolonization, interwoven with the unfolding of other axes, in *uneven, unequal* relations with one another. (361)

They try to differentiate the various axes that the postcolonial subject uses to define herself/himself in different locations such as India, England and the USA. In an 'autobiographical riff' Lata Mani raises the issue of the biographies of the 'theorists most associated with the term'—Said, Bhabha and Spivak—and considers how she could use these biographies as one of the strategies in her explorations of the differences which are contained by the term postcolonial. This would mean that she explores the 'historical-intellectual and political biographies' of these three theorists, "tracing the disjunctions between their own formulation of the issues and the politics of their reception within the Western academy." (350)

One could make use of this strategy in a different way in a different context, remembering that the axes of postcolonial studies are 'unequal and uneven' in differently specific locations. My wish to position Shashi Deshpande in postcolonial arguments—not forgetting the different axes that Frankenberg and Mani mention—is basically a way of reacting from a different location. I agree with Mary E. John when she says that the way theories travel and the way they are received are important for arriving at a useful understanding of postcoloniality.[94] In her proposal to consider theories as being "partial (not relative), composite (not universal)," (38) I find a good argument for my own presentation of the postcolonial theoretical positions.

Selecting one particular example of a novelist from India, who herself restricts the milieu of her stories to a particular class and gender, has in it all the elements of a provincial, essentialist kind of literary criticism. Nevertheless, upholding only the familiar and the local is not the purpose of this study. If postmodernism reacted against universalizing and globalizing issues, recent developments in the field of postcolonialism show that theorists now are reacting to postmodernism differently. Going back to Mary E. John, we tend to agree with her that it is possible to pay attention to theories as they travel without compelling them to be either wholly global or completely specific.[95] She questions the very notion of considering theories as unbiased articulations which have nothing to do with institutions and wants instead to conceive of a theory as being composite, "made up of a network of assumptions, disciplinary affiliations, historical sedimentations, and global connections that have never been fixed or uniform but that evolve in an uneven, power-laden flux." (38) Taking the same example as I have, where Spivak reads the work of the Subaltern Studies Group deconstructively, John tries to make clear what she means by the partial nature of a theory. Spivak's consideration of strategy, in particular, becomes an instance, in John's view, of how travelling theories stumble when they enter new territories:

> It is when a theory recognizes its entrance onto territory for which concepts are not ready at hand, starts to stumble over the new ground, that a theory can be said to be traveling well. Inserting the additional concept of strategy—not determined in advance—is one way of coming to terms with the partial nature of the theory one working within—in this case, de-

> construction's partiality for levels of abstraction that bypass more specific issues. (43)

In a way this is an answer to the postmodernist tendency of reacting to universal theories by deflecting the question of universality. Considering theories as being partial and composite is a very attractive proposal and in fact prevents such easy divisions of location as West and non-West. Yet, one has to remember that very often, theories travel only in one direction.[96] John's formulations are nevertheless very useful if we recognize that she calls for attention to specific issues, and also that the concept of travelling theory does not exclude the idea of change—change that occurs depending on the specificities of the place that receives these theories.

This is a good starting point for debunking any consideration of postcolonial theorizing as something that applies universally to all the postcolonial locations. The question of the politics of location has to be seen in the light of the question of the politics of representation. Stuart Hall talks about the necessity for shifting emphasis on the 'politics' of representation because he too, just as John sees a theory as being composite, sees questions regarding representation in a culture as being 'formative' and not merely 'expressive.'[97] What I see as a common element in these two arguments is the flexibility of these theoretical positions to include differences. Hall's comments that the term 'black' should be seen as a construct can be used to interpret various issues connected with the postcolonial subject also. The oppositional positions which question at times the articulations of Said, Bhabha and Spivak arise because of the urgent need to recognise the element of diversity in subject positions:

> What is at issue here is the recognition of the extraordinary diversity of subjective positions, social experiences and cultural identities which compose the category 'black,' that is, the recognition that 'black' is essentially a politically and culturally *constructed* category, which cannot be grounded in a set of fixed trans-cultural or transcendental racial categories and which therefore has no guarantees in nature. What this brings into play is the recognition of the diversity and dif-

ferentiation of the historical and cultural experience of black subjects. (Hall, "New Ethnicities" 443)

My readings of Said and Bhabha show that they have not really succeeded in emphasizing this nature of the postcolonial subjects.[98] In this regard Spivak has been far more careful to recognise the presence of various axes which mark the constitution of subject positions, as her reading of the literary representation of the subaltern text shows us. However, even while she chooses such terms as 'teacher of literature' or 'decolonizing feminist,' resistance to such nomenclatures arise precisely because other teachers of literature situated in other academic institutions feel differently about teaching literature as well as about being decolonizing feminists.

From Exile to a Poetics of Exile?

Pointing out differences in this manner may give rise to the danger that easy binaries such as national vs. global will be revived. However, in the face of the fear that "a more creative space is reserved for 'diasporic' postcolonials, whose political potential is privileged over those who work in the 'third world,'"[99] one has to pick up words such as migration, exile, home and homeland once again and see if they too denote differences rather than homogeneity in one way or the other. It is true that migratory experience has been the dominant mood of the last few decades. It is also true that the migration of the elite into western academic circles and the coincidence of postmodernist thinking has greatly enabled the discourse of the marginalized and of those in exile.

Even then it is necessary to remember the many layers and contexts of exile. While the experience of hybridity, the experience of belonging to the minority in the country which one has adopted, shares many elements with the experience of the refugees of war or of the migratory workers in the Gulf, it is not possible for us to imagine that we can exchange "the individualistic poetics of exile for a collective politics of refugeehood."[100] At the same time, it should also be remembered that for some, movement to another location is a matter of choice. The option of leaving 'home' may not be open for many. It is also true that having "to speak from 'where they are,' . . . is often an equally ideologically or politically or emotionally fractured space."[101]

This takes us once again to the question of the politics of representation, or rather the politics of identification. The internal divisions of what the term 'postcolonial' might mean, show differences have to be reckoned with at all stages. These differences have to be recognized as a measure of caution; and at the same time it has to be remembered that the specificities of location and contexts become significant because "postcolonial theory will live up to expectations only if it constantly reevaluates its own biases and makes an effort to dispel them."[102] Having used the word "expectations" here, I am conscious that for centuries this word has been wedded to Western expectations and perceived standards of judgement and criticism defined in terms of a Western agenda. However, since I have attempted to read against the grain throughout this project, I wish to stress that in using this word here I am focusing on the *intra*-textual nature of the postcolonial enterprise, which draws sustenance from many sources, rather than from some perceived 'objective' standard, which all too often functioned to justify the racist standards of scholarly judgement.

Having said this, I must digress a little, as a measure of caution as well as to acknowledge further the other possible elements of difference in postcolonial criticism. When the editors of *The Empire Writes Back* make postcolonial such a broad descriptive term that it includes even settler colonies like Australia, USA and Canada, the need to specify who is postcolonial was felt much more than today. Now in the light of the discussions made above and in the light of the fact that the postcolonial critics have been generally writing from the institutional context of the first world, there is a need to look at the claims of Australia for being considered postcolonial. Even though I am wary of using such terms as first world, or third world, I would like to mention here Stephen Slemon's proposition for considering literatures of the second world as postcolonial.[103]

What interests me is his call for considering such a formulation as the second world as a *reading position*[104] because he fears that the increased importance given to the subject in the third world by the postcolonial critics who are located in the first world only repeats the old models of binarism. In his view, writers from the Second World have already internalized such binaries as the colonizer and the colonized, the self and the other, and, he claims, this shows why there has been very little postcolonial critical writing; instead there is what Stephen Slemon would like to call postcolonial creative writing because many writers from Australia have tried to come to terms with these binaries in their creative writings and have been actual sites of ambivalence. It must be said here that Slemon does not claim that Canada and Australia are postcolonial the same way as India, for example. Moreover, the question of the relationship between the settlers and the aboriginals is already an important issue for any discourse that considers Australia as a postcolonial location.[105]

Slemon himself is more interested in locating resistance as the important mode of writing in postcolonial literature. He is obviously not in favour of considering all 'third world' literature as resistance literature. While accepting that the postcolonial concept of difference must take into consideration the different nature of postcolonialism in such a location as Australia, while remembering that even when we talk of the post-apartheid South Africa, we need to interrogate a simplified, unifying idea of postcolonialism, I would still like to maintain that to be postcolonial need not be to look for only resistance. As we have already seen, in many societies colonialism worked together with the existing structures of power and these structures continue to function in different forms, in officially 'independent' societies.

Conclusion

In conclusion, I would like to state once again that there is one particular characteristic which we could point out as being a defining aspect of postcolonial criticism. It is the act of re-reading from a postcolonial perspective. Said's idea of the construction of the orient immediately raised the objection that he himself was dealing with a monolithic concept of the orient. On the other hand, Bhabha's preoccupation with poststructuralist and psychoanalytical models which show that the colonial power was already a power divided and that the colonized subject through mimicry and ambivalence already contained resistance to the unquestioned colonial authority could also be seen as something which later leads him to privilege the experience of the exile and that of the minority figure.

By raising the question 'Can the subaltern speak,' Spivak is already putting the assumptions of the two earlier mentioned critics into question; however, her own rhetorical question has led to many productive debates in postcolonial criticism. Understanding in postcolonialism only the text of resistance, understanding in the text of resistance, only that which can be easily recognized as the text of resistance, Benita Parry shows her unhappiness with Spivak's formulation of the subaltern's inability to speak:

> For Spivak, imperialism's epistemic bellicosity decimated the old culture and left the colonized without the round from which they could utter confrontational words; for Bhabha, the stratagems and subterfuges to which the native resorted, destabilized the effectivity of the English book but did not write an alternative text—with whose constitution Bhabha declines to engage, . . .[106]

Spivak's own arguments in reaction to this kind of criticism has already been mentioned in the earlier section of this chapter. The act of writing, of creating can itself be an act of liberation which contains in it elements of resistance. I tend to agree with the editors of *Women Writing in India* that "[p]atriarchies, reconstituted in the interests of Orientalism, imperialism, the Enlightenment, nationalism, among other forces, provide the horizon within which the text articulates its feminist challenges,"[107] and, I would add, its postcolonial reactions.

Having in mind this background to the postcolonial critical practice, and remembering also that Shashi Deshpande has worked in a postcolonial context in a sense that contains all these differences, I proceed to read some of the novels written by Shashi Deshpande in the following chapter. In their introduction to the Second Volume of *Women Writing in India* the editors say "[s]ince the work of those who wrote in English would be more easily available to the reader," they included only rare pieces from the nineteenth and early twentieth centuries in English.[108] However, in their list of prominent women writers writing in English who do not get representation in their volume on the 20th century India, they mention Shashi Deshpande. To some extent I disagree with the claim that all those works which are written in English are easily available to readers. It is possible that Shashi Deshpande's novels can be read in a 'postcolonial manner' where the possibility of using such terms as subaltern and hybridity lead us not only to a different reading of Deshpande but also that of postcolonialism.

NOTES

1. Michel Foucault, "Two Lectures," *Power/Knowledge: Selected Interviews and other Writings 1972-1977*, ed. Colin Gordon (New York: Pantheon Books, 1980), p. 83.
2. Michael B. Naas, "Introduction: For Example," in Jacques Derrida, *The Other Heading: Reflections on Today's Europe*, trans. Pascale-Anne Brault and Michael B. Naas (Bloomington: Indiana University Press, 1992), p. xiv.
3. Gyan Prakash, "Orientalism Now," *A Review of Reviews, History and Theory*, 34, 3 (1995):199.
4. Edward Said, *Orientalism* (1978; New York: Vintage Books, 1994), p. 40.
5. Robert Young sees here a basic dichotomy in Said's description of the construct 'Orient' which did not have any connection with the 'real' Orient and the use of this representation of the Orient for political purposes. See *White Mythologies* (London: Routledge, 1993), p. 129.
6. See for example, Robert Young, *White Mythologies*, pp. 126-32; James Clifford, *The Predicament of Culture: Twentieth-Century Ethnography, Literature, and Art* (Cambridge: Harvard University Press, 1988), p. 264.
7. Edward Said, "Representing the Colonized: Anthropology's Interlocutors," *Critical Inquiry*, 15 (1989): 205-25.
8. Aijaz Ahmad, *In Theory* (London: Verso, 1994), p. 221.
9. Edward Said, "Orientalism Reconsidered," *Literature, Politics and Theory: Papers from the Essex Conference 1976-84*. ed. Francis Barker et al (London: Methuen, 1986), pp. 210-29. His objectives

in writing *Orientalism* have been clearly stipulated in this article. The most important of the issues addressed in his book are, "the representation of other cultures, societies, histories; the relationship between power and knowledge; the role of the intellectual; the methodological questions that have to do with the relationships between different kinds of texts, between text and context, between text and history." (p. 210)

10. Gyan Prakash, "Orientalism Now," A Review of Reviews. *History and Theory*, 34, 3 (1995):205.
11. Said, "Representing the Colonized: Anthropology's Interlocutors," *Critical Inquiry*, 15 (Winter: 1989) 212.
12. This phrase is used uncritically by Said. See his "Introduction: Secular Criticism," *The World, the Text, and the Critic* (1983: London: Faber & Faber, 1984), p. 3.
13. Said, "Orientalism Reconsidered," p. 225.
14. Compare this with the view expressed by Ngugi wa Thiong'o on the nature of literature: "because of its social character, literature as a creative process and also as an end is conditioned by historical social forces and pressures: it cannot elect to stand above or transcend economics, politics, class, race, or what Achebe calls 'the burning issues of the day' because those very burning issues with which it deals take place within an economic, political, class and race context." See Ngugi wa Thiong'o, "Literature and Society," *Writers in Politics: Essays* (London: Heinemann, 1981), p. 6.
15. Said, *Culture and Imperialism*, p. xii. Whenever the citations are from the same book successively, then page numbers are included in the text itself.
16. In my opinion, *Culture and Imperialism* is some kind of a sequel to Orientalism. His position in the world of literary criticism and his reactions to the fact of literary theory retreating into 'the labyrinth of "textuality",' are already clearly stated in his *The World, the Text, and the Critic*.
17. This point has been picked up by Aijaz Ahmad in *In Theory*, pp. 207-8. Connecting Said's voyage in to the immigrants and the visitors, Ahmad criticizes Said's sweeping generalization about an "adversial internationalization."
18. I agree with James Clifford when he says, "A radical critic of a major component of the Western cultural tradition, Said derives most of his standards from that tradition." Clifford, *The Predicament of Culture*, p. 275.
19. Said, *Culture and Imperialism*, p. 76.
20. Robert Young thinks that through this kind of pleading for discrimi-

nation, Said is lamenting in 'Leavisite tones.' See *White Mythologies*, p. 133.

21. Though comparatist methods are looked at with suspicion quite often, this method of reading texts could also be used in a very profitable manner. For an exciting manner of using comparative technique in scholarly work see Wendy Doniger's *The Implied Spider: Politics and Theology in Myth* (New York: Columbia University Press, 1998).
22. Said, *Culture and Imperialism*, p. 259.
23. Bhabha, "Introduction," *The Location of Culture* (London: Routledge, 1994), p. 2.
24. In this regard Bhabha can be termed a good disciple of Lacan. One is reminded here of what Malcolm Bowie says about Lacan and the students of the unconscious. Reading Bhabha can be a very ambiguous attempt at understanding him, reminding us of the words that Bowie uses for Lacan: "Lacan is quite alone in placing a continuous positive valuation upon ambiguity. and in suggesting that students of the unconscious mind, when they become writers, are somehow morally obliged to be difficult." Malcolm Bowie, "Freud and Lacan," *Lacan, Fontana Modern Masters*, ed. Frank Kermode (London: Fontana Press, 1991), p. 3.
25. An important contribution to the role of poststructuralism in the articulation of contemporary literary theory is the book by Mark Poster, *Critical Theory and Poststructuralism: In Search of a Context* (Ithaca: Cornell University Press, 1989).
26. Bhabha is considered "Fanon's closest reader" by Henry Louis Gates, Jr. See Gates, "Critical Fanonism," *Critical Enquiry*, 17, 3 (Spring 1991): 460.
27. Homi Bhabha, "Commitment to Theory," *The Location of Culture*, p. 36.
28. *Ibid*. This passage has also been quoted by Wägenbaur in an essay that is partially in agreement with Bhabha's own theory of hybridity. However, Wägenbaur is critical of what he considers Bhabha's rather utopian idea of hybrid identity. See Thomas Wägenbaur, "Hybride Hybridität: Der Kulturkonflikt im Text der Kulturtheorie," Arcadia, Band 31, Heft 1/2 (1996): 27-38.
29. Bhabha, "The Commitment to Theory," *Location of Culture*, p. 37.
30. Bhabha, "Dissemination: Time, Narrative and the Margins of the Modern Nation," *Location of Culture*, p. 162. This essay also appears in *Nation and Narration*, ed. Homi K. Bhabha (London: Routledge, 1990), pp. 291-320.
31. *Ibid*., p. 292.
32. For an argument that "hybridity has no definition except in relation

to non-hybridity," see Anthony Easthope, "Bhabha, Hybridity and Identity," *Textual Practice*, 12, 2 (Summer 1998): 341-48. Easthope concludes that Bhabha's writing, in terms of desire, "consists of a fantasy of mastery, the mastery of a subject supposed to know, who can remain sure of themselves even when confronted with the appearance of hybridity on all sides—in culture, in texts, in their own subjectivity." (p. 347).

33. Bhabha, "Interrogating Identity," *Location of Culture*, p. 51.
34. Bhabha, "The Other Question: Stereotype, Discrimination, and the Discourse of Colonialism," *Location of Culture*, pp. 66-84.
35. Bhabha, "Representation and the Colonial Text: A Critical Exploration of Some Forms of Mimeticism," *The Theory of Reading*, pp. 93-122.
36. *Ibid.*, See pp. 103 and 105.
37. *Ibid.*, See pp. 106-14.
38. Bhabha, "The Postcolonial and the Postmodern: The Question of Agency," *The Location of Culture*, p. 173.
39. I differ from the view of Thomas Wägenbaur that Bhabha makes postcolonialism out of poststructuralism. See Thomas Wägenbaur, "Hybride Hybridität: Die Kulturkonflikt im Text der Kulturtheorie," p. 32.
40. Bhabha, "The Postcolonial and the Postmodern," p. 175.
41. Bhabha, "Signs Taken for Wonders: Questions of Ambivalence and Authority under a Tree Outside Delhi, May 1817," *Location of Culture*, pp. 102-22. Also in "*Race*," *Writing, and Difference*, ed. Henry Louis Gates, Jr. pp. 163-84.
42. The present mood of communalism, revivalism, and the habit of associating state with religion can be traced back to the nineteenth century "when a more reactive, self-defensive Hinduism began to take shape in response to the consolidation of social theories that saw colonialism as a civilizing influence and as a pathway from feudalism to modern statehood." See Ashis Nandy, "Culture, State, and the Rediscovery of Indian Politics," *Literary India: Comparative Studies in Aesthetics, Colonialism, and Culture*, eds. Patrick Colm Hogan and Lalita Pandit (Albany: State University of New York Press, 1995), p. 258.
43. Obviously such a thought can be traced to the period of nationalist movement itself. Ranajit Guha explains how the *Swadeshi* movement or the movement which contained the "vision of a self-governing and self-reliant nation" was based on the ideas of 'pure' and 'impure.' What was considered 'impure' was not only the foreign but also the sacrilegious. Thus the import of salt and sugar had to be

doubly rejected—because it was not prepared in *swadesh* or one's own country, and because it was supposed to have been adulterated with the powder got from the bone of cows. See Guha, "Discipline and Mobilize," *Subaltern Studies*, Vol. VII, pp. 69-120.

44. See Robert Young, "The Ambivalence of Bhabha," *White Mythologies: Writing History and the West* (London: Routledge, reprinted 1993), pp. 141-56, and Benita Parry, "Problems in Current Theories of Colonial Discourse," *Oxford Literary Review*, 9, 1-2 (1987): 27-58.
45. This figure is from the 1981 Census of India, and is given in *Manorama Year Book* 1994 (Kottayam: Malayala Manorama, 1994), p. 463.
46. Benita Parry, "Problems in Current Theories of Colonial Discourse," p. 52.
47. Bhabha, "Unpacking my Library . . . Again," *The postcolonial Question*, p. 209.
48. Donna Landry and Gerald Maclean, "Introduction: Reading Spivak," *The Spivak Reader*, ed. Donna Landry and Gerald Maclean (New York: Routledge, 1996), p. 3.
49. See Robert Young, *White Mythologies*, p. 157.
50. It is not unusual for her to say that her approach to a story has been influenced by deconstructive practice. See her introduction to the translated version of Mahasweta Devi's "Draupadi" where she lists those aspects of deconstructive practice which interest her. (p. 180)
51. See Gayatri Chakravorty Spivak, "Feminism and Critical Theory," *In Other Worlds*, pp. 77-92.
52. *Ibid.*, p. 79. For an elaboration of this topic see Spivak, "Ghostwriting," *Diacritics*, 25, 2 (Summer 1995):65-84, esp. 66-68.
53. "A Literary Representation of the Subaltern: A Woman's Text from the Third World," pp. 241-68. "Stanadayini," or the "Breast-Giver," is the story of a poor Brahmin woman who becomes a sort of professional wet-nurse and nurses the progeny of her Master and Mistress.
54. "Explanation and Culture: Marginalia," *In Other Worlds*, pp. 103-17.
55. Spivak, "Strategy, Identity, Writing," an interview with John Hutnyk, Scott McQuire and Nikos Papastergiadis in *The postcolonial Critic: Interviews, Strategies, Dialogues*, ed. Sarah Harasym (New York: Routledge, 1990), pp. 35-49. On being asked to elaborate her position on marginality, she says: "I find the demand on me to be marginal always amusing. And as I have said, I'm tired of dining

out on being an exile because that has a long tradition and it is not one I want to identify myself with." (p. 40)

56. "Explanation and Culture," *In Other Worlds*, p. 107.
57. Spivak, "The New Historicism: Political Commitment and the Post-modern Critic," *The New Historicism*, p. 281. This interview also appears in *The Postcolonial Critic*, pp. 152-68.
58. *Ibid.*, p. 281. Another instance of the use of margin as margin—'one on the right, and one on the left'—which after a while becomes a metaphor for poetic activity is seen in Derek Walcott's "Caligula's Horse," *After Europe*, ed. Stephen Slemon and Helen Tiffin, pp. 138-42.
59. A similar observation is made by Ranajit Guha, in his note on the terms 'elite,' 'people,' 'subaltern' etc. in *Subaltern Studies I: Writings on South Asian History and Society*, ed. Ranajit Guha (Delhi: Oxford University Press, 1994), p. 8, when he points out that the term elite can be applied to all the dominant groups—foreign as well as indigenous; and the nature of the indigenous dominant group is heterogeneous in nature and is represented at the regional and local levels. As Guha puts it: "The same class or element which was dominant in one area . . . could be among the dominated in another." (p. 8) The section which deals with these explanations about the indigenous elite groups has been quoted by Gayatri Chakravorty Spivak in her "Can the Subaltern Speak?," in Patrick Williams and Laura Chrisman, ed., *Colonial and postcolonial Theory: A Reader*, pp. 79-80.
60. See "Postmarked Calcutta, India," in *The postcolonial Critic*, p. 77.
61. There is a discussion of the term and its use by the Subaltern Studies Group in "Subaltern Studies: Deconstructing Historiography," *In Other Worlds*, pp. 197-221. In an interview for the Polygraph, she explains how the term was first used by Gramsci to give a non-traditional meaning: "[the term subaltern] is truly situational. 'Subaltern' began as a description of a certain rank in the military. The word was used under censorship by Gramsci: he called Marxism 'monism,' and was obliged to call the proletarian 'subaltern.' That word, used under duress, has been transformed into the description of everything that doesn't fall under a strict class analysis." "Negotiating the Structures of Violence," *The postcolonial Critic*, p. 141.
62. Ranajit Guha, "Preface," *Subaltern Studies I*, p. vii.
63. Spivak, "Subaltern Studies: Deconstructing Historiography," *In Other Worlds*, pp. 197-221.
64. *Ibid.*, pp. 206-7. See also Mary E. John, *Discrepant Dislocations:*

Feminism, Theory, and Postcolonial Histories (Berkeley: University of California Press, 1996), p.38 and especially the section "Traveling Theory." pp. 49-53, where she uses Spivak's "Subaltern Studies: Deconstructing Historiography," and "A Literary Representation of the Subaltern: A Woman's Text from the Third World," to strengthen her own ideas of partiality and compositeness. Mary John's argument is that in the first part of "Deconstructing Historiography," Spivak seems to be neutralizing "the differences between historiography, philosophy, and accounts of political struggle," although there is a turn in Spivak's argument later on where she uses historiography as strategy. p. 43. My reading differs from that of John because, I see Spivak's method of finding discrepancy as a brilliant instance of deconstructive reading.

65 Spivak, "Subaltern Studies: Deconstructing Historiography," p. 209. Perhaps we can say that already in her "Translator's Preface" to Derrida's *Of Grammatology*, she has started thinking along these lines. She finds a geographical pattern in Derrida too: "paradoxically, and almost by a reverse ethnocentrism, Derrida insists that logocentrism is a property of the West. . . . Although something of the Chinese prejudice of the West is discussed in Part I [of *Of Grammatology*],the East is never seriously studied or deconstructed in the Derridean text." See Spivak, "Translator's Preface," *Of Grammatology* (1974; Baltimore: The Johns Hopkins University Press, 1976), p. lxxxii.

66. For a very good analysis of European Enlightenment and its history, see Paulos Mar Gregorios, *A Light Too Bright—The Enlightenment Today: An Assessment of the Values of the European Enlightenment and a Search for New Foundations* (Albany: State University of New York Press, 1992). Mar Gregorios mentions other Enlightenments, European as well as non-Western and tries to provide alternate arguments which do not only depend on the supreme power of reason. He also points out that "no understanding of the European Enlightenment would be adequate if it does not take into account the imperialist context in which that Enlightenment came to be. Europe's sense of triumph at its domination of the world played a key role in generating the basic idea of the Enlightenment. That idea is that humanity is sovereign over the world, a sovereignty to be exercised through bold self-assertion and the use of human ingenuity (reason) to overcome all obstacles." (p. 69)

67. Spivak, "Subaltern Studies: Deconstructing Historiography," p. 209.

68. For a provocative discussion of postmodernism's critique of the subject and an analysis of the negative implications of such a position

for feminism's emancipatory projects, see Seyla Benhabib, "Feminism and the Question of Postmodernism," in *Situating the Self: Gender, Community, and Postmodernism in Contemporary Ethics* (New York: Routledge, 1992), pp. 203-41.

69. Spivak, "Can the Subaltern Speak?" *Colonial Discourse and Postcolonial Theory: A Reader*, pp. 66-111.
70. Spivak, "Subaltern Talk: Interview with the Editors," *The Spivak Reader*, p. 292. A revised version of "Can the Subaltern Talk?" is going to be included in her forthcoming book and it is said to be 'much more straightforward' but without 'the passion and the anguish' of the earlier version. (p. 289)
71. For a discussion of Spivak's use of these two terms in her critique of Foucault and poststructuralist theories, see *Criticism and Culture: The Role of Critique in Modern Literary Theory*, ed. Robert Con Davis and Ronald Schleifer (Harlow: Longman, 1991), pp. 208-11.
72. "Can the Subaltern Speak?," *Colonial Discourse and Postcolonial Theory*, p. 74.
73. "Subaltern Studies: Deconstructing Historiography," p. 218.
74. I am referring to the story "Douloti the Bountiful," written in Bengali by Mahasweta Devi and traslated into English by Spivak. See Mahasweta Devi, *Imaginary Maps: Three Stories*, trans. Gayatri Chakravorty Spivak (New York: Routledge, 1995), pp. 19-93.
75. Spivak, "Woman in Difference," *Outside in the Teaching Machine*, pp. 77-78. This paragraph also appears in an almost unchanged form in her "More on Power/Knowledge," in *The Spivak Reader*, p. 164.
76. Spivak, *In Other Worlds*, pp. 241-68.
77. Spivak, "A Literary Representation of the Subaltern," p. 241. This essay has already been mentioned in Chapter One.
78. My discussion of "A Literary Representation of the Subaltern" is done more with the intention of using this methodology as a tool; just as Spivak uses the elite theories with a text about the subaltern from the third world, so do I wish to put novels from contemporary India, written in English, within the arguments of the postcolonial critics. Who is a postcolonial novelist? How can Shashi Deshpande read differently with the help of postcolonial arguments?
79. See "A Literary Representation," p. 241.
80. *Ibid.*, p. 244.
81. Personally I tend to accept Mary E. John's idea of travelling theory, rather than just stating that elite theories are inadequate. But I also feel that the strategy of Spivak is a necessary strategy—especially in hindering undue eagerness for 'knowing' the other.

82. Spivak, "How to Read a 'Culturally Different' Book," pp. 137-38.
83. See n. 13 in Spivak, "A Literary Representation of the Subaltern," p. 302. Spivak refers to 'Unpublished Intervention,' at the Subaltern Studies Conference, Calcutta, January 9, 1986. Spivak's translation of Mahasweta Devi's stories, *Imaginary Maps* is better organized in the sense that it contains a slightly revised version of a taped interview with Mahasweta Devi. See "The Author in Conversation," *Imaginary Maps*, pp. ix-xxii.
84. See Spivak, "A Literary Representation of the Subaltern," p. 245. Spivak herself points out this as being the 'implicit grounding presupposition' of Benedict Anderson's *Imagined Communities: Reflections on the Origin and Spread of Nationalism.* See n. 15, p. 302. What Spivak terms 'implicit' has been made explicit in the revised version of *Imagined Communities*. In fact, Anderson includes two appendices to the revised version in order to make for what he considers to be flaws in the first edition. In fact, in the earlier version he traces the idea of nation to "both a genuine, popular nationalist enthusiasm, and a systematic, even Machiavellian, instilling of nationalist ideology through the mass media, the educational system, administrative regulations, and so forth. In turn, this blend of popular and official nationalism has been the product of anomalies created by European imperialism." (p. 114) However, he tries to qualify this statement in the newly added chapter "Census, Map, Museum," where he calls the earlier mentioned view as being 'hasty and superficial.' (p. 163) He is now convinced that "the immediate genealogy of [official nationalism in the colonized worlds] should be traced to the imaginings of the colonial state. At first sight, this conclusion may seem surprising, since colonial states were typically anti-nationalist, and often violently so. But if one looks beneath colonial ideologies and policies to the grammar in which, from the mid nineteenth century, they were deployed, the lineage becomes decidedly clear." (p. 163)
85. See also Spivak, "Translator's Preface," *Imaginary Maps*, p. xxvii, where Spivak talks about 'internalized constraints' which are seen as 'responsibility' in the case of the woman who is sold for prostitution in another of Mahasweta's stories. In her "Echo" too, Spivak writes how important it is to 'acknowledge that the woman in culture may be the site of internalized phallocracy.' *The Spivak Reader*, p. 188. This makes any discussion of feminism very complex; unless we tease out the various elements which contribute towards the constitution of a woman, one cannot talk about the representation of the subaltern woman in a text.

86. "Subaltern Talk: Interview with the Editors," *The Spivak Reader*, p. 289.
87. Spivak, "How to read a 'Culturally Different' Book?" in *Colonial Discourse/Postcolonial Theory*, ed. Francis Baker et a. (Manchester: Manchester University Press, 1993), p. 138. Also in *The Spivak Reader*, pp. 237-66.
88. Jacques Derrida, "Sending: On Representation," trans. Peter and Mary Caws, *Representation, Discourse and Desire: Contemporary Australian Culture and Critical Theory*, ed. Patrick Fuery (Melbourne: Longman Cheshire, 1994), p. 33.
89. At the other end of this argument is James Clifford's use of the term 'travel' as a term to be used in cultural comparisons. He wishes to make a translational use of the term, that is, he wishes to use this general term strategically and contingently in cultural studies. See Clifford, "Traveling Cultures," *Cultural Studies*, pp. 96-116.
90. These terms are from Rey Chow. Reacting to the great importance attached to the question, "Who speaks?," Chow argues that theorists are also in search of objects, to be specific objects of oppression. See Rey Chow, "Listening Otherwise, Music Miniaturized: A Different Type of Question About Revolution," *The Cultural Studies Reader*, ed. Simon During (1993; London: Routledge, 1995), p. 384. Even though no names are mentioned in this article, Chow seems to be indirectly attacking the importance Spivak attaches to the question "Can the Subaltern Speak?" Is Spivak's subaltern a case of 'portable object of oppression'?
91. Rey Chow, "Listening Otherwise, Music Miniaturized," p. 384.
92. Ruth Frankenberg and Lata Mani, "Crosscurrents, Crosstalk: Race, 'Postcoloniality' and the Politics of Location," *Contemporary Postcolonial Theory: A Reader*, ed. Padmini Mongia (London: Arnold, 1996), pp. 347-64.
93. Frankenberg and Mani refer to Grossberg's use of the term postmodern conjuncturalism. "The Formation of Cultural Studies: An American in Birmingham," *Strategies* 2 (1989): 138.
94. See Mary E. John, Chapter 2. "Partial Theories/ Composite Theories," *Discrepant Dislocations*, pp. 29-68.
95. See also Vivek Dhareshwar, "Toward a Narrative Epistemology of the Postcolonial Predicament," *Inscriptions*, 5 (1989): 135-57, for a discussion of 'traveling theories' and his suggestion for the initiation of a poetics of 're-turn.'
96. Robert Dixon gives an example of a postcolonial writer who travels in the other direction. See Dixon, "'Travelling in the West': The Writing of Amitav Ghosh," *Journal of Commonwealth Literature*,

31, 1 (1996):3-24. Mentioning that Amitav Ghosh's search for the documents dealing with the Indian slave of the Egyptian merchant led Ghosh to Philadelphia, Dixon says "[t}o recover the subaltern consciousness, Ghosh has leaned not French but village Arabic; instead of affiliating his text with high theory, he has spent years reading ancient manuscripts and talking to Egyptian peasants." (p. 22) Dixon's description of the writer who is "travelling in the East" (p. 22) is an indirect method of criticizing some of the prominent postcolonial critics who are working in the Euro-American academies and are making use of theories formulated by French thinkers.

97. Stuart Hall, "New Ethnicities," *Stuart Hall: Critical Dialogues in Cultural Studies*, eds. David Morley and Kuan-Hsing Chen (London: Routledge, 1996), p. 443.

98. I am generally in agreement with Robert Young's analyses of these two postcolonial critics. See Robert Young, *White Mythologies: Writing History and the West* (1990; London: Routledge, 1993). Young's questions about Bhabha's method of interpreting archaeological documents in terms of historical resistance are very pertinent especially when questions of difference and specificities require us to be equally vigilant of the past as well as the present. Young reacts to Bhabha's use of the concept of mimicry as a mark of resistance already there in the prime time of colonialism: "Is Bhabha describing a forgotten moment of historical resistance, or does that resistance remain inarticulate until the interpreter comes a hundred and seventy years later to 'read between the lines' and rewrite history? And precisely what reality can such a reading between the lines hope to change? Is it a question of locating previously undetected moments of pre-nationalist subaltern resistance that can now be produced and charted by the critic?" (p. 149) I do not fully agree with the hidden notion that rewriting history should always 'hope to change' the present. Nevertheless, it must be stated that even when Bhabha recognizes the presence of contradictory elements in marginalized groups, the importance he attaches to the migratory experience prevents him from paying attention to the specific differences which arise due to geographical and institutional differences.

99. Ania Loomba and Suvir Kaul, "Introduction: Location, Culture, postcoloniality," *The Oxford Literary Review*, 16, 1-2 (1994): 13.

100. I have taken these words from Una Chaudhuri's "The Poetics of Exile and the Politics of Home," in *Literary India: Comparative Studies in Aesthetics, Colonialism and Culture*. ed. Patrick Colm Hogan and Lalita Pandit (Albany: State University of New York

Press, 1995), p. 146. Taking the example of the British film *Sammy and Rosie Get Laid*, Una Chaudhuri argues that the link between home and the sense of belonging is disrupted in this film, indicating at the same time that postcolonial immigrant experience is not the same always.

101. Ania Loomba and Suvir Kaul, p. 13.
102. Rosemary Jolly, "Rehearsals of Liberation: Contemporary Postcolonial Discourse and the New South Africa," *PMLA*, 110, 1 (January 1995):24. Jolly is reacting here to Derrida's "Racism's Last Word," (see Henry Louis Gates, Jr., ed. "*Race*," *Writing and Difference*," pp. 329-38) because she finds that Derrida's text "calls on the (non-South African) audience to be subjects who perceive racism as a global problem and simultaneously poses apartheid as (South African) object that is unfit by virtue of its spectacular otherness." (p. [illegible]) in her argument considering South Africa as postcolonial without sufficient interrogation demands that the elements of difference among the racist groups be overlooked. This is counter-productive to the discourse of postcolonial theories.
103. Stephen Slemon, "Unsettling the Empire: Resistance Theory for the Second World," *Contemporary Postcolonial Theory: A Reader*, ed. Padmini Mongia, pp. 72-83.
104. *Ibid*., p. 80.
105. See Bob Hodge and Vijay Mishra, *Dark Side of the Dream: Australian Literature and the Postcolonial Mind* (North Sydney: Allen and Unwin, 1990). Pointing out that till 1967, 'Australian literature' did not include Aboriginal texts, they say that their own book might appear as being overbalanced in a reverse manner. However, the authors feel that this was the only way they could have done justice to their "conception of Australian society as split around this particular fissure. It is a lapsed colonial power locked in an unresolved and undeclared struggle with the original possessors for legitimacy and land, producing a neocolonial form of literature from a neocolonial mentality that is still obsessed with the exploited Other. Into this complex is embedded a flourishing oppositional postcolonial development in politics, culture and literature. Unless this new symbiotic form is recognised to exist, the contradictions in it can hardly be understood, much less resolved in any fruitful way." ("Preface," p. xiv)
106. Benita Parry, "Problems in Current Theories of Colonial Discourse," *The postcolonial Studies Reader*. ed. Bill Ashcroft, Gareth Griffiths and Helen Tiffin (London: Routledge, 1995), p. 37.

107. Susie Tharu and K. Lalitha, "Introduction," *Women Writing in India: 600 B.C. to the Present*. Vol. I: 600 B.C. to the Early 20th Century (London: Pandora, 1993), p. 12.
108. Susie Tharu and K. Lalitha, "Preface," *Women Writing in India*, Vol. II: *The Twentieth Century* (London: Pandora, 1993), p. xxiii.

Postcolonial Arguments and Novels of Shashi Deshpande

The birth of the novel coincided with the European colonial project; it partook of and was part of a discursive field concerned with the construction of a universal and homogeneous subject. This subject was held together by the annihilation of other subject-positions. The novel is an imperial genre, not in theme merely, not only by virtue of the historical moment of birth, but in its formal structure—in the construction of that narrative voice which holds the narrative structure together.

Firdous Azim, *The Colonial Rise of the Novel*

I think my present work is to show how in fact the limits of the theories of interpretation that I am working with are revealed through the encounter of what can be defined as 'non-Western material.'

Gayatri Chakravorty Spivak, in an interview with
Elizabeth Grosz, *The Post-Colonial Critic*

There is also the fact that the kind of writing some women were doing in English, (Raji Narasimhan, Jai Nimbkar, myself) charting the inner landscapes of women, was something new. But being neither 'about India' nor Western-readership oriented, it was ignored. The advent of Rushdie and his imitators/admirers marginalised our kind of writing even more.

Shashi Deshpande, *Postkoloniale Literaturen: Peripherien oder neue Zentren?*

Novel as a Colonial Genre

If the genre of novel itself can be considered colonial in its origin, we cannot wash away its association with colonialism by providing it with a postmodern or a postcolonial shade. It is very tempting to consider certain types of novels as being worthy of postcolonial considerations or as being postmodern in nature while disregarding many others for not fitting into this framework. The fear of choosing something which even distantly smells of realistic mode of representation seems to be great in many of the modern critical tendencies and this fear has resulted in the neglect of certain authors and their works. As Gayatri Chakravorty Spivak rightly comments, there seems to be a general feeling that much of the so-called third world literature is realistic in nature and therefore not really worthy of critical attention.[1] Is a novel unworthy of attention just because it is not innovative in its narrative structure? Is there a reason for this seeming attraction for a particular mode of writing? Even though the word 'postcolonial' gives rise to different shades of meaning, one can still claim a novelist to be postcolonial for the simple reason that she/he is born in a politically independent country. Moreover, if the genre itself can be considered 'imperial,' a consideration of the postcolonial implications for any form of novel writing cannot be an absurd idea.

If the genre of novel has imperial beginnings, the realistic mode is all the more entrenched in a colonial past. However, there are different modes of realistic writing. In a very interesting essay, Emily Apter suggests that there is a technically brittle form of writing which she identifies as 'colonial realism' which is in fact a "belated Orientalism of the late nineteenth and early twentieth centuries that may be qualified as both psychological and ethnographic in its painting of modern life."[2] What is of interest here is the fact that the author identifies different kinds of realism. There is also another way of using realism—of using that colonialist mode as a tool of negation. According to Abdul R. JanMohamed, this is one of the reasons for the use of realism by African writers.[3] Before rejecting those who use realism as a mode of writing because of its association with colonialism, it is necessary to find out what is at work behind such a choice.[4]

Having said this, I would like to go back to the two texts quoted at the beginning of this chapter. These two quotations indicate, in a way, why I wish to discuss Shashi Deshpande using the post-colonial discourse. First of all the inextricability of the novel form from the empire is ground enough to consider any novel's relationship with the colonial and neo-colonial influences. Secondly, if one wished to follow Gayatri Spivak's methodology, it is possible to place literary texts in the context of various arguments. My idea is to read Shashi Deshpande having in mind the arguments of the three major postcolonial critics—Said, Bhabha and Spivak—as well as those of others who take part in postcolonial discourse. Nevertheless, it is not an attempt to prove that Deshpande is a post-colonial novelist. The methodology I have used is that of Spivak. If Spivak placed the Third World text in the context of 'alien' arguments, I place my texts in postcolonial arguments. The discussions in the previous chapters have shown us that the statements made about culture and about the literary genre novel need to be altered if we are to take into consideration the socio-cultural and economic specificities that characterize the world of Shashi Deshpande's novels.

If the growth of the novel genre was linked to the enterprise of the expansion of British empire, so was the centrality of the narrating subject. Firdous Azim, while discussing the novel form, especially its manifestations in the nineteenth century as the colonial genre, finds relationship between the growth of this genre and the strengthening of English as a pedagogical subject. Thus connecting this form of creative writing with the colonial discourse involves, for Azim, bringing out the multi-faceted nature of this relationship. Not only in terms of the selection of its themes, but also in terms of 'the formation of subject-positions, and of the formation of a pedagogical subject,' the novel form is clearly linked with colonialism.[5] For Azim, the role of the teacher teaching English literature is significant because, if on the one hand, she is aware that as a pedagogical subject English was introduced during the colonial regime with a specific purpose, on the other, she is equally conscious of its popularity among the women students in the Indian subcontinent.[6]

What I find useful in reading the novels of Shashi Deshpande is Azim's acknowledgement of the need for 'differentiated' reading. I suggest this kind of reading even for a native writer who chooses to write in English. Thus a discussion of Shashi Deshpande's works in the context of postcolonial discussions is valid on three counts:

a) her choice of the genre which originated and was strengthened in the imperial period and the choice of the language;
b) her own reference to many nineteenth-century English writers;
c) her adherence to the scheme of using a similar narrating subject in all the novels discussed here (except in her *A Matter of Time*).

However, Deshpande, unlike the many other postcolonial novelists, refuses to dwell on the issues of nationalism, caste and hybrid cultures. Yet I feel that the concerns expressed by the postcolonial discourse move beyond these obviously postcolonial themes.

At this juncture, it is necessary to present once again some of the arguments of these postcolonial critics mentioned in the previous chapter. However, these arguments are partly meant to justify my intention of considering Shashi Deshpande in the light of postcolonial criticism. Through a case of selective reading of the works of Said, Bhabha, Spivak and the other writers, I have tried to set the context for a discussion of the novels of Shashi Deshpande. However, I wish to identify broadly the particular strands of arguments that I wish to use in the following pages. I focus mainly on Said's idea of contrapuntal analysis, Bhabha's concept of hybrid and ambivalent cultures and Spivak's concept of the 'gendered subaltern.' This however does not mean that the other views will be completely left out.

All these arguments have ultimately contributed towards the following observation: the postcolonial discussions show that literature and reading literature cannot be separated from other areas such as culture and politics.[7] One argument that Said repeatedly puts forth is that one could not study the great novelists of the Empire as if they were detached from the Empire. Talking about imperialism, Said comments that although the 'era of high imperialism' is over, "the meaning of the imperial past is not totally contained within it, but has entered the reality of hundreds of millions of people, where the existence as shared memory and as a highly conflictual texture of culture, ideology, and policy still exercises tremendous force."[8] That colonialism has left its trace on the cultures of its ex-colonies is one of my arguments for selecting Shashi Deshpande's novels for analysis here. The inevitability of the influence of colonialism and the improbability that colonialism did not in any way affect her social milieu make it a good enough argument for taking up her novels for discussion along with the postcolonial arguments.

The role of a woman writer, in the context of feminist literary criticism and that of postcolonial criticism, has come under greater scrutiny. The various ways of reconstructing a tradition for women writers in different societies is an indication of this interest. Is it possible to say that any woman writer writing in a postcolonial society cannot 'escape a feminist reading and a postcolonial reading' or, is it possible to make a generalization that a woman in a postcolonial society is 'doubly alienated'?[9] Shashi Deshpande herself alludes to a double-bind, even though she does not make any reference to postcolonialism, when she says: "To be a woman writing in English is to be doubly damned, for this writing is 'elitist.'"[10] In a country like India, where in the image of woman, modernists, as well as fundamentalists, see an agent who carries traditional values, a woman novelist, writing in English could be the site of conflictual expectations.[11] She is expected to write like a woman making use of a genre and a language which is associated with former colonizing country. Can this site of conflicts be connected and related to postcolonial criticism? One way of situating Deshpande in contemporary postcolonial discussions is to begin with a few biographical details.

Shashi Deshpande, the Novelist

Born in Dharwad, a smaller city of Karnataka, Shashi Deshpande moved to Bombay later, where she completed her graduation. She lives in Bangalore at present. One can see these movements between city and smaller hometowns in her novels too. These movements, in fact, give shape to her metaphor of home—the parental home and the home after marriage. Author of many short stories and children's stories, she started her career as a novelist with the publication of *The Dark Holds No Terrors* in 1980.[12] If one were to talk about intertextuality in her works, two streams of elements are dominant there. First, her constant reference to the characters from one of the two great Indian epics, *Mahabharata*, and second, the knowledge of English literature that her characters exhibit and share.[13] Literature is a well-liked subject for her characters—there is always somebody teaching literature or someone writing it.

The use of writers belonging to the generally recognizable 'English Literature' area and the parallel juxtaposition of events and interpretations of the epics, especially that of *Mahabharata*, the epic which tells us about the great battle between two sets of cousins, *Pandavas* and the *Kauravas*, remind us of Spivak's use of the story of Echo. If the silencing of Echo in such areas as psychoanalysis has inspired Spivak to 'give speech' to her, the method of Echo, who only repeats the words that are given her, provides the decolonizing feminist with an instance that shows how she can be an 'echo' without being a narcissist about her own condition, without loving herself. In many cases, as we shall see, Deshpande seems to be echoing/reflecting situations where women, especially women who have to earn their living as 'household help' figure in, without really remarking on such situations. It has been my argument that these attempts at echoing should be taken seriously.

While discussing Echo in Ovid, Spivak mentions how she read *Mahabharata* with an ethical philosopher, who pointed out to her that this epic represented the tradition of practical ethics, by containing 'narrative instantiations of ethical problems.'[14] In addition to echoing the every day life of a middle-class woman, of her 'maid'—though occasionally—Deshpande's novels mention these narrativizations from *Mahabharata*. We could even say that just as Spivak has picked up the instance of Echo, so does Deshpande pick up the case of Duryodhana, one of the *Kauravas* to narrativize the loneliness of one of her characters. Though this appears as the existential loneliness of a human being, it could be read as the loneliness of the gendered subaltern who has been silenced by patriarchy as well as a daughter who has freed herself through liberal education.[15] Yet in this narrativization of the loneliness of the individual, which we read almost always when her protagonists conclude their narration, also passes a comment on the obvious decision of her women to go on with life as well as on what can be considered real and illusion.[16] 'Philosophical' as they might sound, these re-narrativizations of the ethical problems which appear in the Indian epics, resist the use of the nomenclature 'realist writer' to describe Deshpande.

In the above paragraph, I have intentionally picked up the story of Duryodhana because, I would like to connect this approach to the epics with that of Rudyard Kipling. Kipling, reacting to an English version of the same *Mahabharata* by Babu Protap Chundra Roy, gives an extract from the account of "Arjuna's slaughter of the troops of Duryodhana" as an example of the "barbaric" hand:

> Page upon page might be filled with extracts equally profitless; and appealing, exactly as much as this one, to the Western mind. The fantastic creations of the Hindu Mythology have as much reality in their composition and coherence in their action, as the wind-driven clouds of sunset. They are monstrous, painted in all the crude colours that a barbaric hand can apply; . . .[17]

The racism of the 'crude colours that a barbaric hand can apply' finds a retort in the way in which the imperialistic genre of novel has been transformed by this writer. It is her ability to use both the indigenous as well as the colonial narrative modes that sets her work free from the burden of blind adherence to a colonial form of writing.

This chapter analyses the major novels of Shashi Deshpande using the perspectives that have crystallised in the earlier sections of this work. I begin the analysis of several works of the novelist Shashi Deshpande with some generalisations because they are essential for shaping some of my arguments. To begin with, Shashi Deshpande can be considered a postcolonial novelist because she is writing in post-independence India. This kind of narrowing down of the definition is necessary in order to include her in the category of postcolonial novelists. The term 'postcolonial novels' has already started raising a certain kind of expectation. I defy such definitions by including Shashi Deshpande under such a category. Her narrative mode of social realism and her avowed interest in limiting herself to small social landscapes, especially that of either joint family or a nuclear family, her preference for a narrator who uses the first person narration, the absence of issues which directly deal with questions regarding nation, imperialism, neocolonialism or the conflicts and differences between cultures could act as resisting blocks in claiming her to be either postcolonial or postmodern. The feminism depicted by her novels may not be palatable to many because almost invariably her novels seem to end where they began—with only a changed protagonist who has followed the tortuous route of self-examination and self-realisation. No structures are changed and no changes are visible in the private sphere of home in this fictitious world. Yet if one begins an analysis of her works by conferring the adjective postcolonial to her, we are simplifying the connotations of the term to a simple denotation specifying time and the event of political independence and this simplification puts the novels in tension with the theories. How would the postcolonialists react if this kind of fiction were to be confronted by their theoretical articulations?

At this juncture, it would be worthwhile to look at the nature of the novels written by Shashi Deshpande. One striking feature of her novels, as already mentioned, is that the re-presentation of a woman belonging to a particular class of the Indian society is very 'realistic.' If one wanted to, one could read a good allegorical representation of the middle-class, upper-caste gendered subject who is caught in the struggle between the traditional and the 'modern/western' mode of thinking and living. In at least two of her novels, the huge traditional house with its joint-family structure, and the love-hate relationship of the female protagonist with this house and the power which is associated with this house, symbolises this conflict.[18] This is again an aspect of her work which a certain section of her readers will straightaway recognise and react to in a nostalgic manner. But more than the symbolic theme in the novels, what touches some of the Indian women readers in these novels is the 'story' of the female protagonist, a story which seems to have been written and re-written in all her novels with such concern and conviction that one needs to pay more attention to these novels than simply discarding them as being naively representative.

Can Shashi Deshpande bear the burden of a postcolonial analysis? Can one make a case for Shashi Deshpande? The idea is not to build a case for Shashi Deshpande or to see her crumble hopelessly beneath an essential theoretical mode called postcolonialism. This study will try to read the novels of Shashi Deshpande in the light of the different critical writings which have generally come to be considered postcolonial. It will try to see what such terms as subaltern and mimetic representation can mean in the context of a text which does not seem to raise any question of political import. Deshpande has been accused of making an 'everywoman' of her protagonist and universalising the condition of the female figures presented in her novels by drawing similarities among these different characters.[19] However, what is more obvious than a universalising tendency is her preoccupation with one particular woman who seems to be present in all her novels. It is because of this apparent repetition of the plot and the character type that I propose to read her novels as a form of fictional testimonial that subverts the realistic mode rather than as a realistic novel in the conventional sense of the term.

However, these considerations regarding the structure and contents of her novels should not make us forget that a novel is also a cultural artefact. Said makes it very clear that the novel form as a cultural form was implicated in colonialism in its hey day. Even the selection of a realistic mode of writing then affiliates one to this tradition of novel writing which seems to have thrived in the nineteenth century. Although Said seems to be more interested in bringing out the colonial connections of Jane Austen, Dickens and Thackeray, his objective seems to gain global proportions. According to him

> this global, contrapuntal analysis should be modelled not (as earlier notions of comparative literature were) on a symphony but rather on an atonal ensemble; we must take into account all sorts of spatial or geographical and rhetorical practices—inflections, limits, constraints, intrusions, inclusions, prohibitions—all of them tending to elucidate a complex and uneven topography.[20]

To read Shashi Deshpande in this manner is to make an attempt to add to the uneven topography of postcolonialism. It is actually to show that postcolonial discussions of literature should remain an atonal area that this novelist has been selected for analysis.

Reinterpretation, not only of the modern works in Western literature, art and philosophy, but also of the canons, is what is required in the field of literary criticism. According to Said, this will give rise to a 'revised direction and valence' to writers such as Conrad and Kipling. (*Culture and Imperialism* 60) Even though Said does talk about micro-politics, of 'modes of power,' the overall nature of his arguments is more general and that of a humanist. This is of course rooted in his conviction that imperialism was a major influence on the Western culture. At the same time, the common experience of being the victims of imperialism is seen as something that binds humanity together and in this respect, Said does not really subscribe to the postmodern theoretical positions which are against unifying, generalizing statements. He talks in terms of the 'whole of secular human history,' which almost creates the effect of simplification because one cannot talk about the 'whole' any more without being uneasy about such grandiose terms:

> If I have insisted on integration and connections between the past and the present, between imperializer and imperialized, between culture and imperialism, I have done so not to level or reduce differences, but rather to convey a more urgent sense of the interdependence between things. So vast and yet so detailed is imperialism as an experience with crucial cultural dimensions, that we must speak of overlapping territories, intertwined histories common to men and women, whites and non-whites, dwellers in the metropolis and on the peripheries, past as well as present and future, these territories and histories can only be seen from the perspective of the whole of secular human history.[21]

Although the present work does not wish to see the literary territory from the 'perspective of the whole of secular human history,' it does wish to show that overlapping is inevitable, even if one could not always point out interdependence.

As has already been discussed in Chapter Three, Said suggests that the canons of the centre should be read contrapuntally with the works coming from the margin. Thus the binary exists even though Said's vision for the future is more utopian in nature. In a very strange way, the 'here' and the 'there' that Said talks of in the colonial situation can be seen in the world of the female protagonists of Deshpande too. Once again one feels the presence of such concepts as 'we' and 'they.' However, these two terms are not arranged in a hierarchical manner and the 'we' is further reduced to the 'I' of the narrator. Moreover, in her novels, the influence of one strong colonial institution, namely, English Literature, can be clearly felt. This strengthens on the one hand, Said's argument that any culture represents a culture of innumerable borrowings, but on the other hand, the novels themselves are demonstrations of the specificity of culture in the life of a middle-class educated woman coming from a particular caste and religious background.

This kind of cultural specificity makes the use of theories of Homi Bhabha in reading Shashi Deshpande problematic. Added to this they are basically realistic representations of social experience where the mimetic ability of language is rarely questioned and the subjectivity of the protagonist looms large in narration. What Bhabha does in all his formulations is to question the teleological nature of history, the authority of the subject and the possibility of mimetic representation. How can the element of ambivalence and hybridity be found or created in a world (the world of the novel) where there are very few structural intrusions from other worlds? How can these contradictions be contained if we were to read Deshpande with the help of Bhabha? Is there any justification for doing so?

It is useful here to go back to Bhabha's arguments that culture is not an epistemological object but "an enactive, enunciatory site."[22] Even the contemporary scene of cultural studies can be then considered as having a complex enunciatory nature. What justifies my unusual juxtaposition of theories of Bhabha and the novels of Deshpande, is the fact that the 'signs' that construct the varied range of histories and identities are often different and incompatible:

> [The enunciative position of contemporary cultural studies] attempts to institutionalize a range of transgressive discourses whose strategies are elaborated around nonequivalent sites of representation where a history of discrimination and misrepresentation is common among, say, women, blacks, homosexuals and Third World migrants. However, the 'signs' that construct such histories and identities—gender, race, homophobia, postwar diaspora, refugees, the international division of labour, and so on—*not only differ in content but often produce incompatible systems of signification and engage distinct forms of social subjectivity*. (Bhabha, "The Postcolonial and the Postmodern" 176, emphasis mine)

It is my intention to pick up in Deshpande, what Bhabha calls 'distinct forms of social subjectivity,' and to say that she also contributes to a certain kind of 'transgressive discourse.' If the two volumes of *Women Writing in India: From 600 B.C. to the Present*[23] are any evidence for women writing in India even before their so-called liberation during and after the colonial times, there is a strong reason to construct this transgressive discourse by using the novels of Shashi Deshpande too. It is important to remember here that incompatible systems of signification can exist together but not in the same way as liberal pluralism conceives of a multicultural existence.[24]

In a strange way, these novels resist the theories stipulated by Homi K. Bhabha. Even though the predominant sign which 'construct the histories and identities' of the protagonists in these novels is their gender, this sign can be read at different levels. The privilege of class, that of liberal education and that of birth in the upper caste (even though it is not overtly present) not only splits this sign but puts the woman having these privileges in opposition with the woman who has no education, the woman who comes from that section of the society which is obviously disadvantaged. Thus it is not enough, as Bhabha does, to recognize the difference in content but to recognize that marginalization can occur even among the marginalized group—women in a patriarchal society—and that the agents of such a marginalization are very often women themselves.[25]

Moreover, these novels seem to have more in common with Jane Austen's apparently self-contained world. Culture, whose enunciation takes place between the boundaries, at the interstices, is not felt so prominently here as, perhaps, one would feel it in the world of Rushdie's novels. The world of Deshpande's novels is a world that is rooted in a certain idea of tradition, of culture and even though there exists a kind of conflict between tradition and the changed values, it does not really suggest transnational or translational elements because nowhere do we really see this culture coming into conflict with any 'other' form of culture. There seems to be an assumption about the uniform nature of culture. How do we read a postcolonial novel where the postcolonial subject is not a minority figure but belongs to the culturally prominent section of the society?

The closed world of Shashi Deshpande is not completely inaccessible to those who uphold postmodernist approach as against a traditional realistic representation. The cultural signs which occur in her texts belong to the dominant culture and especially to that of a middle-class Brahmin household. But is it possible to trace in these novels representation of the social experience without taking recourse to such concepts as the transparent reality of empiricism and the intentional mastery of the 'author'?[26] Does the first person narration of her novels—with occasional slipping into third person narrative—pose problem to any consideration of her as being a postcolonial novelist?

Having said this, one must explain what one means by a postcolonial mode of writing or why one has to talk about a postcolonial mode of writing at all. If we go back to what Spivak says about the generalisation regarding the realism of much of third world literature, and if we maintain that much of the hesitation regarding the realistic novels of the third world stems from a lack of knowledge of the connotations of the local language, then what do we say about the novels which are being written in English and which choose the mode of realistic representation? Do we reject them as being failures because they have not been able to achieve formal or linguistic innovations? Or do we consider them as failures because of their inability to radically question the power-relationships that exist within and without the postcolonial state? Do we wait till a post-colonial critic like Spivak talks about a Mahasweta Devi and makes this name familiar to all those who are interested in postcolonialism?

I wish to insert here a statement made by Gayatri Chakravorty Spivak in her discussion of the literary representation of the subaltern: "'Stanadayini' can offer no precise answers, no documented evidence. Taught as a text for use, it can raise constructive questions, corrective doubts."[27] The aim of this project will be to raise constructive questions and corrective doubts.

Such a process can begin with the question: 'Who is the subaltern in these novels?' Again and again her novels reveal the inability of the woman to speak and the positive movement is always the movement towards speech, towards the breaking of 'that long silence.' We could link these female characters with the statement of Gayatri Chakravorty Spivak that the subaltern cannot speak.[28] But the varieties of subalternization makes it difficult to categorise these women so easily. Is the protagonist of *That Long Silence* Jaya, whose relationship with her husband is marked by silence—especially after he is exposed as having misappropriated money—a subaltern? Is Mira the poet in *The Binding Vine*[29] who marries a man repulsive to her and dies after giving birth to this man's son, a subaltern? In both cases, the inability to speak does not mean an inability to articulate. Both of them write, but what they write does not really affect their husbands. Could they be simply termed subaltern because they also occupy the gendered subject positions? Or, in such cases, should we also take a look at the variations in the so-called subaltern subjects? What one cannot and should not forget while reading Shashi Deshpande is the fact that her female protagonists come from a privileged class and caste of the society. Yet this does not mean that their privileged situation frees them of the limitations imposed by their gender.

Loneliness of the Gendered Subject
Looking for the Subaltern in *The Binding Vine*

Talking about Mahasweta Devi's 'Stanadayini,' Gayatri Chakravorty Spivak says that it is the loneliness of the gendered subject which is staged in this short story.[30] How does Shashi Deshpande deal with the loneliness of the gendered female? As already mentioned, Shashi Deshpande has been shown as a writer who tries to universalise by drawing comparisons among different types of women. This statement can be justified to some extent even in her novel *The Binding Vine*. Her mode of representative writing goes here alongwith a technique of weaving together stories from the past and the present as well as stories of different women.

Basically it is the story of Urmila, 'the clever, sharp-tongued' woman, as the back-cover of the book characterises her, and it represents the process of her coming to terms with the death of her small daughter. The network of familial relationships which is evident in her other novels, is also present here. It is presented in a manner which seems to be 'natural' for the story of an Indian woman. It is mixed with other stories, gossip and narrations. Thus Urmi's narration of her own story is interwoven with carefully selected stories of other women—some belonging to the family, some belonging to the larger society, who accidentally draw her into their own narrative structures.

However intricate this network of familial relationships may be, the reader is struck from the beginning with the importance given to the individual in this novel. The outside world, represented in the story of Kalpana, a victim of rape, justifies the personal crisis and finally convinces and strengthens the narrator's own feelings. The narrator, Urmila, is a subaltern if we consider her as a gendered subject. But she also occupies that in-between area where she is enabled to talk because of her class, her 'education,' her role as a college lecturer, her unique position of being married but yet not being married (because her husband Kishore is absent for long periods of time).

Urmila takes upon herself the act of introspection, of speaking for Mira and Kalpana who are the women who 'cannot speak.' But this speaking on behalf of others takes place only after a crisis in her own life—the death of her daughter Anusha. It is this crisis as well as her lonely attempt to come to terms with the death of a daughter that sets her apart from the other woman Priti, who takes great interest in the issues bothering the women of the Indian sub-continent. The novel is consciously raising many questions about the women in Indian society, and the story of the rape victim who belongs to a totally different class is not just a subplot. But there are also many things which seem to be incidental, to have been mentioned in passing, which still question the choice of one story— the story of Kalpana—as a story in support of the narrator's own movement towards some kind of self-fortification. It will be very interesting to trace these tangential figures in the narrative pattern of the novel *The Binding Vine*. Before such an attempt is made, it is necessary to read the story of Mira along with the story of Urmila.

Mira is the mother of Kishore, Urmila's husband. Mira is also a poet whose poems did not reach the public. Since the poems did not seem to be meant for the public eye, the assumption made here by the narrator is that they are autobiographical, that they, along with her diaries, are a testimonial to her tortured existence as the wife of a man whom she despised. One could wonder about the fictionality of the autobiographical mode. But the narrator tackles this question as well. She questions the plausibility of Mira's poems reflecting her emotions. Such a questioning does not last long because Urmila has access to Mira's diaries too—the diaries which are 'strictly private and confidential,' diaries which thus bear the seal of authenticity[31]:

> What memories of her own life did this poem bring back for Akka? Did they say it of her and her husband too? 'A couple just like Laxmi-Narayan'? Or were her tears born of pure pity for Mira, the frightened girl who feared 'the coming of the dark-clouded, engulfing night?' And how was she so sure the experience was Mira's own? *I* know, because it's here, in her diary, the clay out of which she shaped her poem. (66)

The note of authenticity that the diaries bear has been shattered by the most unexpected behaviour of Akka, the second wife of Mira's husband. After Mira's death he married Akka only because he wanted a mother for his son. But Akka too gets a daughter from him: a daughter who was never noticed by the father. What is interesting here is the similarity between the attitude of the script-writer friend of Priti, who talks about the story of 'rape in marriage' and the details given in the back-cover of the Virago edition of the novel. According to this summary of the novel, which is also meant as an appetiser for the prospective buyer/reader of the book, Urmila, the narrator, "becomes caught up in the discovery of her long-dead mother-in-law's poetry, written when she was a young woman subjected to rape in her marriage."

This gives rise to many questions: Why has Mira been granted this higher position of being a martyr/victim? Urmila does concede that after Akka breaks down it is not Mira's story which occupies her but Akka's act of breaking down—an unprecedented act, according to Urmila. Akka, who didn't cry when her crying would have been termed 'natural,' cries now and the narrator is left with an unanswerable question: 'why had she broken down now?'

It is this mute questioning which makes it clear that Mira has been selected because of her ability to articulate: to write poetry, to write confidential diaries. It is this act of writing which ennobles her, which makes the reader of those diaries a confidant. It is through this act of writing that the story of Mira gets preference over the story of Akka, who must have had a worse marriage because her husband married her to get a mother for her son. Why is there no talk about 'rape in marriage' in the case of Akka?[32]

It is at this stage that one notices the complicity between people like the script-writer, Priti, the film-maker with her 'feminist' views and the politics of publishing. In order to get published, and to get published in the West, should the preoccupation of the third-world woman novelist be such themes as rape in marriage? Or is it a term sifted from the many other terms in the novel in order to find a market for the book? Urmila's account of the man is not so crude as the version presented by the back-cover.

> And yet Priti would have made (Mira) beautiful. Perhaps she's right; a heroine has to have beauty. And the man? Perched beside Priti, on her feminist soapbox, I know what I'd have had to make of him: a brutal, insensitive man. Perhaps he was insensitive; but brutal? (52)

Contrasted with her apparent trust in the diaries, this questioning then goes against the grain of 'rape in marriage' theory. The argument in favour of the truthfulness of the diaries is erased by a philosophical interpretation of truth. In the same context Urmila also makes a very intriguing statement about truth. "What is the truth? Is there such a thing as the truth at all, I've often wondered . . . ." It is this realisation that makes her create a story out of Mira, that persuades her to read this story which was Mira, through her photos, her poems and her diaries. To talk about this Mira and then to talk about Kalpana[33] cannot be the same thing. Kalpana, "also the victim of rape" is not a victim of rape the same way as Mira. With Kalpana and her mother, we enter a completely different world where one could really talk about the gendered subaltern. What is depicted here is again the loneliness of the gendered female until the issue of rape becomes an issue of concern for the journalists, for the feminist groups and for the father of the girl.

Although the story of Kalpana touches Urmila forcefully because it is also the story of the daughter-who-would-have-been. The narration of this story is the most effective in its exposure of the fear of a woman belonging to Shakutai's class. It reveals the paranoiac fear of a woman who is caught in the circle of strict morality that her society demands of her. Kalpana is one of those girls whose morality is decided by her class. "Girls of that class," says the police officer who reports the case as being an accident. But Shakutai in the beginning refuses to accept that her daughter could have been raped. Shakutai's—"don't tell any one, I'll never be able to hold up my head again, who'll marry the girl, we're decent people."—reveals the control that a traditionally patriarchal society has on the women in India. It is a statement which combines many issues and reveals the frightening importance given to chastity of the woman and to the necessity of marriage in order to fulfil the life of a woman.

It is ironical that the same Shakutai is finally manipulated by Urmila into telling her story to journalists in order to prevent Kalpana from being transferred to another hospital. In the face of the fervent pleas of Shakutai, the actions and words of the doctor Bhaskar, of the journalist Malcolm and even Urmila's act of persuading the mother to let the public know of the injustice caused to her daughter seem too cruel. It ultimately looks as if all of them are endorsing the view of the police officer: "girls of this class." For the rational and 'educated' doctor, the journalist and the lecturer, women like Shakutai must be incomprehensible, with their fear of the daughters not getting married or with their fear that they would not be able to 'hold up their head again.'

In such a societal framework, with its traditional rigidity and economic disparity, it is not so much that the girl is expected to be chaste as that the girl is to be considered chaste. Shakutai's 'don't tell anyone' is more of a plea that the rest of the world be kept in the dark about the rape of her daughter.[34] It is this fear of society and the expectations of this society which dominate the lives of women like Shakutai, and it is the same fear which makes living almost impossible for them, thus giving them the status of the subaltern. The false confidence given by a scientific education as in the case of the doctor or by his post in the police department as in the case of the police officer, or by her convictions as in the case of Urmila, is unknown to them.

It is in this light that Urmila's final observations become problematic. That Shakutai could get on with her daily chores in spite of her traumatic experiences which she had, leads the narrator to think of the *Chakravyuha*—the strategic positioning used in the great battle of *Mahabharata*.[35] To think that there is no way out of this 'burden of belonging to the human race' is to give an extremely bleak picture and this does not go well with the impression of Urmila which one gets earlier in the book. Or is Urmila incapable of measuring the extent of fear that Shakutai has for the expectations of the society? At the end, Urmila's reference to the 'spring of life' somehow does not give the reader the note of harmony, which perhaps, it is intended to give.

> I race through my chores in the next one hour—cooking, getting ready for college, looking through my timetable, my notes, preparing Kartik's lunchbox. This is how life is for most of us, most of the time; we are absorbed in the daily routine of living. The main urge is always to survive . . .
>
> But what terrible things we do in the process of surviving. And yet, I think of Vanaa, heavily pregnant, sitting by me, holding my hand during the pains before Kartik was born, I remember Kishore's face when he first saw Anu, I think of Akka crying for Mira, of Inni's grief when Papa told her

> about his illness, of Papa's anguished face watching her, of the touch of grace there was in Shakutai's hand when she covered me gently at night while I slept, of the love with which she speaks of her sister, of Sandhya . . .
>
> Is this it, 'the spring of life' Mira was looking for? (203)

From Shakutai's own account of Kalpana, she was not satisfied with the daily routine of a girl belonging to "that class." Shakutai's logic as summarised by Urmila is simple and there is a causal relationship between the various things which happen: "She was stubborn, she was self-willed, she dressed up, she painted her lips and nails and so this happened to her." Urmila gets angry when the mother seems to be suggesting that it was all her daughter's fault. This anger at the unjust way in which the rape victim is handled, however, clashes in the end with her act of winding off of the story without a further reference to Kalpana.

For Kalpana the main urge was not just to survive and the daily routine was obviously much more than cooking or getting ready for college. The subaltern seems not only to be silent at the end, but even a sympathetic woman who tries to soothe the mother, who gets angry with the injustice of all this, who in her own way tries to help is unable to reach this silent subaltern. It is here that we will have to go back to the words of Shakutai: "Women like you will never understand what it is like for us."(148) In spite of the crisis in her own life and the sympathetic leanings of Urmila, is the chasm between the two classes to which these two women belong too great to give rise to dialogue?

The impossibility of representing the subaltern, that Spivak speaks of, is seen here in the incommensurability of the experiences of these two women which in turn is a result of the wide gulf created by the differences in their contexts. Yet we see that the silence of the subaltern operates at different levels here. If the mute image of the raped woman shows us the difficulty for a feminist in reaching across to the subaltern woman—especially the woman in pain—the silenced story of Akka, who intrigues and yet does not get a chance shows us that the form of subalternization of the woman changes even when the socio-cultural context is the same. Akka does not have the privilege of being a writer. Does the woman who belongs to the middle-class upper-caste context lose her voice because there is no medium through which she can represent herself?

Yet it is true that Urmila is not like Priti. She cannot be rejected as the liberal feminist with fixed ideas of feminism. The distinction is made clear from the beginning. Both of them belong to the same section of society. But they differ in their ability to be sensitive, to be even self-critical. Again, what is fascinating is the author's ability to register the fears and the joys of the subaltern. There has already been a reference to those gendered subjects who are incidental to the narrative of this novel. The narration of the scene where Urmila goes and watches the movie which is being telecast talks a lot about this ritual of week-end screenings of the regional movies as well as movies in the national language. And the realism of the family collected around the TV is so true that one cannot but admire the writer's sensitive observation, and the irony hidden beneath this representation:

> I have a sudden understanding of Rekha's fascination with this movie world, so far from her life as a drudge in people's homes. She is already rapt, though it's only the commercials as yet; when the movie begins, she will be wholly lost, ready to give the response it demands. Vanaa and I settle down and we are all of us grouped about the TV as usual—Inni elegantly dressed, as if prepared to go out, Rekha, on the floor by her, Vanaa sprawling comfortably, the two younger children about her. (31)

The household drudge sitting on the floor close to the ladies of the house who are comfortably placed and elegantly dressed, is too familiar a picture for many Indian readers. In fact, it is so familiar that the irony behind the image of Rekha sitting on the floor and forgetting herself in the dream world offered by the commercial movies in India may go unnoticed by the reader. It is this sensitivity in representation which ought to get noticed by the critics of the realistic mode of writing. The subtle irony here is not to be taken as a questioning of the structures of Indian society with its expanding middle class; but it is at least critically registering—echoing, as Spivak would say—the equanimity with which social structures can be taken for granted.

Priti, who takes interest in the feminist issues is lucky because she has come back to India. "I thank God everyday that I can leave this drudgery to someone else" (36), says Priti, while she helps Urmila wash the dishes. For Urmila this remark by Priti might signify one more instance of her shallow interests, but Priti is not the only one who leaves the drudgery to others. Both Urmila and Vanaa, good examples of women who have been partially liberated because of their professions, their educational qualifications and because of their urban existence, have been able to become what they are because there has always been someone else to do the difficult and irritating household chores.[36]

Her attention to the minor details of day-to-day life, reveals to us that in a country like India, it is not simple for a woman to be interested in causes and issues. It is not simple because very often talking about justice to one group of individuals involves exploiting another group of individuals. That the author notices this aspect of the woman belonging to her own class is something which should not be overlooked. Urmila can go to the hospital every day and be with Shakutai because her mother and Rekha are there to look after the irritating daily routine chores. Vanaa can work in the hospital because there is a Hirabai to look after her children. These are the people who are tangential to the narrative but who are as silent in the narrative as the raped girl herself.

It is the silence of these tangential figures which needs to be explored further. When societal structures so tightly fashioned, when rumours are feared more than actual events (as in the case of Shakutai), the luxury of commitment to a cause is allowed mainly to those who are willing to overlook their own roles as the exploiters. The apparently symbiotic relationship between the maid servants and the career women does not hide the unequal power relationships inherent in this system. This relationship of imbalance does not only rest on money, but also on the ability to talk, to articulate. A Mira's story becomes mysterious, intriguing and worthy of the label 'rape in marriage'—worthy of being considered an issue—because it is written, because she is a poet unlike Akka, and Akka herself is absolutely silent about her marriage to the same man. Mira's story is built upon the silence of Akka.

In the same way, the narrative which gets heard—it could be a book which consciously considers a woman's life, it could be a narrative of feminism, it could be a narrative asking for the re-structuring of the society, it could be a narrative demanding radical questioning—is also a narrative which is built upon silence. To belong to the class that cannot afford the gadgets which are taken for granted in the First World, and still to be interested in getting heard is then impossible without one's turning away from the silence of another section of the society. In such a situation, even an act of registering the silence becomes important and in the narrative of *The Binding Vine*, it is the silence of the subaltern which needs to be heard.

Moments of Recognition in *That Long Silence* and the Problematic of Recognition

It is already mentioned in the earlier sections of this work that Bhabha rejects certain modes of critical theories which are dependent on the representation of reality.[37] He is of the opinion that much of the criticism dealing with Third World Literature in English looks at the problem of representing the colonial subject at the mimetic level. According to him the universalist criticism of Leavis as well as nationalist criticism are representationalist theories where knowledge is seen as the recognition of the given objects. I would like to quote his critique of the universalist criticism because as a writer Shashi Deshpande has been seen as someone who is universalising the woman in the Indian context:

> Universalism does not merely end with a view of immanent, 'spiritual' meaning produced in the text. It also interpellates, for its reading, a subject positioned at the point where conflict and difference resolves and all ideology ends. It is not that the Transcendental subject cannot see historical conflict or colonial difference as mimetic structures or themes in the text. What it cannot conceive, is how it is *itself* structured ideologically and discursively in relation to those processes of signification which do not then allow for the possibility of whole or universal meanings.[38]

Rajeswari Sunder Rajan, in the article already quoted, critiques Shashi Deshpande by saying that the author is trying to universalise the problems of women in the third world through the character of Jaya, the protagonist of *That Long Silence*:

> The force of Deshpande's indictment of women's lives lies in the way she is able to *universalize* their condition, chiefly by drawing similarities among Jaya and a variety of other female figures, including characters from Indian history and myth; and among three generations of women in her family (Jaya, her mother, her grandmother); among different classes of women (Jaya, her maid Jeeja); among different *kinds* of women of the same class and generation (Jaya, her cousin Kusum, her widowed neighbour Mukta). So compellingly realistic is this rendering that no Indian woman reader can read this novel without a steady sympathetic identification and indeed, frequent shocks of recognition. (Rajeswari Sunder Rajan 78)

When read from the perspective of the tangential figures in the novel, we could construct a varied reading of the novel even when the first impression seems to notice the universalisation of the woman. It is interesting to read these two observations together. Bhabha's stand against universalist criticism is based on the fact that it overlooks the essential discontinuity which prevents the possibility of any kind of mimetic representation. It is also his observation that such a kind of critique allegedly ends up with content criticism or moral intuition or even image analysis. If we do not resort to this kind of image-analysis, if we bear in mind the plausible constraints that the classes to which these different women belong, their educational status, it is still possible to read their indictment in a different way.

Despite the critical contempt it would 'naturally' receive for being realistic, and in spite of the theoretical stance about the impossibility of an unmediated representation, as is obvious, in many of the novels in English and in the regional languages in India, realism is the favoured mode of writing a novel. To exclude these novels because of their representative nature might lead to some kind of critical prejudice and it will not be very helpful to entertain such prejudices when one talks about postcolonialism. On the other hand, to take up such novels for analysis will also invariably lead to a discussion of such things as the content, image, character, and so on. Rajeswari Sunder Rajan claims that the 'postcolonial features' of the two works selected by her (one of them being *That Long Silence*), is based on their being 'representative of a specific post-independence historical moment.' And she makes it clear that her discussion is based more on their representativeness. It is in this context that she talks about the indictment of women by Shashi Deshpande.

I would like to draw upon Bhabha's observations on universalist criticism and say that the same argument holds true for the novelist too. To have the vision of representing reality in an unmediated manner is not possible anymore. Therefore, even when a novelist wants to 'universalise the condition of the women,' it will not be possible for the novelist. One cannot then, possibly say that the novelist is 'able' to universalise the condition of the women. What one has to accede to Shashi Deshpande here is that the realism of her novel is successful in making the Indian woman reader 'read this novel (with) a steady sympathetic identification and indeed, frequent shocks of recognition.'

It is with this term—shocks of recognition—that I would like to describe the effect of the novel *That Long Silence* in particular and the other novels of the novelist in general. There are moments in the novel where the irony is subtle but so 'realistic' that it will certainly produce a completely different reading in somebody who is a part of the Indian societal and cultural structures than in somebody who wants to identify with the larger universal concept of being a female and therefore being exploited universally. In spite of the possible criticism that this observation is based on critical provincialism, I would like to quote from the novel here:

> Looking at those women, I had begun to think with contempt of Ai's slapdash ways, and how she could not even hem properly. It was all her fault, I had thought; she had prepared me for none of the duties of a woman's life. So that when Prema had said, 'Mohan, you have a button miss-

> ing,' I had not realised that I was expected to feel ashamed, to take the shirt immediately and sew on the missing button. To me it had seemed a conversation between Prema and Mohan, nothing to do with me at all. And so I had been silent even when Sudha, a spoilt and pert girl, had added, 'Poor Monanna, looks like he'll have to fix his own button.'
>
> 'Certainly not!' Prema had retorted. 'Here, Mohan, give it to me.'
>
> It had not occurred to me that this too had been intended as a reproach, even though Prema had made it explicit by raking me from head to toe with an elder-sister-of-your-husband look . . .
>
> These women of Mohan's family were right, I had decided. I would pattern myself after them. That way lay—well, if not happiness, at least the consciousness of doing right, freedom from guilt. (83-84)

This is a shocking moment of recognition for a woman reader who has been broadly shaped by the dominant and obvious form of patriarchy. She recognises this as a 'normal' situation in many families. This is a recognition of the micropolitics that is operative within many of the Indian families which are supported by and support in turn patriarchal relationships.

It is through these moments of recognition that one more interesting aspect of the patriarchal set-up is revealed: the perpetrators of the power structures within the family circle are most often women, and it is the relationship of one woman to another woman mediated through a man that reinscribes the power of a woman over another woman. These are the women who have internalised patriarchy. Once again it goes back to the issue raised in the earlier section of this work: marriage, which so often gives rise to exploitation, is also sought after with obsession because it offers this possibility of exerting power. However, this is not to state that Shashi Deshpande is exploring a universal truth. What I would like to suggest is that the term 'moments of recognition' is a very important term when we talk about the social realism of her works. It is a term which goes against the theory of universalism and yet makes it possible for women belonging to a certain section of the society to say, "we have known this" and thus give rise to some kind of sympathetic reading.

This feeling that we have known the micropolitics of home makes it difficult for us to characterise her feminism as being completely influenced by western feminism.[39] The very structure of the dominant part of the Indian society which makes it possible at one stage for a woman to exert power over another woman, even while being the subject of subjugation herself, is something which prevents any attempt at universalising. Added to this, the differences between the classes are so great that the condition of women belonging to different classes cannot be universalised in spite of these moments of 'universal' recognition.

Once again, in this novel we see that the protagonist is able to be what she is because she has been created with a skill to express herself, to write. This given position of the writing-thinking-ennobled middle-class woman allows the protagonist to think the way she thinks. However, the concluding section of the novel seems to be once more drawn rather hastily. The narration once more seems to be echoing the *Chakravyuha* theory of Urmila in *The Binding Vine*. One cannot come out of this circular formation, unless one dies. It is as if the conflicts faced by Jaya, the protagonist of *That Long Silence* are resolved in the form of some kind of individualism, which is perhaps possible only to somebody like Jaya, with a superiority inferred upon her because of her ability to write.

I once again go back to my earlier position that even to write, to have enough time to write, to have enough money to buy time, is a luxury in Indian society, especially in a class which Shashi Deshpande seems to be representing. But Shashi Deshpande's protagonists are often aware of their dependence on that other class of women who, by offering their own services at a cheaper rate, make it possible for such creativity to exist.[40] There are really no solutions being offered by the novels. The *Chakravyuha* theory seems to be so ingrained in Deshpande's novels that there is no possibility for an easy solution.

It is surprising how many of the critics reading Deshpande, have shown little interest towards these female characters occupying the borders of her stories, without whom the main characters would not have gone into these tortuous route of self-examination. The critical readings of her novels that are available to us show that there is a kind of monolithic concept which all of them are talking about: the Indian woman—she is the one who is torn between tradition and modernity, she is the one who is in search of self-identity, she is the one who tries "to give shape and content to [her] individual existence in a sexist society."[41]

Does the undifferentiated question on the construction of gender in Indian society make it impossible to read Deshpande's novels in any other way than the present readings that are available to us? Can we read Shashi Deshpande contrapuntally, having in mind that postcolonial search for the subaltern, for the hybrid figure, for the element which crosses borders? The following is an attempt to read one of Shashi Deshpande's novels contrapuntally. Contrapuntal reading can take place when one text is read in juxtaposition with other literary and non-literary texts. I would restrict myself to the reading of some of the critical texts that deal with Deshpande's novels. Said mentions such contrapuntal reading especially when he talks about the academic subject called 'literary criticism.' It is his fear—a fear that is understandable if we know his scepticism at least about certain versions of theory—that the 'various national or systematically theoretical schools' offer 'partial analysis' that encourages him to suggest 'the contrapuntal lines of a global analysis, in which texts and worldly institutions are seen working together . . .'[42] I do not embark upon such a project all at once. I just wish to show how the notions of self-realisation which were expressed in early forms of western feminism have shaped the attitude of the critics towards the novels of Shashi Deshpande. I choose Deshpande's first novel, the one 'dearest' to her,[43] *The Dark Holds No Terrors* for such contrapuntal reading.

'A Wife Reconceptualised as Woman and an Individual': Reading *The Dark Holds No Terrors* Contrapuntally

Any reading which claims to an amount of difference also calls for a discussion of that from which it is proposing to be different. What happens when the arguments of those who are labelled as postcolonial critics are confronted by a set of interpretations which still accepts the traditional concept of the author as the authoritative, omnipresent presence? Do these interpretations too exhibit the nervous tension of finding a meaning in the literal text which is in accordance with the social expectations? Is it possible that the consolidating vision of the nineteenth century novelist which Said talks of, is also present in a subversive manner in the interpretations of the novels of Indian women novelists? Deshpande's *The Dark Holds No Terrors* is her first published novel and as in the case of her other novels, the protagonist is a woman. Saru, the daughter with whom the mother never reconciled, especially after the death of her younger brother, defies her mother, goes to a city, studies to become a doctor and marries the man she chooses herself.

It is once again a story of introspection. Saru, a successful doctor, finds that her husband, an English lecturer who once aspired to be a poet, is as split as Dr. Jekyll and Mr. Hyde. A loving father and a caring husband during the day who, with evident pride shows off his doctor-wife to his colleagues, turns into a monster in bed, abusing her and bruising her, creating such terror in her that she finds no voice to scream for help. During the day, there is no evidence in his behaviour to suggest anything that should be a cause for anxiety. There are only bruises which show that the night has been real. Her inability to protest, to find out what was actually wrong, prevents her from doing anything about this problem till she finds out that her mother who had spurned her all these days had died of cancer.

Saru goes back to her father's house after many years because her marriage had alienated her from her mother all these years. It is here, living with her father and Madhav, the young student who stays with the father, that she tries to come to terms with the various events in her life. It is here that all the tortuous introspection goes on. What is interesting, however, is that this introspection cannot be compared to a journey which reaches a goal, which gives the sense of something that has been fulfilled. This is not a *Bildungsroman*. Saru, the protagonist, who is looking for someone with whom she could share her fears, finally tells her father everything, in a manner that reminds one of the ancient mariner in Coleridge's *The Ancient Mariner*, who compels the wedding guest to listen to his story.

It is true that in this novel, the figure of mother—more than that of the mother-in-law, who is conventionally seen by the women writers as a dominating figure—takes an ambivalent shape. There is very often a sense of frustration, of non-comprehension, of resistance in the daughter when she thinks of the mother. However, this complex relationship between the mother and the daughter cannot be simplified as hatred nor can it be claimed that her heroines are 'anti-matriarchal.'[44] The ambiguity of Saru's relationship with her mother is not taken into consideration by many of the critics who have taken up this novel for interpretation. Most of the readings of this novel seem to be driven by the compelling desire to make woman an autonomous being. The protagonist of one novel is sufficient reason for generalizing about the category 'woman':

> The woman in order to achieve her freedom seeks marriage as an alternative to the bondage created by the parental family. The simple need to be independent eventually becomes a demand of the inflated ego and takes shape as the love for power over others. She resents the role of a wife with the hope that her new role will help her in winning her freedom.[45]

This kind of criticism, on the one hand, holds such tradition-bound notions as 'one should be good to the mother' and on the other, the 'western' individualistic notion of freedom. The insensitivity to the questions of difference, the notion that the Indian woman can be easily defined and identified is in accordance with the dominant nationalistic search for the 'essential Indian subject.'

It is not that certain statements that are applicable in general to the Indian women cannot be made. The presence of a dominant cultural mode does enable us to use certain generalisations. For example, in an earlier section of this chapter, I have mentioned how strongly the necessity to hide the rape of a girl is felt by her mother because she fears rumours, because she too is of the opinion that marriage is essential in the life of a woman. This is perhaps one of the many overarching generalizations which could be made in a patriarchal society like India. But the problem with these overarching generalizations is that they can be used everywhere; that the specific case of one novel, one woman character is made to stand for the generality of a 'real' world of women. This is clearly seen not only in the comments regarding marriage as being a door leading to freedom from parental bondage but also in those interpretations where the protagonist is made to stand for all the women presented in the novel. This, in spite of such extreme notions as that the protagonist is 'anti-matriarchal.'

It is not possible to accept such easy classifications if we remind ourselves of Gayatri Chakravorty Spivak's warning regarding the recovery of the voice of woman through autobiography—'the woman in culture may be the site of internalized phallocracy.'[46] Deshpande's protagonist Saru herself, does not give the reader the feeling that she is anti-mother. Saru, while trying to sort out her own reaction to her husband's split-personality, also tries to come to terms with the unrelenting nature of the mother. Her mother had refused to see her daughter till she died. A feeling that her daughter's irresponsibility was the cause of her son's drowning, strengthened her dislike for Saru. Yet it is Saru's decision to go to a different place, and study medicine, and a little later, Saru's decision to marry Manu, a man whom she herself chose, which act as a turning point in Saru's mother's relationship with her daughter. When her daughter was mentioned, she says, "What daughter? I have no daughter." (109) Saru herself believes at one point that it is because her mother cursed her that she is unhappy in her marriage, and is irreconcilable with her childhood. Yet her search does not end with simple answers like a mother hating her daughter, or a daughter hating the mother.

However, easy resolutions are what some of the interpretations are looking for. Many of the critics who have written about the protagonists of Shashi Deshpande's novels, do so, while eliminating all traces of the other women who are present in the novels.[47] This generalizing tendency is reflected in their analyses too:

> [The woman's] emancipation is not in repudiating the claims of her family, but in *drawing upon untapped inner reserves of strength*. The wife, in the end is therefore not a rebel but a redeemed wife—one who has broken the long silence, one who is no longer afraid of the dark. She is a wife *recon-*

> *ceptualised as woman and an individual*—a marked contrast to the older generation of women around her with their uncomplaining, unresisting fatalistic attitude. Hers is *the dilemma of the new woman that could be resolved* when the claims of selfhood are reconciled with the claims made upon her by the family and society.[48] (emphasis mine)

There is no reference to the pain such difficult expectations cause in a woman. The burden of keeping together tradition and modernity has further complicated the lives of women in India. It is all the more difficult because there seems to be some kind of intellectual sanction for 'drawing upon untapped inner reserves of strength.' There are some obvious conclusions to be drawn here. This interpretation is responding to the need to talk about 'the woman' who has to 'resolve' the dilemma between her claims to selfhood and her respect for the claims made on her by the society and by her family. In this interpretation, for the protagonist, and through her for Deshpande—and if one is not mistaken, for the interpreter too,—the resolution lies in the form of reconciliation.[49]

Reading the novel contrapuntally, where the postcolonial arguments are juxtaposed with these interpretations, one gains a different perspective into the novel. I wish to read Saru, not as a rebellious daughter who is searching for her self-identity, for her freedom, not as an egoist who cannot understand the inferiority complex of her husband, not as the guilty sister who was responsible for the death of her brother, not as a daughter who was never forgiven by the mother, not as a traveller who goes on to a spiritual quest that ends in no resolution, but as a woman who possesses '[w]hite, soft and clean' hands in the beginning of the narration (36) and 'roughened' palms towards its conclusion (165). The roughened hands at the end 'echo' two other silent figures in the novel: that of her mother and of Janakibai. This image of the hand is consciously chosen to cancel all the positivistic and philosophical interpretations. What is of significance to this reading is that Saru recognises her domestic servant Janakibai as the one 'who looks after' all of them; it is because of her that she could possess 'white, soft and clean' hands, and Saru identifies herself with her mother at the end. In fact, the novelist makes sure to bring out the similarity between Saru (at a point when narration is approaching conclusion) and her mother. In pulling out Janakibai from her 'behind the stage' location, and in highlighting the ambiguous representation of the mother, I am intentionally ignoring the more obvious narrative line of the story of the drowned brother, and the story of the husband or the issue of inequality in marriage.

If Jane Austen's casual comment about the plantations of Antigua should not go unnoticed, should not the passing comments about a Janakibai who comes to Saru's house, to look after the children and to look after all of them, be given some more attention? Who is this Janakibai? I could construct an image of Janakibai based on my own observation of the many Janakibais of our country. She is perhaps the slum-dwelling woman who comes early in the morning, cooks, cleans and sweeps the house. She could be the live-in maid who has been abandoned by her husband, or has no one 'to look after her.' She is a 'good servant' who has learnt to look after other children as her own. She is the representative of all the women who belong to this section of the working women category who has no job security whatsoever. Once again, the women at the margins of the narration are the women who make this narration possible by allowing the protagonist to leave the smooth running of her own small family to them. Just as the existence of the plantations made it possible for the novel to exist and to be read in the colonizers' country, just as these colonies made it possible for the colonizers to believe in the existence of a rational human being, so does the existence of these marginal figures make it possible for many women to articulate about the condition of woman.

This does not mean that I am relativizing the complexity of the enterprise of the empire. I only wish to show that while recognizing the lasting presence of colonialism, one has to constantly remind oneself of the existence of minor configurations of power structures. The single metaphor 'woman' even when used in a context where generally woman is marginalised as in a patriarchal society like India, defies generalization. It is only by being aware of the different kinds of women that we could begin to talk about the postcolonial woman. And it is only by being cautious about these jarring notes coming from the margin that one could continue to talk about the postcolonial condition. The notion of margin is not anymore the second component of the binary centre-margin; Deshpande's marginal comments about these figures must be read in terms of Spivak's understanding of the term 'margin'—it is 'the place for the argument, the place for the critical moment.'[50]

In an attempt at making the margin also the place for the critical moment, I allow the mother of Saru to occupy the position of being the marginal. Though Saru herself seems to be obsessed with her mother's unrelenting nature, certain narrative moments make it difficult to read everything in terms of this obsession. Saru's father plays an ambivalent role in the novel. It was he who supported her in her decision to leave her hometown and go to Bombay in order to study medicine. Once again we see how, formal education is identified, at least to some extent with liberation, with breaking the bonds of parental house. For Saru's mother it is also something which indicates postponement of her daughter's marriage, which in turn suggests non-fulfilment of a responsibility. It is the responsibility of the parents to see that a daughter gets married. (144) Defying the mother, father and daughter decide that Saru should go to Bombay, live in a hostel and study medicine. However, this moment which can be read as the moment of liberation for a young woman is simultaneously bound with the restricting 'internalization of phallocracy,' to borrow Spivak's phrase, because the text contains innumerable references to the life of father and mother—a shared life marked by inequality, where inequality itself is sanctioned by tradition and what is normally termed as 'culture.'

Saru herself sees marriage as something that would make her like her mother. It is her wish not to be like her mother that makes her dream of becoming a doctor into a strong ambition, an ambition for whose fulfilment she works very hard. Finally when she gets a First Class in her Intermediate school studies and is sure of getting into the medical college, she tells her family about her intention of becoming a medical doctor. This is one instance which shows us how much the mother and the daughter differed from one another. It is an incident, which, read hastily, could be described as one, where the father is seen as being more liberal and the mother conservative, the father more loving and the mother, an unloving, uncaring woman, who is only concerned about her dead son. Yet there are subtle indications of love as well as of the unequal relationship this mother shared with the father, as the following passage makes it clear:

> I went home and told her nothing but that I had obtained a first class. 'Good,' she said. No more. But that night there was something special for dinner, something fried, something sweet, and I knew she was pleased, though her face told me nothing. And there was no more talk than usual as we had our dinner, Baba [father] and I. She never joined us. I cleared up after we had done, and then she ate, all by herself, in the kitchen. (141)

It is a relationship marked by silence. This silence of the mother, contrasts the eloquence of the daughter's narration. When the daughter asks her father whether he wants to listen to her story, whether they can, as daughter and father, separated in age by thirty years, talk about such things as the relationship between man and woman, he says:

> 'Why not?' he said and his voice came out husky. . . . And then he went on, . . . 'Do you know, Saru, I often feel sorry that we left so many things unsaid, your mother and I. When she lay dying there I wanted to ask her . . . Would you like to meet Saru? Sometimes I think she might have said "Yes." But I never did. Silence had become a habit for us. Now, . . . go on, tell me. Tell me everything.' (199)

Is the mother, then, in addition to being a contrast to the stereotype of an all-forgiving woman, used by the novelist as a margin, as a figure in whom the metaphor 'woman' becomes visibly ambivalent, a figure who exemplifies simultaneously the internalization of discriminatory habits which pass off as custom and tradition (such as waiting for the husband and the children to finish their food before eating herself) and an existence as a silent figure—silent, especially in the presence of her husband.

Ambivalence, then, is an important element that we detect in Saru's attitude towards herself, her mother and towards her husband. It looks as though she is finding some kind of refuge in philosophical consideration. However, the ending of the novel is not clear making it difficult for us to read off any easy meaning from it. It looks as if Saru faces her life once again, but the facts of life have not changed for her. Her dead mother and dead brother are not going to come back to give her any kind of assurance, and she has no idea that her husband Manu will ever understand if she tells him that he is the creator of nightmares in her world.

What strikes us in the story of Saru is, however, how well-defined, and small this world is. This world is a world that is hardly exposed to hybrid cultures, although her reference to the city life, to colleagues and friends do bring us into contact with the external world. It is her life in the small town, where everyone seems to know everyone else that we realize that there is hardly any possibility of talking about cultural hybridity. The novelist has not made any effort to include elements from other cultures. Saru is homebound during most of her stay in her father's house. To use Said's distinction of 'here' and 'there,' the 'here' denoted in Deshpande's novels is the 'here' of parental home.

Yet—as mentioned earlier—the 'here' is not presented in any hierarchical order with the 'there.' The house associated with the childhood offers consolation many times to the protagonists in many of her novels, but this consolation is not to be equated with resolution of doubts and cynicism about this household and all that it stands for. One example where an ancestral house, closed to the outer world culturally, closed also in terms of narration, because very few 'outer elements' enter it during the course of narration, is Deshpande's novel, *Roots and Shadows*, where a prodigal daughter of the house who lives away from it, becomes the only inheritor of the wealth of an old widowed relative who was living there.[51]

Ambivalence, Interstitial Perspective and *Roots and Shadows*

However, before entering the world of *Roots and Shadows*, I would like to go back to Bhabha's conception of culture as that which is occupying the in-between spaces. How meaningful is Bhabha's conception of difference and identity, and his attempt of locating culture in the 'realm of the beyond?'[52]

> The imaginary of spatial distance—to live somehow beyond the border of our times—throws into relief the temporal, social differences that interrupt our collusive sense of cultural contemporaneity. (4)

My reading of *Roots and Shadows* is a way of throwing into relief the 'temporal, social differences' that 'interrupt the sense of cultural contemporaneity' that I get from my association with the current discussions in postcolonial criticism. It is my fear that in talking about the cultural contemporaneity and in using such a phrase as 'the trope of our times,' Bhabha is privileging the condition of hybridity, of exile, even when he notices that these experiences are differential. How does one deal with the world of one family as it is represented in Deshpande's *Roots and Shadows*? In many ways the world of *Roots and Shadows* is similar to the world of Mr. Billy Biswas. But is there something more here than an 'uncanny' representation of daydreams and colonial fantasies that Bhabha finds in *A House for Mr. Biswas*?[53]

I agree with Bhabha that we need to think in terms of going beyond the boundaries. But at times, in literary representations, going beyond could also mean going within those closed worlds where there seems to be no seed of change sprouting into life. For Bhabha, the significance of postmodernism lies in a kind of going beyond, it is going beyond a parochial celebration of fragmentation:

> The wider significance of the postmodern condition lies in the awareness that the epistemological 'limits' of . . . ethnocentric ideas are also the enunciative boundaries of a range of other dissonant, even dissident histories and voices—women, the colonized, minority groups, the bearers of policed sexualities. *For the demography of the new internationalism is the history of postcolonial migration, the narratives of cultural and political diaspora, the major social displacements of peasant and aboriginal communities, the poetics of exile, the grim prose of political and economic refugees.*[54] (emphasis mine)

Agreeing fully with this kind of understanding of internationalism, I would like to present the case of a novel which does not come under this concept, and thereby threatens to reveal in the statement quoted above, the tendency towards generalizing on the basis of internationalism. I would, however, like my argument not to negate Bhabha's own position on the nature of culture, but to supplement it.

Roots and Shadows which received a prize for being the best Indian novel in English of 1982-83, is similar to *The Dark Holds No Terrors* in the sense that it is also the story of a daughter who has come home after a long time. Once again memories of episodes and events from the past intertwine with one another to give us the pictures of childhood, of leaving the house, of marriage and of coming back. Indu, the thinking-writing narrator is the motherless daughter of one of the sons of this huge family, who visits the house only occasionally. She has been brought up by one of the widowed aunts, Atya. The most important figure in this joint family is of course, another widowed relative, who is dominating in nature, who commands respect not only because of her age but also because of her wealth. It is Akka, the rich widow, who makes Indu come back when she is on her death bed, who leaves all her wealth to Indu, even though she knows that there are many well-deserving candidates living in the ancestral house itself.

I have termed this a closed world, mainly because of the old building which houses this huge family. In this huge family—where only the close family 'meant twenty of us' (35)—there are a few aberrant elements: Indu's father, who very occasionally visits the family, Indu's relative Naren, who through his disregard for the norm of the family is almost an outsider to it, the orphan boy, Vithal, who is given shelter and food but is not a part of the family and Indu herself who has defied everything and keeps herself away for ten years from the family. Perhaps she is the one farthest from the family, physically as well as mentally; she has married someone from another caste and lives in a city. During the course of narration, very little happens outside the building. Even for Indu, who had consciously kept herself away from the house for such a long time, the house has always been her home:

> Ten years I stayed away from this house. And yet, each day of these ten years, I woke up to the same sounds. For a few seconds of each day, I was back in this house. But this time it was real. (34)

Thus Indu's attempts at going away, at breaking off from this ancestral house and the joint family, its traditions, has not been very successful. The element of change that has entered her life in the form of her husband and in the form of a different kind of lifestyle, does not indicate hybridity, although change in the form of 'freedom' was what she had hoped for when she left the house and when she got married to Jayant. (14) Her confession of what this change has meant for her reminds us of the postcolonial critique of liberal values such as justice, equality, secularism which have had their origins in the period of Enlightenment:

> The trouble with concepts like individualism, liberalism or secularism is that we think we understand them too well. These are ideas, and ideals, that are increasingly complicit with a self-reflective claim to a culture of modernity whether it is held by the elites of the East and West, or the North and South. We may define them in different ways, assume different political or moral positions in relation to them, but they seem 'natural' to us: it is as if they are instinctive to our sense of what civil society or a civic consciousness must be. Despite their limitations, they have a certain 'universal' historical resonance, a universality that comes from the origins of these concepts in the value-system of the European Enlightenment.[55]

For Indu too, the switching over from the traditional old house to the upper middle class life ("In fact, it is considered vulgar to be affluent. We're the upper middle class." p. 26) has opened up a 'modern,' secular space, whose description in ironic terms question the same liberal values which are mentioned by Bhabha above. Indu thinks that it is the 'real' Indu who is uttering these words:

> 'And when we get together . . . . oh, you should listen to us, Naren. . . . We are rational, unprejudiced, broadminded. We discuss intelligently, even solemnly, the problems of unemployment, poverty, corruption, family planning. We scorn the corrupt, we despise the ignorant, we hate the wicked. . . And our hearts bleed, Naren, for Vietnam, for the blacks, for the Harijans..' Suddenly my enforced calm, my deceptive joviality fell off me and I banged my fist on my own lap. Hard. 'But frankly, we don't care a damn. Not one goddam about anything but our own precious selves, our own precious walled-in lives.' (25)

Hence, in the words of the protagonist herself, the change of location, and the change of lifestyle has not brought any possibility of hybridity in the sense of Bhabha—these are walled-in lives. In the ancestral house itself, its inhabitants lead another kind of walled-in lives, where the older members have remained devout Brahmins and the younger generation makes casual reference to caste. But once again, the traditionalism of the hierarchical society is placed at the same level as the secularism of the middle-class, educated section:

> We Indians can never get away from the caste. If we've rejected the old ones, we've embraced new one. Do I think of myself as a Brahmin? Rarely, if ever. But I'm the educated, intelligent, urban, middle class. We have our own rules, our own pattern, to which I adhere as scrupulously as Atya and Kaki observe their fasts and pujas. (58)

The secular and the religious are put together once again. The secular replaces the religious for this liberal younger generation. But this idea of the secular is as ritualistic, as unambivalent as the religious. It is because of this similarity between her chosen world and her childhood home, that I wish to call the world of this novel a closed world.

In this closed world, Akka, the 'indomitable' (5) old lady who dominated over everyone in the house would be the last person to bring about change. Akka refuses to go to the hospital when she is sick because she wouldn't know what caste the nurses and doctors belonged to. It is this Akka, who comes out as the most ambivalent figure in the novel. It is she who creates a third space of enunciation which makes the closed world ambivalent, and it is she who becomes an agent of change, in spite of her adherence to the norms of this world. She occupies this space, in spite of the general narrative line of the story, which seems to ultimately resolve problems by talking about the 'inner strength' of women. (6)

The story of Akka, a sister of Indu's grandfather, is perhaps considered important because it provides a different aspect to the general picture of Akka that we get through the novel. It also helps Indu see in Akka not just a tyrant but a tyrant with a past. Akka, married to a rich man when she was twelve, was sent to her husband's house when she 'grew up,' a house which turned out to be hell for her. When she attempted to run away from this house she was locked up in a room and allowed to starve. Yet she did not want to be sent to her husband's room:

> The child, they said, cried and clung to her mother-in-law saying, "Lock me up again, lock me up." But there was no escape from a husband then. (70)

Akka's husband had many mistresses, and after being married for many years, is 'crazy' about one woman, for whom he would do anything. He even would have liked to take Akka's jewels and give them to her. Then suddenly he gets a stroke, and is looked after by Akka till his death. What makes Akka a figure that defies our attempts at classifying her is revealed at this point in narration. Akka, who nursed her husband very efficiently finds out one day that through the many incomprehensible sounds, her husband was, in fact, asking that his mistress be brought to him.

> And Akka, calm and cool, said, "Listen to me. It's my turn now. I've listened to you long enough now. She came here. Twice. She wanted to see you. She cried and begged to be allowed to see you just for a short while. I threw her out. You'll never see her again."

> 'And . . . that giant of a man, began to cry. Tears poured down his face. . . . But Akka . . . she just looked at him.' (71)

I am reminded here of Spivak's observation that there are many "quiet proto-feminist mothers. . . . who, working with immense innovativeness behind the scenes, made their daughter's career-freedom possible [and this] must not be obliterated in the accounts of the daughter's struggles."[56] Is Akka the 'proto-feminist' voicing her opinion, or is this just a human drama where the one who is hurt is taking her revenge? Her later role as a dominating rich widow in her brother's household has completely hidden her story of suffering and of revenge. What should we make out of this anomaly in narration? Why does Akka choose Indu, the deviant member of the family to be her heiress? Is it because Indu herself can act as an agent, as the one who has the power to organize the demolition of the old house, that she chooses her? Whatever it is, Akka's story shakes many of our stereotypical views that the Brahmin widow is a sub-human figure.

The hard life that a Brahmin widow has had to face in traditional families is a well-known fact.[57] It is through the money that her husband left her, that Akka ultimately becomes so powerful. This money and her will to order others later, distorts the traditional image of the Brahmin widow and it is in this way that the image itself is rendered ambivalent. Unlike in Bhabha, we see here that woman, in different stages of her life occupies different identities because of different reasons. And we also see how even in a closed world, elements of hybridity can be introduced by the same marginalized figures, if one of the axes which determine them is changed. Caste-wise, Akka is privileged but her status as a widow makes her officially an oppressed person. However, her money, and the position which she held in the family reverse these parameters making it difficult for us to generalize about her and about women like her.

The case of Akka simultaneously supports as well as distorts Bhabha's comments on culture. The linguistic metaphor, or the metaphor of the 'articulation of language,' appears now and again in Bhabha, because, for him, it explains the way culture is enunciated.[58] It is an answer to the cultural binarism which seemed to have operated in the colonial world. The use of this metaphor is Bhabha's postcolonial answer to the postmodern rejection of binarism in the cultural field:

> The epistemological distance between the subject and object, inside and outside, that is part of the cultural binarism that emerges from relativism is now replaced by a social process of enunciation. If the former focusses on function and intention, the latter focusses on signification and institutionalization. If the epistemological tends toward a "representation" of its referent, prior to performativity, the enunciative attempts repeatedly to "reinscribe" and relocate that claim to cultural and anthropological priority (High/Low; Ours/Theirs) in the act of revising and hybridizing the settled, sententious hierarchies, the locale and the locutions of the cultural. (Bhabha, *Postcolonial Authority and Postcolonial Guilt* 57)

It is not simply by inverting the hierarchies that a process of reinscription takes place, but by revising and revaluing. (Bhabha 58) It is this kind of revaluing and revising that we see in the construction of the story of Akka. This Akka, who, like many Indian women believed that husband's first name couldn't be uttered by the wife because this would shorten his life (32) is the same ruthless Akka who does not care to fulfil her husband's request at his deathbed. It is the same Akka who refused to go to the hospital because she does not know the caste of doctors and nurses who work there and who decides to leave all her wealth to her grand-niece. This niece and her father are the two who have broken the purity of the caste by marrying outside the community. Yet she chooses her niece to be the recipient of her wealth. It is because of this money that she received from Akka that Indu wants to take up her writing career seriously. It is thus Akka who becomes the agent of '*revising and hybridizing the settled, sententious hierarchies, the locale and the locutions of the cultural*' in this small world of the family. And this is a family which hadn't had any chance of experiencing migration to another location.

Border crossing, migration are not considered very important elements, because the house is rooted in one place, and the sons who have left the house, come back for occasions like death and wedding. Yet, the house is going to be demolished at the end of the novel and if at all the house had been projected as something which binds, the final symbolism reverts the value attached to rootedness. Even though the world created in this novel is seen as insulated against other cultural influences, by making Indu the inheritor, Akka seems to have posthumously caused change in the household, she seems to have initiated movements, crossing of home boundaries.

Indu, who has been chosen by Akka, is a writer, and she hopes to take up writing once again, but this time not for money as she did earlier. Literature, as mentioned earlier, is a beloved subject for many of Deshpande's protagonists. If English literature, its famous writers are often mentioned by her characters, Deshpande's depiction of the role of English language, and of the education system that enables people to speak English and through this, to achieve social respectability is done ironically.

Speaking English as if it were a Real Language

The role of English language and the power it gives to people belonging to a certain section of society and the cultural elevation which the ability to speak English fluently can guarantee, is a factor to be reckoned with in the Indian middle class today and English remains a language that apparently keeps one in touch with the upwardly mobile class.[59] For a man like Mohan in *That Long Silence*, this language brings the hope of a movement within the rigid structure of the society. It is a movement from the small town to a metropolitan city like Bombay, and it is a movement from being 'uncultured' to being 'cultured.' It is Mohan's desire for a girl who could speak English, or as Jaya's brother puts it, it is his desire for 'an educated, cultured girl' which makes Mohan agree to marry Jaya. His own fantasy for an English-speaking wife arises from the house-warming ceremony of his patron's house where he, for the first time comes across women who could talk the language 'as if it was a real language':

> 'They spoke it as if it was a real language, easily and fluently, you know, quite unlike the English I'd heard till then. They stood in the doorway for a while—from the way our host fawned on them, I imagine they were rich relations. As they were leaving, the girl said something. I can't remember what she said, but I can remember how wonderful it seemed to me to be able to talk like that, to be so . . . so easy and . . . confident and how terrible it was to be shut out . . . to be different . . .' (89-90)

It was Jaya's father (Appa) who sent his children to the convent school (the connotation being that it is a school run by the catholic nuns, in which the medium of instruction is English). It is her father who has the opinion that English is going to be more helpful to his children than 'being good Brahmins' and it is this decision which ultimately makes Jaya 'ready for Mohan.' (90) This identification of English with culture, education, with a liberatory aspect is not peculiar to Mohan. It is something which has afflicted generations in post-independence India.[60] What would all this talk about postcolonial discourse mean to these generations? It is not just Mohan who tries to improve his position in the society by marrying a woman who can speak English. As Jaya herself puts it, Mohan's ideas are amusing 'today when even Jeeja and Tara are planning to send Tara's two sons to an English school' (89).

The power wielded by the English language, by the people who can call themselves 'educated,' who see themselves differently because of their ability to talk this language is a sign that the discourse about colonialism has to read not only the texts of the empire but also the text produced after the official ending of the rule of the empire. If Mohan and his desire to possess respectability and privilege given by the English language is not regarded as positive by the self-critical protagonist Jaya, there are distinct moments in this and the other novels of Shashi Deshpande, when one could clearly point out to the influence of a particular set of books written or translated into English.

As mentioned in the first part of this chapter, the intertextuality of her novels is sustained mostly through the protagonists' readings of the canons of English Literature and their knowledge of the great

Epics and mythologies in Sanskrit Literature. Whether this observation itself points to something else, is a question which needs to be examined and posed in the context of the existing educational system in India today. It is as important a question as the problem of representation or of the impossibility of universal meanings.

An equally important theme is that of the role of a teacher in teaching English literature. How does a postcolonial teacher differentiate between and make use of literature written in English, literature written during the colonial period and literature written in culturally different contexts? It is Gayatri Chakravorty Spivak who chooses the designation 'teacher,' and it is through her that one can initiate a discussion on this issue.

On Teaching Literature in a Multicultural Society

The designation 'teacher' is something that is preferred by a critic like Gayatri Chakravorty Spivak to describe herself. If the introduction of English literature as an academic subject was done first in India, then the teaching of English, and the teaching of literature written in English in postcolonial societies should be an issue of considerable importance to all those who are interested in postcolonial discourses. A similar problem is taken up by Spivak in "How to read a 'Culturally Different' Book?"[61] It must be, however, remembered that she writes about the methodological difficulties involved in teaching a multiculturalist course. Once again, we see the border between literature and culture studies blurring. This essay is meant to offer the students as well as teachers of a multicultural canon "a clue to the roadblocks to a too-quick enthusiasm for the other, in the aftermath of colonialism." (Spivak 248)

The essay assumes that the multiculturalist course is offered in a metropolitan city. The context is quite clearly marked here. However, there are moments when Spivak does use the term 'teacher' or 'postcolonial teacher' or 'metropolitan teacher teaching a multicultural course' in a way that makes us wonder how this postcolonial teacher relates herself to other postcolonial teachers teaching in the other parts of the world.[62] Teaching English and literatures written in India, could any time be considered equivalent to teaching a multicultural canon, especially if literatures of other commonwealth countries are included in the syllabus.[63]

Moreover, the example taken by her—that of R.K. Narayan's *Guide*—is one good example of an author exhibiting the 'will to particularism'[64] and within India itself could be considered 'culturally different' by people belonging to different regions and to different communities. How do postcolonial teachers overcome this difficulty of teaching a text without being too enthusiastic or too negative about the other? This question is very important especially if we take into consideration the ever-increasing communal tension in India.[65] It is very likely that we see disregard for the other in an Indian class-room situation rather than a 'too-quick enthusiasm for the other.' Moreover, in India, we also have to reckon another group of readers, that of students, who read books such as *Guide* not because of any interest in literature, but as part of a compulsory requirement that comes attached to the study of English language. There exists a difference in being a teacher of multicultural course where to be multicultural may be a question of enthusiasm, and being a teacher in a context where multicultural existence—even in its liberal sense—is threatened. This difference gives many of the arguments of the postcolonial critics a shade of generalization, thereby making us conscious that these statements have to be compared, contrasted and modified while discussing literature of a specific cultural matrix.

Reconsidering Representation and Mimicry

I have tried to argue that faced with cultural specificity, particular forms of postcolonial discussion, which can be used to discuss contexts like those created by Deshpande's novels, have to vary from the current discussions on representation, representability, on cultural diversity, hybridity. As Kumkum Sangari puts it succinctly:

> the problems of meaning and representation that beset the 'Third World' are very different from the slippage of meaning and of the 'real' which currently confronts *academic* discourses of Europe and America. To say this is not to claim the possibility of arriving at some essential indigenous truth

> by a more tortuous route, but to insist that the epistemological problem is *itself* a historical one. Both meaning and the need for locating meaning are conjunctural; and it is useful to maintain a distinction between the realized difficulty of knowing and the pre-asserted or a priori difficulty of knowing. And if we agree, then surely the problem of meaning for the 'Third World' is also at bottom entangled in the problems of social and political aspiration and reconstitution; whereas the tenuousness of meaning in the 'West,' equally a product of this historical conjuncture, is one in which the felt absence of the will or the ability to change things as they are can become the voice of the epistemological despair.[66]

Unless this problem is mentioned, even postcolonial discourse will fall into the trap of universalising tendencies. To be interested only in the question of the possibility or impossibility of a representative mode of writing where recognition is the only means of reading will also be faulty, if it is taken as a critical stance. The problem of meaning is entangled with the problem of social and political aspiration and reconstitution.

With the help of the novels discussed in this chapter and by using some of the analytic tools derived from several postcolonial theories, I have attempted to show that the question of subaltern subject position as well as the question of representation need to be dealt with in a diversified and complicated manner, especially when taken up in connection with a specific context. I do not wish to say that in Deshpande's novels one can detect an Indian version of feminism as has been suggested elsewhere.[67] I have been trying to say that some of these critical terms and theories might act as theories of exclusivism and finally lead to another kind of canon formation within the post-colonial situation. Moreover, the understanding that the unmediated representation of realism in fiction is not possible, should not stop one from taking up novels which are branded as being realistic.

It is, however, not to say that the prominent postcolonial critics are writing about a uniform 'Other.' The differences, and contradictions among the 'others' of a society, the blurring of the borders between self and other, are not taken for granted by most of these critics. The discussions presented in this section are meant to supplement the already existing tone of caution which we detect in many of these arguments. Just as the concept of the 'other' is made a complex issue, so can the idea of representation and mimicry be explained at many levels. Bhabha, when he mentions the ambivalence involved in mimicry does not really talk about different versions of mimicry. In her discussion of the politics of identity, Diana Fuss mentions two arguments regarding mimicry which seem to be prevalent in present-day critical arguments:

a) mimicry of subversion, as used in recent feminist theory and

b) mimicry of subjugation, as recorded by Bhabha.[68]

It is her view that these two theories of mimicry can also overlap and that the mimicry of subversion can at times lead to a reinforcement of conventional relations, and the mimicry of subjugation can give rise to resistance and disruption. The politics of mimesis is shaped by the context and also by such questions as 'who is imitating whom and under what conditions':

> When we take into account multiple axes of difference that cross-cut, interfere with, and mutually constitute each other, the dream of a playful mimesis cannot be so easily or immediately recuperated for a progressive politics. Given the various and continually changing cultural co-ordinates that locate identity at the site of both fantasy and power, one would have to acknowledge, at the very least, that the same mimetic act can be disruptive and reversionary at once. (Diana Fuss 25)

One also has to bear in mind this aspect of representation when one talks about novels such as the ones analysed here. The generalisations which could come into being because of the class position of the novelist have to be re-written since there are other elements involved here.

Repetition as a Mode of Representation

Writing about the central ambivalence which constitutes and gives currency to the colonial stereotypes, Bhabha characterizes this discursive strategy as a "form of knowledge and identification that vacillates between what is always 'in place,' already known, and something that must be repeated.'"[69] I would like to make use of this formulation for my discussion of the strategies used by the novelist, in the works which have been discussed in this chapter. Not stereotype, but repetition characterizes her writing, and it is a kind of repetition which not only renders the category 'woman' ambivalent, but also shows that 'what is always "in place," what is already known,' must be repeated. It is this repetition which makes it difficult to categorize her novels as simply being examples of realistic representations. This tendency towards repetition seems to be there despite a desire in the novelist to talk about human predicament, to present 'honest articulations of a painful human experience.'[70]

Thus the desire for conveying a certain meaning is seen even in the novels of Shashi Deshpande. However, it does not always take the shape of the omniscient author who goes around imparting meanings. The desire to create a meaning, to convey a message which outlives the plot of a novel continues in her case in the form of repetition: repetition of character-types, plot construction, social milieu and the literary interests of the female protagonists of her novels. This repetition, and the seriousness with which repetition is made, also gives rise to one more set of meanings. Though they are similar to the meanings one could get from the individual novels, together, they attain the stature of something like a testimonial. I do not wish to suggest here that one can glean out 'true meaning' or 'true experience' out of a testimonial. I would like to emphasise that her very attempt at representing lives of women takes the form of repetition. It is the mode not the meaning that interests me here.

The possibility of naming some of the characters in her novel subaltern, has already been explored in the earlier section I of this work. According to such an argument, it is not possible to term the protagonists of her novel subaltern because of the peculiarly privileged positions they occupy despite their gender and despite their 'awareness' of themselves as being female. This privilege is given by their class, caste, 'education' and also by their ability to read and appreciate the canons of Western Literature, Sanskrit Literature as well as by their ability to articulate. Yet the protagonists could not be termed 'liberated' either. There seems to be something which all the protagonists as narrators are trying to establish and convey. The privilege of their position does not exclude elements of subjugation—of subalternity. It is this ambiguous subalternity which gets a patterned representation in the novels of Shashi Deshpande.

Deshpande herself sees some kind of 'wholeness' in her heroines, which prevents them from disintegrating at the time of crisis.[71] However, it is not only crisis which binds most of her female characters together. There are certain patterns which are repeated; certain plot structures which seem all too familiar to a reader who has already read one or more of her novels. The crisis that is represented in the novel is also the critical point in the marriage of her protagonist.

If one could superimpose her novels upon each other, one would arrive at the common pattern with one or more of the following themes: uneasiness in marriage but a desire to go on with it, the crisis caused by the death of a loved one; the conflict with a mother or a motherly figure; the presence of a male figure outside the marriage, who generally understands the creativity and the sensitivity of the narrator; the wise father or father figure who is good to the daughter; the transition from the joint family structure to the nuclear family, the longings and nostalgic memories which are attached to a childhood spent in the joint family, and so on. Yet, these are not to be dismissed as the "same refrain" and monotonous "monologues."[72] The refrain so produced breaks the myth of the wholeness of the character and thus goes against the argument that it is the individual who is important in her novels. The universalisation of the 'woman' is not brought about by the narration of one story, but it seems to have been achieved by the compelling re-narration which happens in many of her novels. The moments of shocking recognition, however, survive even after these repeated narrations and in spite of the obvious marks of the influence of the western novel, especially the novels of the nineteenth century, on the narrator.

Understanding Time Differently

Although I do not wish to talk about a peculiarly Indian attitude towards time, I want to mention here two instances of literary criticism, where this non-Western concept of time has been highlighted. Dieter Riemenschneider, in his contribution "History and the Individual in Anita Desai's *Clear Light of Day* and Salman Rushdie's *Midnight's Children*," particularly mentions the difference between Rushdie and Desai, which is actually rooted in their different approach to the concept of time. Pointing out how the moral issues are linked with the philosophical in the Hindu concept of time, he reminds us that Rushdie's Saleem perceives history as it is understood in Hindu cosmology, where years in a nation's life are but a fraction in the life of Brahma, the God of creation. In Deshpande's novels too, we see her protagonists pondering over such issues as reality and illusion. Their pondering is more philosophical than moral. This is clearly seen in *A Matter of Time*, where Sumi's husband Gopal, who leaves his wife and his three daughters, to live all by himself, cannot give any reason for his unusual behaviour. Unlike her other novels, in *A Matter of Time* there is no logical cause which has induced Gopal to give up his family life. Surprisingly, both husband and wife react to this crisis as if it were normal, for such a thing to happen in a 'normal' family. There is no animosity between the husband and wife. One year after this kind of life apart from one another, Sumi visits her husband, and her philosophical comments are what I wish to emphasize in order to put across the earlier mentioned concept of time:

> Living with Amma, I've begun to see it differently. A *year*, I mean. For her, it's not just a chunk that gets cut off and then it's over. No, it's all mixed up with the seasons and festivals and flowers and fruits. It's a cycle. Nothing is over, *things keep coming back over and over again*, they're all connected. Ganapathi and the rains, Dussehra and marigolds, Diwali and the wintry feeling, Tulsi lagna and the tamarinds . . . (219, Emphasis added)

This takes me back to what Riemenschneider has to say in connection with Rushdie's Saleem. Considering how years in the life of a man or in the history of a nation are but fractions when considered along with the enormity of the life of Brahma,

> [r]eality is, indeed, illusion within the context of Brahma's life, irrespective of whether we take Hindu cosmology literally in a religious-philosophical sense or understand it as a myth created to grasp the relationship between reality and illusion.[73]

As we have seen in the earlier paragraphs, this attention to repetitiveness, to the circularity of structure, imply that in the novels of Shashi Deshpande, the more general understanding of time as something that traces linear movement, is being constantly rewritten by this other understanding of time which follows circular path.

Another critic who recognizes the use of this kind of circular plot construction, is Adele King. This time it is in the context of the discussion of the portrayal of women in Shashi Deshpande's novels. According to her in these novels, "[t]ime seems to move rather in circles than in straight lines. The conclusions are therefore tentative; there is no end to a circular pattern."[74] But for King it is indicative of the "position of the woman in a patriarchal society—someone without a clear sense of the purpose (. . .) and without a firm sense of her own identity." (King 165) It is not unusual to consider that a circular concept of time does not incorporate change. We have already seen that even though there aren't obvious changes in the protagonists, nor is there complete stasis. It is this ambiguity which enables the women in her novels to envisage change.

It is her book *A Matter of Time* that stands apart from the rest of the previous novels. It is here that we can really see the breaking of the accepted notions of a realistic mode of writing. In this book which is again about a middle-class married woman, the general pattern of her novels is superimposed by the many stories of the women who figure in here. Unlike the other novels where there is clearly one protagonist, here we see both Gopal and Sumi acting as narrators and there is a constant move between the third person and the second person narrative. The complacency of the reader of realist novels is broken here by the innumerable number of names that are mentioned, names that indicate the different scions of the family. Sumi's story only becomes a catalyst that pulls out so many other stories. The narrative continuity is often broken by such comments as "They will not meet again" (224) and "We will leave them there" (246), indicating that the author does not make any attempt to pass this off as a realistic novel. Even the death of Sumi and her father at the end somehow seems to forge the idea of destiny that rules over our lives but which also makes us free to face it with 'dignity and strength.' (246)

What is interesting in this rather new approach to narrative is the way in which a kind of female tradition and continuity is envisioned in the history of a traditional family where the women find no place. For the first time in the corpus of her novels we come across a woman who accepts that she can be away from her husband, who finds an opportunity to re-read and re-write the tale of a princess who marries the son of a gardener, who entertains thoughts of getting a job away from the supportive nexus of relatives and friends. Yet the woman does not last the narrative. She dies at the end making her general use of the circular plot of the novel change into the circular theme of life and death.

Strangely enough, this novel, unlike her other novels records the presence of migratory history. Unlike Bhabha's understanding of the migratory experience, here we see that the experience of migration does not result in any obvious form of antagonistic relationship. It is a case of the new element gradually being accepted by the surrounding context. There is no mention of the borders of culture or of hybrid culture. This family in its wider network of other relationships appears to be as closed as the others.

It is because of the many unusual elements in *A Matter of Time* that I do not wish to group it with the other novels. Going back to the theme of repetition, we have to mention again that the repetitive nature of these novels also threatens the usually accepted and critiqued version of time—and as a consequence, history—as something which is progressive, something which is linear in nature. In other words, it could be associated with Kala Chakra—a concept which sees time as being cyclic. The usual assumption associated with this concept of cyclic time is that it did not include any scope for change. But Romila Thapar in *Time as a Metaphor of History: Early India,*[75] shows how the idea that Indian sense of time was entirely cyclic and did not include the concept of change originated at the turn of the eighteenth century.

It was in fact a part of the process of orientalist othering where complimentarity was stressed and the other was actually what the self was not and in building up an image of the other the complimentary self was being projected in a series of binary oppositions. Cyclic time was considered primitive as opposed to the concept of the progressive linear time. Romila Thapar argues with the help of texts that deal with the ancient scripts and their analyses that the concept of time in India was never entirely cyclic but included various versions of linear time too. More important, there was always the idea of change incorporated into this simultaneous existence of cyclic and linear time. Talking about the other categories of time Romila Thapar says that the "sharp demarcation between cyclic and linear is made somewhat indistinct by these chronological forms which therefore introduce a range of mediatory positions. The dichotomy weakens if there is a recognition that the one does not negate the other and the two can co-exist." (Thapar 9) Her study shows how the distinction between these two supposed polarities become blurred in this different attitude to time.

Perhaps it is this ambivalent attitude towards time, that makes these repetitive structures peculiar to Deshpande. The linear concept of time is rewritten in the composite structure of her novels. We could thus use her novels as tools even in poststructuralist discussions as signs which bring into crisis narrations which are dependent on progressive, unilinear development of stories and events.

Shashi Deshpande's protagonists embody the western concept of the individual as being the knowing narrator. However, this Enlightenment idea of the subject is being rewritten when she rewrites her protagonists in each novel. The blurred existence of the subject as the knowing individual moving towards a self-determined end and the subject as being caught in the cycle of repetition brings to mind the ambivalence of Bhabha. Are the thinking-writing female protagonists of Deshpande the embodiment of this kind of ambivalence?

These protagonists are generally in contrast with the context which can be termed traditional in broad terms. Many of the older women too, likewise, could be called traditional, even when some of them are discussed here as giving rise to ambivalent meanings.

We could therefore consider these women to be representing traditional values, whereby to 'tradition' I am ascribing a set of conditions that are similar to those mentioned by Raymond Williams. Tradition, not as something that refers to the past but as something which refers to the contemporary world. In other words, tradition is

> an aspect of *contemporary* social and cultural organization, in the interest of the dominance of a specific class. It is a version of the past which is intended to connect with and ratify the present. What it offers in practice is a sense of *predisposed continuity*.[76]

Especially in the context of these novels, where technically speaking, women seem to be occupying more space than men, one could say that this kind of 'social and cultural organization' is in the interest of the dominance of a specific *gender*. This version of traditional women then connects with and ratifies the present. The mothers who ate all by themselves after the fathers and children have finished their meal do give a sense of 'predisposed continuity.' Moreover, the novels also conclude with a note that suggests continuity, rather than change. Should we then call Deshpande's novels themselves as being traditional? Such an attempt is also thwarted by the repetitive nature of the stories, of characters. It is therefore that we have to look for a different kind of explanation for this mode of writing.

The repetition of the same kind of story and the reappearance of the same kind of thinking female character—a woman who tries to chart out new roles for herself within marriage and becomes preoccupied with her own self, looks for meaning in the complicated network of family ties, frequently finds woman as perpetrator of the patriarchal system, notices those women who really make the existence of women of her class easier—takes fiction away from the chosen mode of realism. The narrative of repetition then makes its presence felt outside the traditional framework of a realistic novel. It adds a tone of testimony to the fictitious world of the first-person narrations.

Fictional Testimonial

This tone of testimony makes one wonder if her novels too could be described as being examples of *testimonio*. Although John Beverly is very cautious about giving a generic form to *testimonio*, his own account of this form of writing at least shows that it is getting much more attention than before and shows also that it is different from the conventionally accepted genres of literature.[77] It is not possible to claim this kind of nomenclature for the novels of Shashi Deshpande, but the testimonial-like elements present in her novel makes one propose that it is a subverted model of *testimonio* that we see in her writings.

It is my hypothesis that it is the peculiarity of the historical moment and the nature of her class identity which gives rise to this aspect. Unlike the real *testimonio* which "represents an affirmation of the individual subject, even of individual growth and transformation, but in connection with a group or class situation marked by marginalization, oppression, and struggle,"[78] a peculiar ambiguity arises here because of the contradictions which the class differences produce in the identification of the protagonist with the group 'female': "The narrator in *testimonio* is a real person who continues living and acting in a real social history that also continues. *Testimonio* can never in this sense create the illusion of that textual 'in-itselfness' that has been the basis of literary formalism, nor can it be adequately analysed in these terms."[79] In a reversal, the protagonist of the novels of Shashi Deshpande lives on in her other novels and therefore, appears to defy the textual "in-itselfness."

Once again, it is my hypothesis that this peculiarly subverted or, fictional form of testimonial is produced because of the peculiar nature of the middle class woman whom the novelist projects in her novel. Her class and her education give her privileges which prevent her from being identified as subaltern or from completely identifying herself with the women belonging to the class of the maid-servants, but at the same time, there are also elements which bind her to these other women because of the traditionally rigid societal expectations.

NOTES

1. Gayatri Chakravorty Spivak, "A Literary Representation of the Subaltern: A Woman's Text from the Third World," *In Other Worlds: Essays in Cultural Politics* (Routledge, 1988), pp. 267-68. Spivak mentions the tendency to generalise all third-world literature as being still caught in realism and observes that much of this misrepresentation stems from a lack of acquaintance with the language of the original. Although she takes up the specific case of Mahasweta Devi's "Breast-Giver," the idea is something which could be applied to novels which are written by the post-colonial subjects in the English language. In spite of a fear of being a prey to provincialism, one has to stress here that the lack of acquaintance with the milieu of the writer could once again result in some kind of essentialism or exoticism.
2. Emily Apter, "Ethnographic Travesties: Colonial Realism, French Feminism, and the Case of Elissa Rha's," *After Colonialism: Imperial Histories and Postcolonial Displacements*, ed. Gyan Prakash (Princeton: Princeton University Press, 1995), p. 299. This essay, by way of discussion of the works of the Algerian writer of the 1920s, Elissa Rha's, raises the issue of the relationship between 'realistic' fiction as well as stereotypes of the women in North Africa and the early feminist struggles in France. What she terms as colonial realism is noticeable in that period where photographic presentation of the exotic competed with the written presentation. In the fiction of Rha's, Apter detects the break where the 'type' veers into caricature. It is here that this kind of realism reveals the "complex process of 'native' self-representation and self-marketing under the conditions of colonial image-production than about the 'local color' of authentic autochthonous experience." (p. 311) It would not be wrong to say that this complex process of self-representation and self-marketing can be seen at work even now in the world of post-colonial image-production.
3. See Abdul R. JanMohamed, *Manichean Aeshetics* (Amherst: The University of Massachusetts Press, 1983), p. 283. JanMohamed's claim that the very act of writing in English is an antagonistic move is not applicable to Deshpande because she is not addressing her novel such groups as 'colonizers' and the 'colonized.' The colonial situation is never overtly mentioned in her novels. Moreover, his idea of literacy as something which destroys oral culture is not ten-

able in all the sections of the society in India. The written forms have existed for quite a long time now, although oral cultural forms have also existed simultaneously because certain communities were denied access to the written forms.

4. Viney Kirpal, in an interesting attempt at delineating the characteristics of the Third World novel points out how putting these novels in the nineteenth century 'realistic' novels is absurd. See Kirpal, "What is the Modern Third World Novel?," *Journal of Commonwealth Literature*, 23, 1 (1988): 144-56.
5. See Firdous Azim, *The Colonial Rise of the Novel* (London: Routledge, 1993), pp. 30-31.
6. Spivak too makes the observation that the students of English Literature in India are 'mostly women.' See Gayatri Chakravorty Spivak, "The Burden of English," in *Orientalism and the Postcolonial Predicament: Perspectives on South Asia*, ed. Carol A. Breckenridge and Peter van der Veer (Philadelphia: University of Pennsylvania Press, 1993), p. 136.
7. For an interesting presentation of the current discussion literature and its implication to and involvement with other areas like culture studies, see Thomas Wägenbaur, "Hybride Hybridität: Der Kulturkonflikt im Text der Kulturtheorie," Arcadia, Band 31, 1996: 27-29.
8. Edward Said, "Overlapping Territories, Intertwined Histories," *Culture and Imperialism*, p. 12.
9. P.P. Raveendran asks this question while considering the historicity of some of the poems written by the Malayalee poet Kamala Das. See his essay "Text as History, History as Text," *Journal of Commonwealth Literature*, Vol. XXIX, No. 1(1994):51. Another critic who uses this term 'double-bind' is Meenakshi Mukherjee, according to whom the study of literature in India 'a generation ago' meant submitting to the dominant critical mode that had its origin in Anglo-American academic institutions and was male in outlook. See Mukherjee, "The Centre Cannot Hold: Two Views of the Periphery," *After Europe*, ed. Stephen Slemon and Helen Tiffin, p. 41. This view can be contrasted with that of Robin Visel, who talking in terms of a settler colony, says that if the colonized woman is a victim of 'double colonization' then, the white settler woman can be termed 'half-colonized.' To my mind, this kind of categorization and conferring of names sounds too smug and contrived. See Visel, "A Half-Colonization: The Problem of the White Colonial Woman Writer," *Kunapipi*, 10, 3 (1988): 39-45.
10. See Viji Sheshadri and Shashi Deshpande, "Gegenwärtige indo-englische Literatur von Frauen," *Postkoloniale Literaturen: Peripherien*

oder neue Zeiten? hrgs. Liselotte Glage und Martina Michel (Hamburg: Argument Verlag, 1993), p. 102.

11. Rajeshwari Sunder Rajan, referring to a 'new brand of woman' projected by media, shows that the construction of this image of woman has to comply with harmonious mixing of ideas of a 'traditional Indian woman' as well as a 'modern' woman. See her "Real and Imagined Women: Politics and/ of Representation," *Real and Imagined Women: Gender, Culture and Postcolonialism* (London: Routledge, 1993), pp. 129-46. The modern woman projected by the commercial advertisements, TV Serials and other forms of media is represented as balancing 'between (deep) tradition and (surface) modernity.' (p. 133)
12. Shashi Deshpande, *The Dark Holds No Terrors* (1980; New Delhi: Penguin Books, 1990).
13. In an interview, Deshpande says that she is "an admirer of earlier writers Jane Austen, the Brontes, Mrs. Gaskell, Dickens, Trollope . . . " See T.N. Geetha, "An Interview with Shashi Deshpande," in *Indian Women Novelists*, Set III, Vol. 4, ed. R.K. Dhawan, pp. 9-11. This is an interesting connection to the world of English literature because almost all of these writers have been re-read by Said from the perspective of culture and imperialism.
14. See Spivak, "Echo," *The Spivak Reader*, ed. Donna Landry and Gerald McLean (London: Routledge, 1995), p. 178.
15. See the short story "The Last Enemy," in Deshpande's collection of short stories *The Intrusion and Other Stories* (New Delhi: Penguin Books, 1993). Duryodhana, who awaits death at the hands of Bhima, his cousin and one of the Pandava brothers, is acutely conscious of his loneliness, but comes to the conclusion that in death he is victorious, even though in the battle he has been the loser.
16. The story of Duryodhana is used once again in her *The Dark Holds No Terrors* (1980; New Delhi: Penguin Books, 1990), where Saru's mother on her death-bed takes courage from Duryodhana's experience. Saru, the protagonist, herself justifies her decision to 'go on living' based on Duryodhana's realization that ultimately human beings are lonely. I quote from *The Dark Holds No Terrors*: "And then it came to her. It was as if she was vouchsafed a vision, the same one perhaps, that her mother had had when she had heard Duryodhana's story just before she died. Even if it is an illusion, it is the only reality we will ever know. Therefore the only thing is to go on as if it is real, knowing all the while it is only an illusion." pp. 219-20. Though this might seem fatalistic to those who are not exposed to this kind of philosophical reflection, I have mentioned

it to show that other versions of *Weltanschauung* are possible.

17. Kipling, *Kipling's India: Uncollected Sketches 1884-88*, ed. Thomas Pinney (Houndmills: Macmillan Press, 1986), p. 177.
18. *That Long Silence* (1988; Penguin Books India, 1989), and *Roots and Shadows* (1983; Hyderabad: Disha Books, 1992).
19. Rajeswari Sunder Rajan, "The Feminist Plot and the Nationalist Allegory: Home and World in Two Indian Women's Novels in English," *Modern Fiction Studies: Fiction on the Indian Subcontinent*, 39, 1 (Spring 1993): 71-92. Rajeswari Sunder Rajan, in her interesting essay on Deshpande, also talks about the novelist's refusal to undertake a radical social critique. It is her contention that one of Deshpande's novels, *That Long Silence* "offers itself too easily in terms of a contrast between a Western feminism that raises women's consciousness about their oppression, and an indigenous culture that designates her role as solely domestic." (p. 79) My own reading of this novel is that the domestic role played by the woman and her consciousness of oppression are represented in a more complex manner and therefore do not break up into any easy contrast.
20. Edward Said, "Freedom from Domination in the Future," *Culture and Imperialism*, p. 318.
21. *Ibid.*, p. 61. This idea can be contrasted with that of 'subaltern secularism' put forth by Bhabha in "Unpacking my Library . . . Again." *The Postcolonial Question*. See pp. 208-11.
22. Homi K. Bhabha, "The Postcolonial and the Postmodern," *The Location of Culture*, p. 178.
23. Susie Tharu and K. Lalitha, *Women Writing in India: Volume 1: 600 B. C. to the Early Twentieth Century* (New York: Feminist Press, 1991); *Volume 2: The Twentieth Century* (New York, 1993).
24. Bhabha repeatedly distinguishes between liberal ideas of multiculturalism, secularism which have had their origins in the European Enlightenment. His answer to these liberal ideas of tolerant living together is 'subaltern secularism.' See "Unpacking my Library. . . . Again," *The Post-colonial Question*, pp. 208-11.
25. It must be mentioned here that Bhabha does mention the difference in the understanding in Britain among men and women who were involved in the miners's strike of 1984-85; for him, however, this difference in experience, which has arisen due to the difference in gender (even though there is no difference in class) is indicative of the 'hybrid moment of political change,' because there has to be negotiation between the gender and class. See "The Commitment to Theory," The Location of Culture, pp. 27-28.
26. Bhabha, "The Postcolonial and the Postmodern," *The Location of*

Culture, p. 179.

27. Spivak, *In Other Worlds*, p. 258.
28. Gayatri Chakravorty Spivak, "Can the Subaltern Speak?," *Colonial Discourse and Post-colonial Theory: A Reader*, ed. Patrick Williams and Laura Chrisman (New York: Harvester Wheatsheaf, 1993), pp. 66-111.
29. Shashi Deshpande, *The Binding Vine* (London: Virago Press, 1993).
30. Gayatri Chakravorty Spivak, *In Other Worlds*, p. 253. It must be mentioned here that Spivak's use of the term 'subaltern' in connection with the gendered subject can be seen as a conscious reaction to the use of the same term in the series *Subaltern Studies: Writings on South Asian History and Society, Vols. I, II, III*, ed. Ranajit Guha (Delhi: Oxford University Press). In Vol. I, first published in 1982, the editor gives the Concise Oxford Dictionary meaning of the word subaltern as 'of inferior rank,' but continues to say that in the book it will be used as "a name for the general attribute of subordination in South Asian society whether this is expressed in terms of class, caste, age, gender and office or in any other way." In her own appraisal of the three volumes of this series called "Subaltern Studies: Deconstructing Historiography," Spivak, by 'reading against the grain of the text,' makes the observation that the female as the subaltern is excluded in these volumes. According to her, "if the question of female subaltern consciousness, whose instrumentality is so often seen to be crucial, is a red herring, the question of subaltern consciousness as such must be judged a red herring as well." (*In Other Worlds*, p. 218) Later, on the same page she goes on to say, "If the peasant insurgent was the victim and the unsung hero of the first wave of resistance against territorial imperialism in India, it is well known that, for reasons of collusion between pre-existing structures of patriarchy and trans-national capitalism, it is the urban sub-proletarian female who is the paradigmatic subject of the current configuration of the International Division of Labour."
31. Hereafter, wherever I have quoted from her novels, I have indicated the page numbers within brackets immediately after the quotation.
32. The theme of 'rape in marriage' is a recurring theme in Deshpande's novels and short stories. For example, *The Dark Holds No Terrors* (1980; Penguin Books India, 1990). The short story "The Intrusion," in *The Intrusion and Other Stories* (Penguin Books India, 1993), explores a similar theme.
33. I am once again referring to the back cover of the book.
34. Shakutai's fear of gossip is understandable because its truth-like appearance is particularly effective in a society where solidarity-

through-gossip can be easily achieved. I have in mind the comments made by Trinh T. Minh-ha regarding anthropological studies and 'scientific gossip': "The kind of truth [gossip] claims to disclose is a confidential truth that requires commitment from both the speaker and the listener. He who lends an ear to gossip already accepts either sympathizing with or being an accomplice of the gossiper." See Trinh T. Minh-ha, *Woman, Native, Other: Postcoloniality and Feminism* (Bloomington: Indiana University Press, 1989), p. 68.

35. In the great battle between the Pandavas and the Kauravas, Abhimanyu, one of the sons of the Pandavas, is defeated because of the Chakravyuha formation. Once the warrior makes his way through the circular positioning of the enemy soldiers, he cannot come out of this labyrinthine formation. As Urmila puts it here, "Abhimanyu had to die, there was no other way he could have got out." (p. 202)

36. This difference in the position of women occupying different classes of the society is not always taken into consideration by women's movements too. Drawing our attention to the fact that "much feminist research and practice has been contained within the colonial and nationalist historical paradigms of reform and reawakening," Kumkum Sangari and Sudesh Vaid claim that many of the urban reforms that demand equality for women at home and in the work place "show little concern with class inequality." See Sangari and Vaid, ed., "Introduction," *Recasting Women: Essays in Colonial History* (New Delhi: Kali for Women, 1989), pp. 24-25.

37. Homi K. Bhabha, "Representation and the Colonial Text: A Critical Exploration of Some Forms of Mimeticism," *The Theory of Reading*, ed., Frank Gloversmith (Brighton: The Harvester Press, 1984), pp. 92-122.

38. Rajeswari Sunder Rajan, *Modern Fiction Studies*, 39, 1 (Spring 1993):104.

39. Rajan, "In Deshpande's novel this tension leads to a focus on women's issues—implicitly regarded as common to all women—even as the writer's consciousness about women's oppression is attributed to promptings from western feminism." *Modern Fiction Studies*, 39, 1 (Spring 1993):77.

40. A similar observation is already made by Rajeswari Sunder Rajan in the article quoted earlier. She in turn draws upon the observation of the well-known Kannada writer and teacher of English Literature, U.R. Ananthamurthy that the major division in Indian society is between the literate few and the illiterate majority so that any book-reading public is always already an elite group: "'The Search for an Identity': A Kannada Writer's Viewpoint," in *Dialogue: New Cul-*

tural Identities, ed. Guy Amirthanayagam (London: Macmillan, 1982). Rajeswari Sunder Rajan herself says that the "(w)omen novelists writing in English in India therefore necessarily inhabit a rarefied realm; . . ."

41. See Prasanna Sree Sathupathi, "Conflict and Identity in Shashi Deshpande's Novels," *Indian Women Novelists*, Set III, Vol. 4, pp. 12-19.
42. Said, *Culture and Imperialism*, p. 318.
43. See "Author's Note," *The Dark Holds No Terrors.*
44. S.P. Swain, "Shashi Deshpande's *The Dark Holds No Terrors*: Saru's Feminine Sensibility," *Indian Women Writers*, Set III, Vol. 4, ed. R. K. Dhawan, p. 34. The author does not make clear what this feminine sensibility is. However, it is mentioned that the mother stands for the traditional and the old while the daughter for the modern and the new. The desire to convert Deshpande's heroines into everywoman is expressed in this case too. The further claim that the mental journey of the protagonist is "an initiation into the mystery of human existence," (p. 39) only gives a philosophic appearance to the many clich/s which appear in the text of the critic.
45. Prasanna Sree Sathupati, "Conflict and Identity in Shashi Deshpande's Novels," *Indian Women Writers*, Set III, Vol. 4, p. 17. It is interesting to see that the question of identity is central here. However, the debates which are associated with the identity-question are not at all taken into account. It is as if the talk about the identity of the woman has moved one full circle.
46. Spivak, *The Spivak Reader*, p. 188.
47. Or, as mentioned earlier, they go to the other extreme of seeing no difference in characterization, of saying that she universalizes the condition of her protagonist and a 'variety of other female figures.'
48. Kamini Dinesh, "Moving out of the Cloistered Self: Shashi Deshpande's Protagonists," in *Margins of Erasure: Purdah in the Subcontinental Novel in English*, pp. 204-5.
49. I am once again reminded of the brilliant analysis of the representation of the new brand of woman by Rajeshwari Sunder Rajan in "Real and Imagined Women: Politics and/of Representation," *Real and Imagined Women*, pp. 129-46.
50. Spivak, "The New Historicism," p. 281.
51. Deshpande, *Roots and Shadows* (1983; New Delhi: Disha Books, 1992). All the page numbers provided for citations are from this edition and are mentioned in the text itself.
52. See Homi K. Bhabha, "Introduction: Locations of Culture," in *The Location of Culture*, pp. 1-18.
53. See Bhabha, "Representation and the Colonial Text," *The Theory*

of Reading, especially pp. 114-20.

54. Bhabha, "Introduction," *The Location of Culture*, pp. 4-5.
55. Bhabha, "Unpacking my Library . . . Again," p. 208.
56. Spivak, "How to read a 'Culturally Different' Book" p. 149, n. 14.
57. Even in narrations that represent the Brahmin widow as bound by all the restrictions that a traditional Hindu Brahmin society can conceive of subversion and opposition can be seen. See for example M.K. Indira, *Phaniyamma*, trans. Tejaswini Niranjana (1976; New Delhi: Kali for Women, 1989).
58. See Bhabha, "Postcolonial Authority and Postcolonial Guilt," *Cultural Studies*, ed. Lawrence Grossberg, Cary Nelson and Paula A. Treichler, pp. 58 and 59. The ideas developed in this essay seem to have been used for the writing of two longer essays in *The Location of Culture*: "The Postcolonial and the Postmodern: The Question of Agency," pp. 171-97 and "How Newness enters the World: Postmodern Space, Postcolonial Times and the Trials of Cultural Translation," pp. 212-35.
59. Compare this with Spivak's comment about education being an instrument of upward class-mobility. Spivak, "How to Read a 'Culturally Different' Book," p. 138.
60. Shakuntala Bharvani sees Jaya as being representative of the girls belonging to the middle-class families in post-Independence India. According to her the duality which one can see in such a woman arises because of the desire to get English liberal education on the one hand, and to remain conservative on the other. See "Some Recent Trends in Modern Indian Fiction: A Study of Shashi Deshpande's *That Long Silence*, Shashi Tharoor's *The Great Indian Novel* and Amitav Ghosh's *The Shadow Lines*," in *Indian Women Novelists* Set I, Vol. I, p. 149.
61. Spivak, "How to read a 'Culturally Different' Book?," in *Colonial Discourse/Postcolonial Theory*, ed. Francis Baker et al (Manchester: Manchester University Press, 1993), pp. 126-50. This essay also appears in *The Spivak Reader*, pp. 237-66.
62. At this point I would like to draw attention to the Interview "The Post-colonial Critic," in *The Post-colonial Critic: Interviews, Strategies, Dialogues*, pp. 67-74. There is a clear indication that her interviewers Rashmi Bhatnagar, Lola Chatterjee and Rajeshwari Sunder Rajan wish to differentiate themselves from Gayatri Chakravorty Spivak. Their terms of differentiation of her as being the 'post-colonial diasporic Indian who seeks to decolonize the mind' and themselves as native intellectuals (for the sake of convenience, they say) is not acceptable to Spivak (p. 67). She constitutes all

of them as being 'post-colonial intellectuals.' The problem with this kind of categorization is that the attempt of the interviewers to convey the conditions under which they teach English literature especially to women, does not receive serious attention from Spivak.

63. This idea can be contrasted with that of Meenakshi Mukherjee, who says that "in India at least there is a general obliviousness of the political complexities and cultural contradiction inherent in the situation of an English teacher in a postcolonial classroom . . . " See Mukherjee, "The Centre Cannot Hold: Two Views of the Periphery," *After Europe*, ed. Stephen Slemon and Helen Tiffin, p. 42.

64. Frantz Fanon, *The Wretched of the Earth*, p. 192. This phrase is used by Abdul R. JanMohamed to explain the cultural specificity exemplified by the realism of Chinua Achebe's novels. JanMohamed sees this as a method of negation of the colonial depiction of the natives as savages. See JanMohamed, *Manichean Aesthetics*, p. 283.

65. To compare Spivak's way of treating a culturally different text with that of a Third World teacher teaching First World texts, see Zakia Pathak, "A Pedagogy for Postcolonial Feminists," in *Feminists Theorize the Political*, ed. Judith Butler and Joan W. Scott (New York: Routledge, 1992), pp. 426-41. Even though there are a few generalizations such as 'canonized criticisms' (p. 427), 'our feminist identity'(p. 429), 'Orientalist reading of the Orient' (p. 423), the essay offers new insights into the not-so-often-discussed predicament of the teachers of literature in India. Their attempt to connect the texts which they teach—especially the *Book of Job* and Eliot's *Murder in the Cathedral*—to the political and religious uproar in India caused because of controversies about the location of some important Mosques, makes an interesting reading.

66. Kumkum Sangari, "The Politics of the Possible," *Interrogating Modernity: Culture and Colonialism in India*, ed. Tejaswini Niranjana et al (Calcutta: Seagull, 1993), pp. 245-46.

67. Ranjana Ash, "The Search for Freedom in Indian Women's Writing," in *Motherlands: Black Women's Writing form Africa, the Caribbean and South Asia*, ed. Susheila Nasta (London: The Women's Press Limited, 1991). I am not sure if it could really be claimed as an Indian version, or if one could claim anything as being an Indian version of feminism; but this is how Ranjana Ash describes Shashi Dehshpande's earlier novel *Roots and Shadows*: "In Deshpande's important treatment of what one might call Indian 'feminism' in her novel, *Roots and Shadows* (1983), she shows that the self is not a simple construct: . . . " (p. 16) Even going by the basic paradigms of realistic representation it is hard to arrive at the

following reading of *That Long Silence* which has been given by Ranjana Ash: "For Jaya too there must be a search for her *dharma* and then to follow it: to be a true partner, listening, speaking and understanding that she and Mohan are combined in their mutual *dharma*." (p. 170)

68. Diana Fuss, "Interior Colonies: Frantz Fanon and the Politics of Identification," *Diacritics,* Vol. 24 Nos. 2-3, 1994, pp. 25-42. For another interpretation of 'mimicry' as a liberating force, see Peter Hughes, "Last Post: Alternatives to Postmodernism: A Review Article," *Contemporary Studies in Society and History*, 38, 1 (January 1996): 182-88.
69. Bhabha, "The Other Question," *The Location of Culture*, p. 66.
70. Shashi Deshpande, "Gegenwärtige indo-englische Literatur von Frauen: Eine Perspektive," *Postkoloniale Literaturen*, p. 102.
71. Shashi Deshpande, in an interview, "Breaking that Long Silence," Suman Gopinath, *Sunday Herald* section of the Bangalore-based newspaper *Deccan Herald*, September 25, 1994. Answering a question regarding the sense of loss which recurs as a theme in her novel and about her women who seek 'relentless self-definition,' she says, "The sense of loss is true, but it does not end with loss. The loss that the women experience works as a kind of catharsis and is very necessary for them. A lot of people have said that my women characters are helpless, weak women, but I don't agree. You have to see that there are moments of crisis in their lives and at this point, they might disintegrate. But they do recover and this comes mainly from an innate understanding of the wholeness that lies within themselves."
72. Madhu Jain, *Book Review: The Intrusion and Other Stories by Shashi Deshpande* (Penguin India, 1993). Review published in *India Today,* March 15, 1994, p. 220.
73. Dieter Riemenschneider, "History and the Individual in Anita Desai's *Clear Light of Day* and Salman Rushdie's *Midnight's Children*," *The New Indian Novel in English: A Study of the 1980s*, ed. Viney Kirpal (New Delhi: Allied, 1990), p. 196. It is amusing to see how Riemenschneider's observation that Rushdie's Saleem is influenced by the Indian philosophical understanding of time and history stands in contrast with the view of Makarand Paranjape that in *Midnight's Children* a "large, inclusive, profound, and wise philosophical outlook" is missing. See Paranjape, "Inside and Outside the Whale: Politics and the New Indian English Novel," p. 221, in the same volume.
74. Adele King, "Shashi Deshpande: Portraits of an Indian Woman,"

The New Indian Novel in English, p. 165.

75. (Delhi: Oxford University Press, 1996).
76. Raymond Williams, *Marxism and Literature* (Oxford: Oxford University Press, 1977), p. 116.
77. John Beverly, "The Margin at the Center: On Testimonio (Testimonial Narrative)," *Modern Fiction Studies*, 35, 1 (Spring 1989:11-28. My hypothesis that Shashi Deshpande's novels have the nature of a testimonial is based upon the observation of the author of this article that in a *testimonio* it is the intentionality of the narrator which is paramount: "The situation of narration in *testimonio* has to involve an urgency to communicate, a problem of repression, poverty, subalternity, imprisonment, struggle for survival, and so on, implicated in the act of narration itself." (p. 14) However, the detailed charting out of different aspects of testimonio also make it clear that a comparison between what this article means to be *testimonio* and what the novels of Shashi Deshpande create, can only be a forced and artificial one. Yet, the fact remains that the novels do give rise to some kind of effect which resembles that of the testimonial.
78. *Ibid*., p. 23.
79. *Ibid*., p. 25.

A Margin so Thick with Context[1]

Fortunately, in every age there are readers who prefer the margins to the center.

Tzvetan Todorov, *Genres in Discourse*

For me, literary criticism is promotion as well as understanding, a response to the writer to whom there is often no response, to folk who need the writing as much as they need anything. I know, from literary history, that writing disappears unless there is a response to it.

Barbara Christian, "The Race for Theory"

Much as the colonizer and colonized can no longer be examined as totally autonomous entities, so must critical discourse recognize its imbrication in the fields of its analyses. The postcolonial condition is neither territorially bound nor more the property of one people than of the other: instead, its inevitably retroactive narrative allows for the inclusion both of its colonial past and of the function of criticism at the present time as necessary corollaries to the telling of its stories.

Sara Suleri, *The Rhetoric of English India*

This is a work which has two focal points: postcolonial discourse and the novels of Shashi Deshpande. It has used the postcolonial discourse while reading Shashi Deshpande's novels and at the same time exposed the limitations of these texts when they are used in an unqualified manner. It has provided one specific example of a novelist and her works to show that the postcolonial arguments need to be constantly revised when they are confronted by the peculiarities of the local configuration.

Sanctification of the Local?

It has taken a particular direction and tried hard neither to be too general, nor to be too specific. Perhaps it has become clear that my sympathy is with what one could call postmodern thinking because this way of thinking refuses to generalise. But does this way of thinking also mean that the local is glorified? Does the very local colour of Shashi Deshpande's novels project the idea of provincialism and an uncritical anti-West stand? To answer in the affirmative will defeat the purpose of this project. How important, therefore, is the role of the local in this study? It is worthwhile to quote the warning words of Andrew King and to remind ourselves of the dangers of giving too much importance to the local:

> The argot of postmodernism, words and phrases such as "pluralism," "diffusion of power," "loss of legitimacy," and "colonization," is the language of transition, a transition from a house that is on fire to one that has not yet been constructed. Anyone who ponders on this strange and highly stylized jargon will note that it savagely denigrates the very idea of nation, but resanctifies the local and personal spheres. A resurgency of ethnicity, of biological, regional, linguistic, and cultural associations, looks like a journey back to less abstract social forms and a rediscovery of the comfortable and the familiar.[2]

Has this study been shaped by a desire to rediscover 'the comfortable and the familiar'? Will 'the language of transition' mentioned above only lead to a lack of purpose, a lack of direction? Should talking about 'colonization' lead only to a resanctification of the 'local and personal sphere'?

Recapturing the Arguments

At this moment there is a need to go back to some of the statements made earlier in this study. It must be stated again that specifying the local is not an indication of its sanctification. This is especially true of postcolonialism. Postcolonial discourse, sharing the mood of postmodernism and questioning the continuation of hierarchies, does not merely suggest a reversal of the many binaries which exist in the conemporary world. The postcolonial arguments, taken to their limit, must also recognise the local power configurations. This recognition prevents any kind of simple sanctification of the local. In the concluding paragraphs of his essay, Andrew King mentions the fear of some that in the postmodern world, "the best the intellectual can hope for is to be a shamanistic guardian of the local shrines." (21) It is my hope that this work has contributed towards a refutation of such an image which the interest in the local can instigate. To show that this is a study that pays attention to the local without glorifying it, a recapturing of the arguments is called for.

As the title of my project suggests, the most important aspect of postcolonialism as far as this study is concerned, has been the act of reading—to be specific, the act of rereading. Postcolonialism is basically a shift in perspective. Not only postmodernism or deconstruction, but also the growing importance attached to cultural studies and feminist studies, contributed towards the setting that made possible a discourse which came to be known as postcolonial studies. These prior theories had been reactions, in one way or the other, to the universalizing humanistic world view where one perspective—to put it crudely, that of the white male—obliterated other perspectives which were equally legitimate. Initially postcolonial literary critical activity began as a reading and questioning habit. As in the other contemporary theoretical stances, it is hard to isolate postcolonial literary theories as something that is purely literary in nature. In fact, there is no such thing as a clearly definable literary theory in this area. It is an interdisciplinary field sometimes encroaching upon what can be identified as anthropology, history or culture studies. Opposition to colonialism itself is not new. In the words of Robert Young

> [w]hat has been new in the years since the Second World War during which, for the most part, the decolonization of the European empires has taken place, has been the accompanying attempt to decolonize European thought and the forms of its history as well. It thus marks that fundamental

> shift and cultural crisis currently characterized as postmodernism.[3]

Even though the need to attempt this kind of decolonization was more strongly felt after the publication of Said's Orientalism in 1978, Young feels that one could already say that this shift was achieved with Fanon's *The Wretched of the Earth* which was first published in French in 1961.[4] The settlers, the colonizers, had become the objects of investigation for Fanon, and ironically it was up to Sartre to act as the intermediary and to introduce Fanon's perspectives to the Europeans:

> For the fathers, we alone were the speakers; the sons no longer even consider us as valid intermediaries: we are the objects of their speeches.[5]

Here it is still the dichotomy between the self and the other which is functioning. It is as yet the shift in the roles, a reversal of the subject-object positions, that is being spoken of. Sartre's 'we' and 'they' are two distinct groups while in Fanon himself, even though the distinction between the colonizer and the colonized is clear, the national bourgeoisie, by its "will to imitation,"[6] mimics the colonizer, thereby blurring the sharp lines which divide the colonizer and the colonized.[7] Perhaps the most interesting aspect of Fanon for this study is the way Fanon examines how the culture of the native gets represented. Fanon already mentions those issues which were to become later the core of Said's *Orientalism*—the negation of the culture of the dominated people:

> The interest of this period for us is that the oppressor does not manage to convince himself of the objective non-existence of the oppressed nation and its culture. Every effort is made to bring the colonized person to admit the inferiority of his culture which has been transformed into instinctive patterns of behaviour, to recognize the unreality of his 'nation,' and, in the last extreme, the confused and imperfect character of his own biological structure.[8]

Said differs from Fanon to the extent that he says that the Orient who became the subject for academic areas of study such as Orientalism was a construct which in its turn guided production of governmental policies as well as literary representations.[9] What is important for Said is the transformation of the Orient, as that which is alien, into that, over which geographical claim is extended.[10] His method of showing this transformation has been one of re-reading the texts from this period. Such a method has suggested to the postcolonial critics a new way of interpreting because literatures of the colonizing countries could be read from a different perspective now. It is perhaps at this stage that one has to mention that category called Commonwealth Literature. Although Said himself appears to hold Commonwealth Literature positively, its constitution does not really call for a re-reading of the works of, say, Jane Austen.[11]

Commonwealth Literature does give importance to the diversity of the different cultures which are held together through their past attachment to the empire. It marks a stage where the individual literatures feel the need to be brought together in comparative terms.

However, in Commonwealth Studies, questions of identity and authenticity become crucial to the discussions; the exposure of the presence—or of the silenced presence—of the native in the literature of the colonial period was never its preoccupation. Yet, one has to admit that this was one of the early fora where an attempt was made to differentiate literatures—even if on a smaller scale—from the *Literature*. The 'desire' to create a national literature, however, could not resist the temptation of comparing itself with the English literature, and comparison, in such a case, always created a kind of hierarchical categorization. And those who wish to continue to cling to the concept of commonwealth literature without exposing it to the arguments of the postcolonial critics will only state once again that the great tradition of English literature is enriched by the presence of commonwealth literatures:

> It is increasingly being realized that literature being written in Australia, New Zealand, West Indies, South Africa, Canada, Nigeria, and India is in no way *inferior* and that the writ-

> ers in these countries have contributed *substantially and significantly to the modern English literature.*[12] (emphasis added)

First of all, the above statement shows the strong urge to justify and to defend. A kind of relativization is being acknowledged here and the comparative elements which are upheld by this kind of understanding of literature then function only in terms of relative positioning of the different literatures in comparison with the modern English literature, or an idea of English literature. The danger of comparing literature in this manner lies in the fact that such a situation is similar to earlier attempts at contrasting the civilized and the savage; the creation of the savage was a needed antithesis to the idea of the civilized in Europe of the nineteenth century.[13]

The comparative aspects of cultures on which colonization has left its mark is still in the foreground in *The Empire Writes Back.* In this sense the book represents a certain uneasiness with the term 'Commonwealth Literature' but not with its conception which is based upon an acknowledgement of the elements of commonness. This commonness is a result of the impact of imperialism felt by the different cultures of the world. One could thus say that the early use of the word 'postcolonialism,' as in the case of *The Empire Writes Back*, is a slightly different projection of the same ideas which fed into the creation of the term 'Commonwealth Literature.' This use of the term postcolonialism to include settler colonies and the ex-colonies like India has been questioned in various ways.[14] The prefix, however, cannot be taken anymore as an indication of the temporal aspect, where we understand 'post' as something which comes after.

The context of literary theory in the contemporary period itself is greatly influenced by the poststructuralist, postmodern perspectives. Therefore, it is difficult to conceive of a unified body of the postcolonial citizens who are bound together by a past experience of subjugation.[15] Moreover, it is becoming increasingly clear that the kind of domination which the period of colonization represented continues to be present in the contemporary societies in many different parts of the world and in many different ways. In this setting the term postcolonial develops connotations which make it an ally with the postmodern.[16] It would not be wrong to say that this association with the other post-words made postcolonialism rather fashionable and highly visible.[17]

The present study is based on an understanding of the term 'postcolonial' which draws on both the earlier term 'commonwealth' as well as the more complex use of the 'post'—as something which involves the past as well as the present. The selection of Shashi Deshpande, in fact, is based more on a recognition of a category called ex-colony. The assumption is that Shashi Deshpande is postcolonial because she has been working in a postcolonial world, where the term 'postcolonial' refers to the official ending of the colonial period. From this simplistic position, however, the study has tried to draw out elements which use as well as critique some of the positions of the postcolonial critics.

As the previous chapters show, one of the most striking aspects of this field of discourse called postcolonialism has been the dissonance among the postcolonial critics and the diverging interpretations of the term itself. There is no single interpretation which is acceptable to a large number of critics. Questions such as 'Who is a postcolonial?' or 'When did the postcolonial begin?' have continued to contribute to the debate about the use or misuse of the term.[18] What strikes one in all these arguments is the desire to define and redefine the spatio-temporal nature of the postcolonial situation. The differences of opinion as to who forms the postcolonial are, no doubt, of value if we consider the entire body of writing which can be termed postcolonial critical theories. However, if these discussions regarding the postcolonial are to be used as literary critical devices, it is necessary to clarify some of the confusion such discussions have given rise to.

There is no confusion, however, amongst these discordant voices about the irreversible impact of colonization on the different subjugated cultures. What is being questioned, displaced and sometimes still assumed is the binary colonized/colonizer, and what is being re-read is the narrativization, in histories as well as stories, of the very complex nature of colonization. Stuart Hall's differentiation of postcolonial as a useful term in the discourses on colonization and the present globalization is also an answer to the many detractors who point out the negating confusions the use of the term can create. The argument behind postcolonial discussions is not that colonization continues to repeat itself. The argument is for reconsidering the official version of colonization:

> It is, rather, that colonisation so refigured the terrain that, ever since, the very idea of a world of separate identities, of isolated or separable and self-sufficient cultures and economies, has been obliged to yield to a variety of paradigms designed to capture these different but related forms of relationship, interconnection and discontinuity. This was the distinctive form of dissemination-and-condensation which colonisation set in play. It is in privileging this missing or downgraded dimension in the official narrative of 'colonisation' that the discourse of 'post-colonial' is conceptually distinctive.[19]

One could, in fact, say that the work of Said contributed towards privileging the missing elements of the official version of 'colonization.' What does not come out clearly in the works of Said, however, is the blurring of the lines, the presence of destabilizing factors in the colonial enterprise itself. Bhabha, in his many articles has tried to use psychoanalytical elements and poststructural arguments to show the ambivalence that was at the centre of the colonial enterprise and exposes the myth behind its imagined, unified power. Even the stereotype, that is taken in the traditional literary critical discussions to be a trope which denotes fixity and one-sided characterization, is shown by Bhabha to contain an ambivalent element which hides within it both fantasy and defence.[20]

By invoking the element of ambivalence in the narrativization of colonization itself, Bhabha is dislocating the binary colonized/colonizer. However, this is not to be understood as either the negation of the differences between the two groups nor as the disavowal of the anti-colonialist movements. Once again, Stuart Hall has described this critical context where the binary does not operate anymore as "a move from one conception of difference to another," (Hall 247) a move which involves the transition to the 'postcolonial.' According to Hall, the transition to the postcolonial is also obliging us

> to re-read the very binary form in which the colonial encounter has for so long itself been represented. It obliges us to re-read the binaries as forms of transculturation, of cultural translation, destined to trouble the here/there cultural binaries for ever. (Hall 247)

Homi K. Bhabha, with his insistence on the presence of ambivalence and with his interpretation of culture as that which happens at the interstices, the place in between the borders, is then pointing out to the impossibility of thinking in terms of such binaries any more. Narration and representation from the margins of a society have great significance for Bhabha. And it is the element of hybridity in cultural questions which interests him. Even though in Bhabha's theories of hybridity and ambivalence, differences are not erased, nor relativized, the problem of other structures of power which operate within the so-called 'margins' do not get elaborated in his writings. But a re-reading of colonization as called for by the term 'postcolonial' makes it clear that different levels of power play existed during the colonial period, and hence different configurations are possible in the various postcolonial societies because of these different axes of power structures.

The peculiar patterns of power structures become clear especially if we consider the question of the subjectivity of woman in postcolonial discussions. Just as travel writings by women from the colonizers' world are being re-read, so are the archives being searched for instances of women writing from the colonized world. Such attempts show that within the frameworks of patriarchy and colonialism, women wrote under complex restraints. The approach to women who wrote under such restrictive situations has changed. In countries like India, patriarchal structures and the colonial machinery, worked hand in hand in a peculiar way. It is now a commonplace insight that the elite and the colonizers were quite often accomplices in creating subjugated positions for women. Thus the re-reading of colonization through postcolonialism has given rise to many complex configurations although its global significance has been understood differently. To quote Stuart Hall again:

> Colonisation, understood or re-read in this sense, was only intelligible as an event of global significance—by which one signals not its universal and totalizing, but its dislocated and differentiated character. That is to say, it had to be understood then, and certainly can only be understood now, in terms, not only of the vertical relations between coloniser and colonised, but also in terms of how these and other forms of power-relations were always displaced and decentred by another set of vectors—the transverse linkages between and across nation-state frontiers and the *global/local* inter-relationships which cannot be read off against a nation-state template. (Hall 250)

These cautious remarks remind us that everything cannot be "read off against a nation-state template," even when one wishes to take part in the post-colonial discussion. It is important for the post-colonial reader/critic to be vigilant when she re-reads and constructs texts. Gayatri Chakravorty Spivak points out that even if one talks about history from the perspective of the subaltern peasant insurgent, one could be overlooking the subaltern woman in the same narration. What is of interest in such an observation is the suggestion that even the category subaltern is not without its heterogeneous content. This is, of course, acknowledged by the authors of Subaltern Studies. Spivak's critique, however, is that there is an effacement of the subjectivities of the peasant women in these studies.

If Stuart Hall talks about the global/local relationships and about transcultural movements, Spivak, through specific examples, connects the local and the global. From the general discussion of a question, she narrows down to the specific instance and by revealing the complexity of the issues even at the local levels, she wishes to caution us against any hurried approach to multicultural courses. Spivak's preference for the term 'teacher' also explains her way of dealing with texts. Her example of placing a Third World text in the context of first world theoretical arguments shows the limitations of many elite theories when they are used to analyse the different configurations that determine the politics of the local. Spivak's example has been made use of in this study.

What has been the point of alluding to the specificity of Shashi Deshpande, and how can one retain this position of paying such attention to the local without being an essentialist? In what manner is this study a critique of postcolonialism as well as an attempt to contribute to the body of postcolonial literary criticism? To search for answers, one has to find the methodology which is at work here. I hold that in postcolonial discourse in general, and in the present study in particular, the methodology has been one of reading from a different perspective. Said, Bhabha and Spivak, as well as all the other critics who write from other positions, have resorted to the method of reading different texts associated with colonialism or with a postcolonial nation, from an angle which had remained unexplored for a long time, because of the undue importance given to the need for preserving universal critical standards. It was only with the onset of the critique of universal values that other perspectives came to be considered as acceptable perspectives.

Postcolonial critical writings have demonstrated that when reread from the perspective of the colonized, the complicity between culture and imperialism stands exposed. Accepting the fact that this methodology of reading the colonial texts differently has given rise to many fruitful debates, I would like to point out once again that postcolonial critics like Spivak have always stressed the need to be cautious when pursuing approaches that also call for comments on the cultural imbrications of the texts. I have tried to argue in the previous sections of this work that the question of location can change the structure of priorities in our arguments. Without this question, Postcolonial discourse can become one more version of 'formation' that Raymond Williams writes about.[21] Both the importance given to the minority cultures, the significance of occupying hybrid positions, may have to be articulated differently in each location, because the elements which contribute to the cultural dynamics of a place may have different attributes in different locations.

Taking Spivak's warning to be cautious seriously, I arrived at the argument that the micropolitics represented in the world of Shashi Deshpande, even if it does not shed light on colonialism directly, helps us see the question of the subaltern in a different way. The privilege of education and of class do not always rescue the woman from a subaltern position in a society where a woman has to struggle to make her position as the subject apparent. Yet we must remember that there are strange configurations being drawn because of the different axes drawn by class, caste and gender.

These configurations become clearer only when we pay attention to the fact that reading or re-reading can be used as a very powerful tool when we want to be cautious in our approach to the multicultural literary courses. Reading Shashi Deshpande in the context of postcolonialism and reading postcolonial theoretical formulations in the context of the fictive world of Shashi Deshpande's works, have to benefit each other mutually. This can be done only when we accept Todorov's argument that reading is as much a construction as the world of the fiction itself:

> After constructing the events that make up a story, we then give ourselves over to the task of reinterpretation, which allows us to construct the work's characters on the one hand, the system of ideas and values underlying the text on the other. This reinterpretation is not arbitrary; it is controlled by two series of constraints. The first is implicit in the text itself: it suffices for the author to spend a little time teaching us how to interpret the events he evokes. . . . Such an interpretation, present in the text of the book, thus has a double function: on the one hand, it teaches us the cause of a particular fact (exegetic function); on the other hand, it initiates us into the interpretive system that will be the author's throughout the book (metaexegetic function). The second series of constraints comes from the cultural context . . . . These cultural constraints, which are nothing but the commonplaces of a social group (notions its members deem plausible), are modified over time, which makes it possible to explain the different ways earlier texts have been interpreted.[22]

What is of importance for this study is that the construction of reading, which is analogous to the construction of characters, as Todorov would say, is subject to the constraints that come from the cultural context; or, in other words, there are 'local cultural codes that make personal experience articulate.'[23] Here, however, I would like to add that the constraints might vary not only in terms of difference in the chronological aspect—"the different ways earlier texts have been interpreted." In the context of India, the multicultural and multireligious reality gives rise to different kinds of readers. Even when the different social configurations are bound together in some ways, it is difficult to speak of "the commonplaces of a social group." In Deshpande's texts which appear to be pecualiarly insulated from other cultural elements, the social group whose commonplaces are *recognizable* is the middle-class, liberal educated, upper caste community. Yet this small group is over-arched by the other, larger constraint in the form of the patriarchal society with its own expectations and ideas that are seen as 'commonplace.' This idea of 'commonplace' emerges from the interpretations that talk repeatedly of the 'autonomy of the woman.'[24] The constant search for the autonomy of woman forgets that even in the homogeneous context of patriarchal society, women themselves occupy heterogeneous contexts. What is of interest in this kind of heterogeneity is the manner in which the women react to the different constraints. Thus, not only Shashi Deshpande's protagonists, but the other women, some whose silences are pointed out by the author and some who are silenced by her, also indicate the many constraints that are present within an apparently homogeneous context.

These silent figures, sometimes belonging to the same group as the protagonists in her novels, sometimes belonging to the group of women who have to work as housemaids to earn their living, make many of the observations made by critics like Said in a different context peculiarly significant. Said's suggestion that novels of Jane Austen should be read *contrapuntally*, in the context of Shashi Deshpande's novels means that the thinking, writing protagonists of her novels also have to be read *contrapuntally*. This, in turn, means that a number of elements which problematize the construction of the subjectivities of such women in terms of illiteracy, ideological brainwashing in patriarchal societal structures, the problem of dowry, the complexity of the issue of caste, economic status, will also have to be taken into account. This kind of reading will then deconstruct the assumed uniformity of Said's Orient, reminding us that his questions regarding the consolidating vision of the novelist will have to be asked in the postcolonial context too, lest we forget that simple binaries do not exist.

Nation, narration, history and past whose complexities are revealed in Bhabha's works do not really seem to be part of the world of Deshpande's novels. The exception is her latest novel, *A Matter of Time*,[25] which one could term the most postmodern of all works. In this novel, she uses a more self-conscious style. It is a novel where the history of a family, its migration to an alien land, and its retention of the mother tongue are all mentioned. I find particularly significant, the importance that is given to history and historians:

> Historians, even the most brilliant of them, are like magicians. With flamboyance they draw attention to what they want you to see, take it away from what they want to conceal. 'Look!' they will say, 'the Queen of Spades.' And you see the Queen of Spades. All else is concealed in the darkness of a deliberate deceit. (*A Matter of Time* 99)

The present study, however, is more concerned with her earlier works, especially those novels which have been considered for postcolonial discussions in spite of an absence of issues such as nation. Even though there are movements towards metropolitan cities, hybridity is not a theme in any of these earlier novels. Life in the city is always contrasted with the ancestral or parental home which in itself stands for 'closedness'—there is very little migration and there is very little hybridity here. Yet these are the most important issues for postcolonial critics like Bhabha. Even Stuart Hall is trying to avoid criticism when he qualifies the notion of diaspora:

> The notion that only the multi-cultural cities of the First World are 'diaspora-ised' is a fantasy which can only be sustained by those who have never lived in the hybridised spaces of a Third World, so-called 'colonial' city. (Hall 250)

Are only those who occupy the hybridised space worthy of being taken into consideration in postcolonial discussions? Retrieval of an original ethnic background can be problematized even in a small town, and even in the monolithic house of Shashi Deshpande's novels. But the world of women, living in these quarters cannot truly be described as a hybridised world. Surprisingly, the outside elements which sneak into this closed world are the elements of liberal education which the protagonists receive, and very often these are elements drawn from a formal study of English Literature. This observation is particularly interesting if we recall the work of Gauri Viswanathan, *Masks of Conquest*, which investigates the role of English Literature in India, and in which she points to "the irony that English literature appeared as a subject in the curriculum of the colonies long before it was institutionalized in the home country."[26]

Yet the impact of liberal education, which is itself one of the results of the colonial period, has not always made a difference in the world of many of the women whom the patriarchal system forces to live in a kind of *zenana*—even where there is no continuation of the *purdah*—because emotionally they live a cloistered life.[27] These women, though marginalised, do not live in the interstices. Moreover, many of these women within the emotional or physical *purdah* are capable of occupying sub-structures of power. This shows that Bhabha's critical terms cannot be used without qualification in all postcolonial contexts. The privileging of the migratory experience and the hybridised existence has been rewritten by Bhabha in a recent essay, where he recognises that control of the minorities may be "exerted by state institutions against minority groups, or by patriarchal and *class* structures within minority communities themselves."[28] Based on the novels of Shashi Deshpande, however, I have argued that control is exerted even within the marginalised group—'women'—by patriarchal and class structures, and very often women themselves are agents exerting power because of the patriarchal and class structures themselves.

The peculiar functioning of the class and caste structures are brought out by Gayatri Chakravorty Spivak's discussion of the Bengali short story, "Breast Giver." Just as the Brahmin wet nurse belonging to the lower class makes it difficult to answer the question, "Who is a subaltern gendered subject?," so do the many women in Deshpande make a definition of the subaltern woman a difficult task. The life of a Brahmin widow and the life of an untouchable woman could both be representations of subjugated existence. In Deshpande's novels, the most important attribute of many of the women characters seems to be silence. Whether it is the forced silence of a rape victim or that of a dead woman, silence is present in many forms and often there is a desire to break 'that long silence' of these characters in her novels.

Spivak's question "Can the subaltern speak?" is not always useful if we deal with only the protagonists of these novels, because they are able to transform their silences through writing in most of the cases. Many of them write poems, plays and columns for women's magazines. On the periphery of the lives of these women, enabling them to pursue the luxury of writing, however, there are those other women who are denied speech—by the society in which they live, the family of which they are members, and at times by their author as well. These are the postcolonial subaltern subjects whose subjectivites have been denied, and these are the silent presences in literatures of our times whose speech acts have to be completed in the sense that they need to be heard. Just as the editors of *Women Writing in India* have made the works of women writing over the centuries accessible in a collection at a time when the traditional subjugation of women in India is getting more attention in the mass media, so will a postcolonial approach to Deshpande's women make known the silent women who are waiting to be heard. What the narrator says about the written family history in *A Matter of Time* is usually true of the women who remain in the background in Deshpande's novels: "Of the women, there is nothing. They are only an absence, still waiting to be discovered." (*A Matter of Time* 95)

The problems involved in teaching multicultural studies in First World academic circles, as pointed out by Spivak, are not always the same as the problems faced by teachers teaching literatures—written in English as well as in the regional languages—in a multiethnic context like India. However, the overarching presence of a particular kind of social expectation, makes reading/teaching the texts of women writers result in the search for self-realization and liberatory conclusions in novels. This is clearly revealed in the body of critical writing which has appeared around Shashi Deshpande's novels in India. As mentioned earlier, the search for an autonomous woman, or for the ending where a protagonist has achieved self-realization, marks the patterned response to Deshpande in many of these essays, even though her novels leave the readers feeling that there has not been a major change in the life of the female protagonist at the end. It is the process of self-evaluation which reveals the pressure of social expectations and it is an attempt to come to terms with an immediate crisis in life which distinguishes these novels from novels of self-realization.

The approaches which search for the motif of self-realization, might give us the feeling that Deshpande's novels represent a kind of *Bildungsroman*. But I consider this kind of approach to be basically flawed; it suggests that once the protagonist realizes that there is a real self behind the many stifling faces she presents to the world, she can be true to her self and thereby rescue herself from succumbing to the pressures of the society. That the idea of this true 'self' is often shaped by the context is not given much importance in such deliberations. What frightens one in these novels is the 'reality' of the role play which these women are forced to accept and the realization by the protagonists themselves that it is all role play. Neither the critical appraisals, nor the author herself, consider role play as a construct—at least in literature—which can be something more than a mere stifling experience. They believe that behind her roles, there is a sense of identity which becomes available to the protagonist through a process of self-realization. In an interesting discussion on the nature of role play, Bettina Friedl states that the positive qualities attributed to the portrayal of self-realization, when analysed, reveal that there is always an assumption being made about an essential identity.[29] Even when her women characters recognize themselves in their different roles, role-play itself has not been taken up by Deshpande as a narrative technique. Nor do her characters see in role play any kind of liberating experience. This shows that they believe in an essential identity which these thinking/writing women try to bring out.

The will to put forth the idea of identity is seen in the recasting of similar characters in many of novels, the analogous stories of her female characters, the compulsive return to the past events which have shaped their lives and their ways of thinking, and the confessional and self-questioning tone of narration which looks like monologue in many parts of the novels, had made me suggest earlier that these novels could be treated as fictionalised versions of testimonials. The creation of such a terminology should not, however, give rise to the idea that every specific writer has to be fitted with a specific mode of writing. Perhaps this could be considered as the starting point for further research along this line. This also explains why the realistic mode of writing is still a favourite mode with many writers. It is not the kind of realism that we see in Victorian novel. The mode has been used subversively.

For those who think that this is a case of "an excessive propensity to treat as significant elements which might be simply fortuitous,"[30] my answer is that the elements that I have drawn out gain their significance in the context of the arguments that I have presented. To believe that a certain mode of writing was blindly used amounts to claiming that there was blind imitation. Yet in the case of Deshpande we have seen that this mimicry is an ambivalent repetition, to use Bhabha's concept. There has been the production of a hybrid subversive form of writing in this case. It is subversive because the novelist through her corpus of novels defies the conventions that are assosciated with the realist mode of writing.

In Conclusion

The title "The Enterprise of Reading Differently," in itself suggests that the basic methodology involved in postcolonial discourse is one of re-reading. First of all, it involves re-reading or reading differently, the different aspects of narrativization, in histories as well as literatures, and it also involves a re-reading of archival materials as well as cultural manifestations. The second major attribute of postcolonial discourse is the constant questioning of the appropriateness of the term itself; this, in my view, has contributed productively to the discussion. Thirdly, due to the special debate, one cannot really characterize postcolonial mode of writing based on certain themes which in turn are recognized as postcolonial. Finally, instead of talking about postcolonial themes in literatures, one should perhaps mention a postcolonial approach to the works.

What this study has done, then, is to investigate the novels of Shashi Deshpande by way of postcolonial arguments. Even though it began with the presupposition that Deshpande could be claimed as a postcolonial writer because chronologically she belongs to post-independence India, it is clear now that the term postcolonial can no longer be used in such a reductionist manner. Moreover, this study has, to some extent, answered the criticism that some of the positions—such as subaltern, hybridity—can function as universalizing concepts, by showing how these concepts need to be qualified and modified in the context of the world of the novels of Shashi Deshpande. One of the most significant corollaries of this argument is that the specificity of the local has to be borne in mind, even when differentiated arguments are presented, even when the postcolonial critics talk about the necessity to be cautious. If the study has shown differences among the 'emigrated natives' and the 'natives,' it is because it acknowledges that

> [o]ur particular location, mediated as it is through language or history or social ideology, brings with it privileges or deprivations that affect our relationships with others and our relation to the world. . . . The claim is that our location is an objective feature of the world in which we live, the world as it is constituted precisely by various 'positions' of power and powerlessness.[31]

Novels dealing with women in a particular sociological location have been presented in this study so that Postcolonial Studies retains its commitment to recognition of heterogeneity among the postcolonial societies and also as a hurdle in the path of all those who show a 'too-quick enthusiasm' for postcolonial discourses. Seen from a different perspective, this study, through its analyses and discussions of different positions within the field of Postcolonial Studies, has tried to find out what a postcolonial reading method can yield when we approach literary texts borrowing certain important concepts as 'subaltern,' 'hybridity,' 'cultural difference' or 'contrapuntal reading.' The methodology followed here can be described as a conscious imitation of Spivak's manner of 'placing' a Third World woman's text in 'alien'/elite arguments. Here I have considered the major arguments of the postcolonial critics as 'alien' because Shashi Deshpande does not deal with what seems to be obvious themes for postcolonial discussions such as nation, exile, neocolonialism, border crossings, hybrid existence.

At this point it must be stressed that in addition to highlighting the interpretative use of postcolonial theories in literary criticism, this work has tried to avoid the pitfall of creating models for post-colonial literary works which are then upheld as being worthy of consideration within postcolonial discussions. Hopefully, both post-colonial studies and the critical response to Shashi Deshpande, have benefited mutually through the mediation of this project of reading differently.

The purpose of this study will be fulfilled, if it has ultimately contributed one more different voice to the atonal area of studies called postcolonial studies. Narrowing down its focus from the very broad, highly controversial category 'postcolonial' to the highly specific and particularized world of the novels of Deshpande, it has tried to say that any attempt at generalizing the 'postcolonial' experience has to be rejected because the colonial experience has not been uniform everywhere. I agree fully with Kwame Anthony Appiah that "even identical colonial policies identically implemented working on the very different cultural materials would surely have produced widely varying results."[32]

I wish to go one step further and claim that even where there is an amount of similarity in the cultural materials, differences and different combinations are created because of difference in the different social axes which determine an individual's identity. In this criss-cross of different axes, it is possible that the oppressed of one configuration becomes the oppressor in a different configuration. This is best exemplified by the women of Shashi Deshpande, especially by many of her less-important women characters. By paying attention to them, especially to those who do not seem to be educated, to be 'thinking-writing' women like her protagonists, I have tried to establish the validity of the statement made by Trinh T. Minh-ha with regard to the Third World women:

> . . . to simply denounce Third World women's oppression with notions and terms made to reflect or fit into Euro-Ameri-

> can women's criteria of equality is to abide by ethnographic ideology (. . .), which depends on the representation of a coherent cultural subject as source of scientific knowledge to explain a native culture and reduces every gendered activity to a sex-role stereotype.[33]

I have tried to show that even woman, woman coming from a particular cultural background, remains an ambivalent subject—not coherent—who is both a victim and an agent, depending on the axes which determine her position in the society. This should not be taken to mean a kind of exoticization of the 'other.' because, one of the main purposes of this study has been that of problematizing the idea of the 'other' in the general field of literary studies. The other is not that which occupies the margin and provides it with context. For, as Homi K. Bhabha evocatively points out:

> The 'other' is never outside or beyond us; it emerges forcefully. within cultural discourse, when we *think* we speak most intimately and indigenously 'between ourselves.'[34]

NOTES

1. From Gayatri Chakravorty Spivak, "Poststructuralism, Marginality, Postcoloniality and Value," *Literary Theory Today*, p. 221. The passage containing this term has already been quoted in Chapter One.
2. Andrew King, "Postmodern Forerunners," *Postmodern Political Communication: The Fringe Challenges the Center*, ed. Andrew King, Praeger Series in Political Communication (Westport: Praeger, 1992), p. 20.
3. Robert Young, *White Mythologies: Writing History and the West* (1990; London: Routledge, 1993), p. 119.
4. *Ibid.*, p. 119. Another important work which influenced the critical discourse coming from the perspective of Caliban, which records the presence of neocolonialism in the 'Free World,' and which calls for coalition of the oppressed is the essay by Roberto Fernandez Retamar, "Caliban: Notes Towards a Discussion of Culture in Our America," trans. Lynn Garafola, David Arthur McMurray, Robert

Marquez in *Massachusetts Review*, 15 (Winter-Spring 1974): 7-72.

5. Jean-Paul Sartre, "Preface," in Frantz Fanon, *The Wretched of the Earth*, trans. Constance Farrington (1961; London: Penguin, 1990), p. 9.
6. Fanon, *The Wretched of the Earth*, p. 130.
7. Yet, Fanon's way of handling gender issues has been criticized. See for example, Gwen Bergner, "Who is that Masked Woman? or, The Role of Gender in Fanon's Black Skin, White Masks," *PMLA* 110, 1 (January 1995):75-88 and Ketu H. Katrak, "Decolonizing Culture: Toward a Theory for Postcolonial Women's Texts," *Modern Fiction Studies*, 35, 1 (Spring 1989): 157-79, esp. 160-65.
8. Fanon, *The Wretched of the Earth*, p. 190.
9. Said's description of Orientalism, if taken without qualifications can give rise to a "uniformly passive oriental world." Shyamal Bagchee argues that the confrontation between the East and West was not always one-sided by giving examples from expatriate British poetry. See Bagchee, "Writing Self/Writing Colony in *situ*: Expatriate British Poetry in India," *Ariel*, 23, 4 (1992):7-32, esp. 9-11.
10. See Said, *Orientalism*, pp. 210-11. It is because of this endeavour to 'take over' of the geographical space of the Orient that the nineteenth century and the canons of literature produced in this period become important for Said.
11. See Said, "Figures, Configurations, Transfigurations." *From Commonwealth to Postcolonial*, ed. Anna Rutherford (Sydney: Dangaroo Press, 1992), pp. 3-17. Said's apparent enthusiasm for Commonwealth literature and his argument for considering English as the world language (p. 3), is attacked by Aijaz Ahmed in his "Orientalism and After: Ambivalence and Metropolitan Location in the Work of Edward Said," *In Theory*, pp. 159-220. See esp. pp. 211-17.
12. R.K. Dhawan, "Introduction: Indian Women Novelists," *Indian Women Novelists*, Set I: Vol. I, ed. R.K. Dhawan (New Delhi: Prestige Books, 1991), p. 7. Unfortunately, the many volumes produced in three sets over the period 1991-1995 do not really take into account postcolonial perspectives. Even when he claims that "Indian fiction which happily has liberated itself from the constrains of nationalism and pan-Indianism," Dhawan is in favour of a critical framework of its own for Indo-English fiction. (p. 9).
13. See Robert J.C. Young, *Colonial Desire: Hybridity in Theory, Culture and Race* (London: Routledge, 1995), p. 35. Young discusses how civilization began to be considered in terms of difference, which in turn needed the invoking of the non-European racial-cultural elements.
14. Linda Hutcheon, for example, feels that the label 'postcolonial' cre-

ates complications that "involve the historical and national contexts in which literature is produced and received, as well as the gender, class, religious, and racial specifities of colonial (and imperial) experiences." See Hutcheon, "Colonialism and the Postcolonial Condition: Complexities Abounding," *PMLA*, 110, 1 ((January 1995): 8.

15. My use of colonization and imperialism have been rather flexible in the sense that at times they have been used as synonyms. I am however, aware of the distinctions which can be drawn here. Marc Ferro, while identifying the early phase of colonialism as expansionism, connects the later phase with imperialism. And imperialism, according to him, showed the following primary impulses: "to colonize, to civilize, to spread one's culture, to expand." See Ferro, *Colonization: A Global History* (London: Routledge, 1997; French edition 1994), p. 11.
16. This alliance between postcolonialism and postmodernism is questioned by critics. See for example, the review of *The Empire Writes Back* by M. van Wyk Smith, "Colonial and Post-Colonial Literatures," *The Review of English Studies*, 44, 175 (August, 1993): 393-99.
17. I would like to claim here that many of the poststructuralist and postmodernist interpretations bear similarities to the postcolonial positions. But these 'analogies'—to borrow a word from Henry Louis Gates, Jr.—are not to be considered as weak points in this kind of discourse. I would like to echo what Gates has to say in this regard about black theory: "My use of this sort of analogy is designed to show the many-faceted nature of contemporary criticism, and not to suggest limitations or lacunae in Black theory"—or in this case, in postcolonial discourse. See Henry Louis Gates, Jr. *The Signifying Monkey: A Theory of African-American Literary Criticism* (1988; Oxford: Oxford University Press, 1989), p. xxiv.
18. It is not unusual to see antagonism among intellectuals who have migrated to USA, not only because of their claim or non-claim for the term postcolonial but also due to what postcolonial critics obviously stand for. Unfortunately this kind of antagonism is often rooted in misunderstanding rather than deeply felt differences. One example for this is Bharati Mukherjee whose distrust of Said, Spivak and Bhabha has already been mentioned earlier. In her "Beyond Multiculturalism: Surviving the Nineties," *Journal of Modern Literature*, Vol. 20, No. 1 (Summer 1996): 29-34, we see her often voicing views some of which are almost similar to the ones put forth by other postcolonial critics, but from a completely antagonistic position. Even though she does not name anyone, it is clear who she is referring to when she says, "some India-born, upper-middle-class

Marxist green-card holders with lucrative Chairs on U.S. campuses." (p. 33) She has no respect for these 'fence-saddlers' because she regards 'the artificial retentions of "pure race" and "pure culture" as dangerous, reactionary illusions fostered by the Eurocentric and the ethnocentric empire-builders within the academy.' (pp. 33-34) Rejection of the idea of 'pure culture' is exactly what many post-colonial critics are doing.

19. Stuart Hall, "When was 'the post-colonial'? Thinking at the limit," in Iain Chambers and Lidia Curti, ed., *The Post-Colonial Question: Common Skies, Divided Horizons* (London: Routledge, 1996), pp. 252-53.
20. Homi K. Bhabha, "The Other Question: Stereotype, Discrimination and the Discourse of Colonialism," p. 75.
21. Williams describes that cultural movements, especially the kind he names 'paranational,' are a peculiar feature of the twentieth century. Taking place, in a metropolitan, internationalized community, a cultural formation, shows signs of conscious breaking away from traditional styles. See Williams, *Culture* (London: Fontana, 1981), especially pp. 57-86.
22. Tzvetan Todorov, *Genres in Discourse*, trans. Catherine Porter (Cambridge: Cambridge University Press, 1990), pp. 44-45. Todorov talks about the representational mode of writing and has in mind the classic texts of fiction. Since Deshpande's novels too could be classified as representational, Todorov's arguments can be used here.
23. I have borrowed this part of the sentence from James Clifford's *The Predicament of Culture*, p. 263.
24. See, for example, P. Ramamoorthi, who claims that 'feminism' is the core of Deshpande's novels because her protagonists quote Virginia Woolf and Betty Friedan. "'My life is my own': A Study of Shashi Deshpande's Women," *Indian Women Writers*, Set I: Vol. V, pp. 37-49. Ramamoorthi writes: "One of the primal and seminal concerns of feminism is to declare that a woman is a being. She is not an appendage of man. A woman is not the 'other'; she is not an addition to man. She is an autonomous being, capable of, through trial and error, finding her way to salvation." (p. 37, emphasis added)

    The conflict of the heroines is seen as an exploration of the possibility of gaining an 'autonomous' existence by other interpreters also. Ujwala Patil in "The Theme of Marriage and Selfhood in *Roots and Shadows*" sees no end for the suffering of the Deshpande heroines: "For Shashi Deshpande, as for her sensitive and intelligent women, Indu, Saru and Jaya, women, though modern, essentially Indian in sensibility, an autonomous self in a society that is largely conventional in its outlook is a myth." (*Indian Women Writers*, Set

I, Vol. 5, p. 136, emphasis mine)

25. Shashi Deshpande, *A Matter of Time* (New Delhi: Penguin Books India, 1996).
26. Gauri Viswanathan, *Masks of Conquest: Literary Study and British Rule in India* (New York: Columbia University Press, 1989), p. 3.
27. See *Margins of Erasure: Purdah in the Subcontinental Novel in English*, ed. Jasbir Jain and Amina Amin (New Delhi: Sterling, 1995). Two of the articles consider Shashi Deshpande's novels: Rani Dharkar's "Marriage as Purdah: Fictional Rendering of a Social Reality" (pp. 49-59) equates marriage to purdah and it "works, in fact, in a more insidious fashion than an actual purdah since it grants an outward semblance of freedom." (p. 50) Kamini Dinesh in her contribution to this collection, "Moving out of the Cloistered Self: Shashi Deshpande's Protagonists," (pp. 196-205) finds analogous movement in Shashi Deshpande's *The Dark Holds No Terrors* and in *That Long Silence*: "Working outside the tradition of purdah as specified in the households where there are architectural divisions into the 'zenana' and the 'mardana,' or the physically cloistered woman, Deshpande focuses on the emotionally cloistered woman who struggles to shed her inhibitions and the subordinated self." (p. 196)
28. Homi K. Bhabha, "Unpacking my Library. . . . Again," *The Postcolonial Question: Common Skies, Divided Horizons*, p. 209.
29. Bettina Friedl, "Metamorphosen des Weiblichen: Lisa Althers Kinflicks und Cindy Shermans (Selbst-)Portraits," *Zwischen Schrift und Bild: EntÜrfe des Weiblichen in literarischer Verfahrensweise*, Christine Krause, Sylvia Mayer, Margret Schuchard und Agnes Speck (Hrgs.), Mattes Verlag Heidelberg, 1994, pp. 159-60.
30. Jonathan Culler, "In Defence of Overinterpretation," *Interpretation and Overinterpretation: Umberto Echo with Richard Rorty, Jonathan Culler and Christine Brooke-Rose* (Cambridge: Cambridge University Press, 1992), p. 122. Culler, however, considers this a "quality to be cultivated rather than shunned." (p. 123)
31. Satya P. Mohanty, "Colonial Legacies, Multicultural Futures: Relativism, Objectivity, and the Challenge of Otherness," *PMLA*, 110, 1 (Spring 1995): 109-10.
32. Kwame Anthony Appiah, "African Identities," *In My Father's House: Africa in the Philosophy of Culture* (New York: Oxford University Press, 1992).
33. Trinh T. Minh-ha, *Woman, Native, Other: Writing Postcoloniality and Feminism* (Bloomington: Indiana University Press, 1989), p. 106.
34. "Introduction," in *Nation and Narration*, ed. Homi K. Bhabha (London: Routledge, 1990), p. 4.

Bibliography

Achebe, Chinua. "An Image of Africa," *Massachusetts Review*, 18 (Winter 1977):782-94.

Adam, Ian and Helen Tiffin, ed. *Past the Last Post: Theorizing Post-Colonialism and Post-Modernism*. New York: Harvester Wheatsheaf, 1993 (1991).

Adam, Ian. "Breaking the Chain: Anti-Saussurean Resistance in Birney, Carey and C.S. Peirce." *Past the Last Post*, ed. Ian Adam and Helen Tiffin, 79-93.

______. "Oracy and Literacy: A Post-Colonial Dilemma?" *The Journal of Commonwealth Literature*, 31, 1 (1996):97-109.

Ahmad, Aijaz. *In Theory: Classes, Nations, Literatures*. London: Verso, 1994 (1992).

______. "Postcolonialism: What's in a Name?" In *Late Imperial Culture*, ed. Roman De la Campa, E. Ann Kaplan and Michael Sprinker, 11-32.

Anderson, Benedict. *Imagined Communities: Reflections on the Origin and Spread of Nationalism*. London: Verso, 1994 (1983).

Appiah, Kwame Anthony. "Is the Post- in Postmodernism the Post- in Postcolonial?" *Critical Inquiry* 17(2) 1991:336-57.

_____. In *My Father's House: Africa in the Philosophy of Culture*. Oxford: Oxford University Press, 1992.

Apter, Emily. "Ethnographic Travesties: Colonial Realism, French Feminism, and the Case of Elissa Rha's." In *After Colonialism: Imperial Histories and Postcolonial Displacements*, ed. Gyan Prakash, 299-325.

Ash, Ranjana. "The Search for Freedom in Indian Women's Writing." In *Motherlands: Black Women's Writing from Africa, the Caribbean and South Asia*, ed. Susheila Nasta, 152-74.

Ashcroft, Bill, Gareth Griffiths, Helen Tiffin, ed. *The Empire Writes Back: Theory and Practice in Post-colonial Literatures*. London: Routledge. 1989.

Ashcroft, Bill et al, ed. *The Post-colonial Studies Reader*. London: Routledge, 1995.

Ashcroft, W.D. "Constitutive Graphonomy: A Post-Colonial Theory of Literary Writing." In *After Europe: Critical Theory and Post-Colonial Writing*, ed. Stephen Slemon and Helen Tiffin, 58-74.

Azim, Firdous. *The Colonial Rise of the Novel*. London: Routledge, 1993.

Bachmann-Medick. Doris. ed. *Kultur als Text: Die anthropoloische Wende in der Literaturwissenschaft*. Frankfurt am Main: Fischer, 1996.

Bagchee, Shyamal. "Writing Self/Writing Colony in Situ: Expatriate British Poetry in India." In *Ariel*, 23, 4 (October 1992):7-32.

Barker, Francis et al, ed. *Europe and its Others: Proceedings of the Essex Conference on the Sociology of Literature July 1984*. Colchester: University of Essex, 1985.

______. *Colonial Discourse/ Postcolonial Theory*. Manchester: Manchester University Press, 1994.

Bell, Michael. *F.R. Leavis*. In *Critics of the Twentieth Century Series*, ed. Christopher Norris. London: Routledge, 1988.

Benhabib, Seyla. "Feminism and the Question of Postmodernism." In *Situating the Self: Gender, Community and Postmodernism in Contemporary Ethics*. pp. 203-41. New York: Routledge, 1992.

Bennington, Geoffrey and Jacques Derrida. *Jacques Derrida*, trans. Geoffrey Bennington. Chicago: The University of Chicago Press, 1993.

Berger, Anne-Emmanuelle. "The Latest Word from Echo." In *New Literary History* 27, 4 (1996):621-40.

Bergner, Gwen. "Who is that Masked Woman? or, The Role of Gender in Fanon's *Black Skin, White Masks*." *PMLA*, 110, 1 (January 1995):75-88.

Beverly, John. "The Margin at the Center: On Testimonio (Testimonial Narrative)." *Modern Fiction Studies* 35, 1 (Spring 1989):11-28.

Bhabha, Homi K. "Representation and the Colonial Text: A Critical Exploration of Some Forms of Mimeticism." In *The Theory of Reading*, ed. Frank Gloversmith, 93-122. Brighton: Harvester Press, 1984.

______. "DissemiNation: Time, Narrative, and the Margins of the Modern Nation." In *Nation and Narration*, ed. Homi K. Bhabha, pp. 291-322. 1990; London: Routledge, 1993.

______. "Postcolonial Authority and Postmodern Guilt/ Discussion." In *Cultural Studies*, ed. Lawrence Grossberg, Cary Nelson, Paula A. Treichler, pp. 56-68. New York: Routledge, 1992.

______. *The Location of Culture*. London: Routledge, 1994.

______. "The Postcolonial Critic: Homi Bhabha Interviewed by David Bennet and Terry Collits." In *Literary India: Comparative Studies in Aesthetics, Colonialism, and Culture*, ed. Patrick Colm Hogan and Lalita Pandit, 237-53.

______. "Unpacking my Library. . . . Again." In *The Post-Colonial Question: Common Skies, Divided Horizons*, ed. Iain Chambers and Lidia Curti, 199-211.

Bharvani, Shakuntala. "Some Recent Trends in Modern Indian Fiction: A Study of Shashi Deshpande's *That Long Silence*. Shashi Tharoor's *The Great Indian Novel* and Amitav Ghosh's *The Shadow Lines*." In *Indian Women Novelists*, ed. R.K. Dhawan, Set I, Vol. I, 20-31.

Boehemer, Elleke. *Colonial and Postcolonial Literature: Migrant Meta-*

phors. Oxford: Oxford University Press, 1995.

Booth, Wayne C. "Freedom of Interpretation: Bakhtin and the Challenge of Feminist Criticism." In *The Politics of Interpretation*, ed. W.J.T. Mitchell, 51-82.

Bowie, Malcolm. *Lacan*. London: Fontana Press, 1991.

Brantlinger, Patrick. *Rule of Darkness: British Literature and Imperialism, 1830-1914*. Ithaca: Cornell University Press, 1988.

Breckenridge, Carol A. and Peter van der Veer, ed. *Orientalism and the Postcolonial Predicament*. Philadelphia: University of Pennsylvania Press, 1993.

Brydon, Diana. "Commonwealth or Common Poverty?: The New Literatures in English and the New Discourse of Marginality," *After Europe: Critical Theory and Post-Colonial Writing*. ed. Stephen Slemon and Helen Tiffin, 1-16.

Chambers, Iain and Lidia Curti, ed. *The Post-Colonial Question: Common Skies, Divided Horizons*. London: Routledge, 1996.

Charsely, Simon. "'Untouchable': What is in a Name?" *The Journal of the Royal Anthropological Institute* 2 (1), 1996:1-23.

Chaudhuri, Una. "Poetics of Exile and the Politics of Home." In *Literary India: Comparative Studies in Aesthetics, Colonialism, and Culture*. ed. Patrick Colm Hogan and Lalita Pandit, 141-49.

Chow, Rey. "Listening Otherwise, Music Miniaturized: A Different Type of Question about Revolution." In *The Cultural Studies Reader*, ed. Simon During, 382-99.

Chrisman, Laura. "The Imperial Unconscious? Representations of Imperial Discourse." *Critical Quarterly* 32 (3) 1990:38-58.

Clarke, Sathianathan. *Dalits and Christianity: Subaltern Religion and Liberation Theology in India* (Delhi: Oxford University Press, 1998).

Clifford, James. *The Predicament of Culture: Twentieth-Century Ethnography, Literature, and Art*. Cambridge, MA: Harvard University Press, 1988.

Clifford, James. "Traveling Cultures/Discussion." In *Cultural Studies*, ed. Lawrence Grossberg, Cary Nelson and Paula A. Treichler, 96-116.

Collini, Stefan, ed. *Interpretation and Overinterpretation: Umberto Eco with Richard Rorty*, Jonathan Culler and Christine Brooke-Rose. Cambridge: Cambridge University Press, 1992.

Collier, Peter and Helga Geyer-Ryan, ed. *Literary Theory Today*. Cambridge: Polity Press, 1990.

Coronil, Fernando. "Beyond Occidentalism: Toward Nonimperial Geohistorical Categories." *Cultural Anthropology* 11, 1 (1996):51-87.

Culler, Jonathan. "In Defence of Overinterpretation." In *Interpretation. and Overinterpretation*, ed. Stefan Collini, 109-25.

Dalrymple, William. "Caste Wars." In *Granta*. 57 (Spring 1997):173-84.

Davis, Robert Con and Ronald Schleifer. *Criticism and Culture: The Role of Critique in Modern Literary Theory*. Harlow: Longman, 1991.

De la Campa, Roman, E. Ann Kaplan, and Michael Sprinker, ed. *Late Imperial Culture*. London: Verso, 1995.

Derrida, Jacques. "Racism's Last Word," ed. *"Race," Writing, and Difference*, ed. Henry Louis Gates, Jr., 329-38. Chicago: The University of Chicago Press, 1994.

______. *The Other Heading: Reflections on Today's Europe*, trans. Pascale-Anne Brault and Michael B. Naas. Bloomington: Indiana University Press, 1992.

______. "Sending: On Representation," trans. Peter and Mary Ann Caws, in *Representation, Discourse and Desire: Contemporary Australian Culture and Critical Theory*, ed. Patrick Fuery, 9-34. Melbourne: Longman Cheshire, 1994.

Deshpande, Shashi. *The Dark Holds No Terrors*. New Delhi: Penguin, 1990 (1980).

______. *If I Die Today*. Sahibadad: Vikas, 1982.

______. *Roots and Shadows*. 1983; Hyderabad: Disha Books, 1992.

______. *That Long Silence*. London: Virago Press, 1988.

______. *The Intrusion and Other Stories*. New Delhi: Penguin, 1993.

______. *The Binding Vine*. London: Virago Press, 1993.

______. "Breaking that Long Silence." *Interview by Suman Gopinath*. Sunday Herald section of *Deccan Herald*, Bangalore, September 25, 1994.

______. "An Interview with Shashi Deshpande." With T.N. Geetha. *Indian Women Novelists*, ed. R.K. Dhawan, Set III, Vol. 4, 9-11.

______. *A Matter of Time*. New Delhi: Penguin, 1996.

Devi, Mahasweta. *Imaginary Maps: Three Stories*, trans. Gayatri Chakravorty Spivak. New York: Routledge, 1995.

Devy, G.N. "The Wind and the Roots: The Problem of Historiography of Commonwealth Literature." In *The History and Historiography of Commonwealth Literature*, ed. Dieter Riemenschneider, 78-90. T'bingen: Gunter Narr Verlag, 1983.

Dhareshwar, Vivek. "Toward a Narrative Epistemology of the Postcolonial Predicament." In *Inscriptions*, 5 (1989):135-57.

Dharkar, Rani. "Marriage as Purdah: Fictional Rendering of a Social Reality." In *Margins of Eraser: Purdah in the Subcontinental Novel in English*, eds. Jasbir Jain and Amina Amin, 49-59.

Dhawan, R.K. "Introduction: Indian Women Novelists." *Indian Women Novelists* Set I, Vol. 1, ed. R.K. Dhawan, 7-26. New Delhi: Prestige, 1991.

Dinesh, Kamini. "Moving out of the Cloistered Self: Shashi Deshpande's Protagonists." In *Margins of Erasure: Purdah in the Subcontinental Novel in English*, ed. Jasbir Jain and Amina Amin. 196-205.

Dirks, Nicholas B. "Introduction: Colonialism and Culture." *Colonialism and Culture*, ed. Nicholas B. Dirks, 1-25. Ann Arbor: The University of Michigan Press, 1992.

______, et al. ed. *Culture, Power, History: A Reader in Contemporary Social Theory*. Princeton: Princeton University Press, 1994.

Dirlik, Arif. "The Postcolonial Aura: Third World Criticism in the Age of Global Capitalism." *Critical Inquiry* 20 (Winter 1994):328-56. Also in *Contemporary Postcolonial Theory: A Reader*, ed. Padmini Mongia, 294-320.

Dixon, Robert. "'Travelling in the West': The Writing of Amitav Ghosh." In *Journal of Commonwealth Literature*, 31, 1 (1996):3-24.

Donaldson, Laura E. "The Miranda Complex: Colonialism and the Question of Feminist Reading." *Diacritics* 18 (3) 1988:65-77.

Doniger, Wendy. *The Implied Spider: Politics and Theology in Myth*. New York: Columbia University Press, 1998.

During, Simon, ed. *The Cultural Studies Reader*. 1993; London: Routledge, 1995.

Easthope, Anthony. "Bhabha, Hybridity and Identity," *Textual Practice*, 12, 2 (Summer 1998): 341-48.

Ferro, Marc. *Colonization: A Global History*. London: Routledge, 1997 (French 1994).

Foucault. Michel. *Power Knowledge: Selected Interviews and Other Writings 1972-1977*, ed. Colin Gordon. New York: Pantheon, 1980.

Frankenber. Ruth and Lata Mani. "Crosscurrents, Crosstalk: Race, 'Postcoloniality' and the Politics of Location." *Contemporary Postcolonial Theory: A Reader*, ed. Padmini Mongia, 347-64. London: Arnold, 1996.

Fuss, Diana. "Interior Colonies: Frantz Fanon and the Politics of Identification." *Diacritics*. 24, 2-3 (1994):20-42.

Galinsky, Karl G. *Ovid's Metamorphoses: An Introduction to the Basic Aspects*. Berkeley: University of California Press, 1975.

Gasch/, Rudolphe. *The Tain of the Mirror: Derrida and the Philosophy of Reflection*. Cambridge, MA: Harvard University Press, 1986.

Gates, Jr. Henry Louis. *The Signifying Monkey: A Theory of African-American Literary Criticism*. Oxford: Oxford University Press, 1989 (1988).

______. *"Race," Writing and Difference*. Chicago: The University of Chicago Press, 1994 (first printed 1985).

______. "Critical Fanonism." In *Critical Inquiry*, 17, 3 (Spring 1991):457-70.

Gilbert, Sandra and Susan Gubar. *The Madwoman in the Attic: The Woman Writer and the Nineteenth-Century Imagination*. New Haven: Yale University Press, 1984.

Glage, Liselotte and Martina Michel. *Postkoloniale Literaturen: Peripherien oder neue Zentren?* Gulliver Deutsch-Englische Jahrb. cher Band 33 (Hamburg: Argument Verlag, 1993).

Gopal, Priyamvada. *Book Review of Women Writing in India*, 2 vols. *The*

Oxford Literary Review. Special Issue: On India: Writing History, Culture, Post-Coloniality 16 (1-2) 1994: 287-94.

Gregorios, Paulos Mar, *A Light Too Bright—The Enlightenment Today: An Assessment of the Values of the European Enlightenment and a Search for New Foundations*. Albany: State University of New York Press, 1992.

Griffiths, Gareth. "Imitation, Abrogation and Appropriation: The Production of the Post-colonial Text," *Kunapipi*, Vol. ix, No. 1, 12-20.

Guha, Ranajit, ed. *Subaltern Studies: Writings on South Asian History and Society*. Vol. I. 1982; Delhi: Oxford University Press, 1994.

______. "Discipline and Mobilize." In *Subaltern Studies: Writings on South Asian History and Society*. Vol. VII, ed. Partha Chatterjee and Gyanendra Pandey, 69-120. Delhi: Oxford University Press, 1993 (1992).

Hassan, Ihab. *The Postmodern Turn: Essays in Postmodern Theory and Culture*. Columbus: Ohio State University Press, 1987.

______. "New Ethnicities." In *Stuart Hall: Critical Dialogues in Cultural Studies*, ed. David Morley and Kuan-Hsing Chen, 441-49. London: Routledge, 1996.

Hodge, Bob and Vijay Mishra. *Dark Side of the Dream: Australian Literature and the Postcolonial Mind*. North Sydney: Allen and Unwin, 1990.

Hogan, Patrick Colm and Lalita Pandit, ed. *Literary India: Comparative Studies in Aesthetics, Colonialism, and Culture*. SUNY Series in Hindu Studies. Albany: State University of New York Press, 1995.

Hohnsträter, Dirk. "Homi K. Bhabhas Semiotik der Zwischenräume-Eine, berzeugende Konzeptualisierung interkultureller Konflikte?" In *Arcadia, Band 31*, Heft 1/2 (1996):62-68.

Hughes, Peter. "Last Post: Alternatives to Postmodernism." *A Review Article. Comparative Studies in Society and History*. 38. 1 (January 1996): 182-88.

Hutcheon, Linda. *A Poetics of Postmodernism: History, Theory, Fiction*. New York: Routledge, 1988.

______. "Colonialism and the Postcolonial Condition: Complexities Abounding." *PMLA*, 110, 1 (January 1995):7-16.

Iser, Wolfgang. *Der Implizite Leser*. 1972; München: Wilhelm Fink Verlag, 1979.

Iyengar, K.R. Srinivasa. "The Literature of India." In *The Commonwealth Pen: An Introduction to the Literature of the British Commonwealth*, ed. A.L. McLeod, 115-41. Ithaca, New York: Cornell University Press, 1961.

______. *Two Cheers for the Commonwealth: Talks on Literature and Education*. New York: Asia, 1970.

Jain, Jasbir and Amina Amin. *Margins of Erasure: Purdah in the Subcontinental Novel in English*. New Delhi: Sterling, 1995.

Jain, Madhu. Book Review: The Intrusion and Other Stories by Shashi

Deshpande. *India Today*, March 15, 1994, 220.

JanMohamed, Abdul R. *Manichean Aesthetics: The Politics of Literature in Colonial Africa.* Amherst: The University of Massachusetts Press, 1983.

Jameson, Fredric. "World Literature in an Age of Multinational Capitalism." In *The Current in Criticism: Essays on the Present and Future of Literary Theory*, ed. Clayton Koelb and Virgil Lokke. West Lafayette: Purdue University, 1987:139-58.

Jeyifo, Biodun. "On Eurocentric Critical Theory: Some Paradigms from the Texts and Sub-Texts of Post-Colonial Writing." *After Europe: Critical Theory and Post-Colonial Writing*, ed. Stephen Slemon and Helen Tiffin. 107-18.

John, Mary E. *Discrepant Dislocations: Feminism, Theory, and Postcolonial Histories.* Berkeley: University of California Press, 1996.

Jolly, Rosemary. "Rehearsals of Liberation: Contemporary Postcolonial Discourse and the New South Africa," *PMLA*, 110, 1 (January 1995):17-29.

Joy, Hepzi R.J. *History and Development of Education of Women in Kerala.* Thiruvananthapuram: Seminary Publications, 1995.

Katrak, Ketu H. "Decolonizing Culture: Toward a Theory for Postcolonial Women's Texts." *Modern Fiction Studies*, 35, 1 (Spring 1989): 157-79.

Kaye, Jacqueline. "Islamic Imperialism and the Question of Some Ideas of 'Europe.'" *Europe and Its Others*, ed. Francis Barker et al, 59-71.

King, Adele. "Shashi Deshpande: Portraits of an Indian Woman." In *The New Indian Novel in English: A Study of the 1980s*, ed. Viney Kirpal, 159-67.

King, Andrew, ed. *Postmodern Political Communication: The Fringe Challenges the Center. Praeger Series in Political Communication.* Westport: Praeger Publishers, 1992.

Kipling, Rudyard. *Kipling's India: Uncollected Sketches 1884-88*, ed. Thomas Pinney. Houndmills: Macmillan Press, 1986.

Kirpal, Viney. "What is the Modern Third World Novel?" *The Journal of Commonwealth Literature*, 23, 1 (1988):145-56.

______, ed. *The New Indian Novel in English: A Study of the 1980s*. New Delhi: Allied, 1990.

______ "Has the Indian Novel been Understood?" In *From Commonwealth to Postcolonial*, ed. Anna Rutherford, 303-15.

Landry, Donna and Gerald Maclean, ed. *The Spivak Reader*. New York: Routledge, 1996.

Levine, George, ed. *Realism and Representation: Essays on the Problem of Realism in Relation to Science, Literature, and Culture*. Wisconsin: The University of Wisconsin Press, 1993.

Levin, Samuel R. "Allegorical Language." *Allegory, Myth and Symbol*, ed. Morton W. Bloomfield. Cambridge, MA: Harvard University Press, 1981, 23-38.

Lionnet, Francoise. *Postcolonial Representations: Women, Literature, Identity*. Ithaca: Cornell University Press, 1995.

Loomba, Ania, and Suvir Kaul. "Introduction: Location, Culture, Post-Coloniality." *Oxford Literary Review*. Special Issue *On India: Writing History, Culture, Post-Coloniality*. 16, 1-2 (1994):3-30.

Lutzeler, Paul Michael. "Der postkoloniale Blick: Deutschsprachige Autoren berichten aus der Dritten Welt," *Neue Rundschau*, 107. Jahrgang, Heft 1/1996:54-69.

Lyotard, Jean-Francois. *The Postmodern Explained: Correspondence 1982-1985*, trans. and ed. Julian Pefanis and Morgan Thomas. Minneapolis: University of Minnesota Press, 1993. Original French Edition 1988.

Mani, Lata. "Cultural Theory, Colonial Texts: Reading Eyewitness Accounts of Widow Burning/Discussion." In *Cultural Studies*, ed. Lawrence Grossberg, Cary Nelson, Paula A. Treichler, 392-408.

______. "The Production of an Official Discourse on Sati in Early Nineteenth-Century Bengal." In *Europe and Its Others: Proceedings of the Essex Conference on the Sociology of Literature July 1984*, ed. Francis Barker et al. 107-27.

Mann, Harveen Sachdeva. "'Cracking India': Minority Women Writers and the Contentious Margins of Indian Nationalist Discourse." In *Journal of Commonwealth Literature*, 29, 2 (1994):71-94.

Manorama Year Book 1994. Kottayam: Malayala Manorama, 1994.

Marathe, Sudhakar, et al, ed. *A Way of Leaving so as to Stay: Papers in Honour of S. Viswanathan*. Madras: T.R., 1994.

Massey, James. *Dalits in India: Religion as a Source of Bondage or Liberation with Special Reference to Christians*. Delhi: ISPCK, 1995.

McClintock, Anne. "The Angel of Progress." In *Colonial Discourse and Post-colonial Theory: A Reader*; ed. Patrick Williams and Laura Chrisman, 291-304. New York: Harvester Wheatsheaf, 1993.

McLeod, A.L, ed. *The Commonwealth Pen: An Introduction to the Literature of the British Commonwealth*. Ithaca, NY: Cornell University Press, 1961.

Michie, Elsie. "From Simianized Irish to Oriental Despots: Heathcliff, Rochester and Racial Difference." *Novel*, 25 (2) 1992: 125-40.

Miller, Hillis, J. "The Two Allegories." In *Allegory, Myth, and Symbol*, ed. Morton W. Bloomfield, 355-70. Cambridge, MA: Harvard University Press, 1981.

Mishra, Vijay and Bob Hodge. "What is Post(-)colonialism?" In *Colonial Discourse and Post-colonial Theory: A Reader*, ed. Patrick Williams and Laura Chrisman, 276-90.

Mistry, Rohinton. *Such a Long Journey*. London: Faber and Faber, 1991.

Mitchell, W.J.T, ed. *The Politics of Interpretation*. Chicago: The University of Chicago Press, 1983.

Mohanty, Chandra Talpade, et al, ed. *Third World Women and the Politics of Feminism*. Bloomington: Indiana University, 1991.

Mohanty, Satya "Drawing the Color Line: Kipling and the Culture of Colonial Rule." *The Bounds of Race Perspectives on Hegemony and Resistance*, ed. Dominick LaCapra. Ithaca: Cornell University Press, 1991, 311-43.

______. "Colonial Legacies, Multicultural Futures: Relativism, Objectivity, and the Challenge of Otherness." *PMLA*, 110, 1 (Spring 1995):108-18.

Mongia, Padmini, ed. *Contemporary Postcolonial Theory: A Reader*. London: Arnold, 1996.

Morley, David and Kuan-Hsing Chen, ed. *Stuart Hall: Critical Dialogues in Cultural Studies*. London: Routledge, 1996.

Mukherjee, Bharati. An interview with Vranda Nabar in *The Sunday Times of India Review*, December 31, 1995: 2.

______ "Beyond Multiculturalism." *Journal of Modern Literature*, 20, 1 (Summer 1996):29-34.

Mukherjee, Meenakshi. "The Centre Cannot Hold: Two Views of the Periphery." *After Europe: Critical Theory and Post-Colonial Writing*, ed. Stephen Slemon and Helen Tiffin, 41-49.

Nandy, Ashis. *The Intimate Enemy: Loss and Recovery of Self under Colonialism*. Delhi: Oxford University Press, 1983.

______. "Culture, State and the Rediscovery of Indian Politics." In *Literary India: Comparative Studies in Aesthetics, Colonialism, and Culture*, ed. Patrick Colm Hogan and Lalita Pundit, 255-74.

Narasimhaiah, C.D. and C.N. Srinath, ed. *A Common Poetic for Indian Literature*. Mysore: Dhvanyaloka, 1984.

Nasta, Susheila, ed. *Motherlands: Black Women's Writing from Africa, the Caribbean and South Asia*. London: The Women's Press, 1991.

Niranjana, Tejaswini. "Whose Culture is it? Contesting the Modern." In *A Way of Leaving so as to Stay*, ed. Sudhakar Marathe et al. Madras: T.R., 1994, 127-52.

Niranjana, Tejaswini, Sudhir and Vivek Dhareshwar, ed. *Interrogating Modernity: Culture and Colonialism in India*. Calcutta: Seagull, 1993.

Ngugi wa Thiong'O. *Writers in Politics: Essays*. London: Heinemann, 1981.

Ovid. *Metamorphoses*, trans. A.D. Melville. Oxford: Oxford University Press, 1986.

Ondaatje, Michael. *The English Patient*. London: Bloomsbury, 1992.

Paranjape, Makarand R. "Inside and Outside the Whale: Politics and the New Indian English Novel." In *The New Indian Novel in English: A Study of the 1980s*, ed. Viney Kirpal, 213-26.

______. "Postmodernism and India: Some Preliminary Animadversions." In *A Way of Leaving so as to Stay*, ed. Sudhakar Marathe et al, 89-109.

Parry, Benita. "Problems in Current Theories of Colonial Theories," *Oxford Literary Review*, 9 (1-2) 1987:27-58.

Pathak, Zakia. "A Pedagogy for Postcolonial Feminists." In *Feminists Theorize the Political*, ed. Judith Butler and Joan W. Scott, 426-41. New York: Routledge, 1992.

Pieterse, Jan Nederveen and Bhikhu Parekh. "Shifting Imaginaries: Decolonization, Internal Decolonization, Postcoloniality." In *The Decolonization of Imagination: Culture, Knowledge and Power*, ed. Pieterse and Parekh. London: Zed Books, 1995:1-19.

Poster, Mark. *Critical Theory and Poststructuralism: In Search of a Context*. Ithaca: Cornell University Press, 1989.

Prakash, Gyan. "Writing Post-Orientalist Histories of the Third World: Indian Historiography is Good to Think." In *Colonialism and Culture*, ed. Nicholas B. Dirks, 353-88.

_______, ed. *After Colonialism: Imperial Histories and Postcolonial Displacements*. Princeton: Princeton University Press, 1995.

______. "*Orientalism* Now." A Review of Reviews. *History and Theory* 34, 3 (1995):199-212.

Rajan, Rajeshwari Sunder. *Real and Imagined Woman: Gender, Culture and Postcolonialism*. London: Routledge, 1993.

______. "The Feminist Plot and the Nationalist Allegory: Home and World in Two Indian Women's Novels in English." In *Modern Fiction Studies*, 39.1 (Spring 1993):71-92.

Rapaport, Herman. "Deconstruction's Other: Trinh T. Minh-ha and Jacques Derrida." In *Diacritics*, 25, 2 (Summer 1995):98-113.

Raveendran, P.P. "Text as History, History as Text: A Reading of Kamala Das's Annamalai Poems." In *Journal of Commonwealth Literature*, 29, 1 (1994):47-54.

Ravenscroft, Arthur. "Foreword." *Commonwealth Literature Periodicals: A Bibliography, including Periodicals of former Commonwealth Countries, with Locations in the United Kingdom*. Compiled and ed. Ronald Warwick. London: Mansell Publishing, 1979, vii-xiii.

Retamar, Roberto Fernandez. "Caliban: Notes Towards a Discussion of Culture in Our America," trans. Lynn Garafola, David Arthur McMurray, Robert Mzrquez, *Massachusetts Review*, 15 (Winter- Spring 1974):7-72.

Riemenschneider, Dieter, ed. *The History and Historiography of Commonwealth Literature*. Tübingen: Gunter Narr Verlag, 1983.

______. "History and the Individual in Anita Desai's *Clear Light of Day* and Salman Rushdie's *Midnight's Children*." In *The New Indian Novel in English*, ed. Viney Kirpal, 187-210.

Rossel, Jacques. *The Roots of Western Europe: An Essay on Interpenetration of Cultures during the First Nine Centuries of our Era*, trans. John M. Lyle. Basel: Basileia Publications, 1995.

Rushdie, Salman. *Imaginary Homelands: Essays and Criticism 1981-1991*.

1991; London: Granta Books, 1992.

Rutherford, Anna, ed. *From Commonwealth to Postcolonial*. Sydney: Dangaroo Press, 1992.

Said, Edward W. *Orientalism*. (With a New Afterword) 1978; New York: Vintage Books, 1994.

______. *The World, the Text, and the Critic*. 1983; London: Faber & Faber, 1984.

______. "Opponents, Audiences, Constituencies and Community," *Postmodern Culture*, ed. Hal Foster. London and Sydney: Pluto Press, 1985. Second Impression 1987.

______. "Orientalism Reconsidered," *Literature, Politics and Theory*, ed. Francis Baker et al. London: Methuen, 1986, 210-29.

______. "Representing the Colonized: Anthropology's Interlocutors," *Critical Inquiry*, 15 (Winter 1989):205-25.

______. "Figures, Configurations, Transfigurations." In *From Commonwealth to Postcolonial*, ed. Anna Rutherford. 3-17.

______. *Culture and Imperialism*. New York: Alfred S. Knopf, 1993.

Sangari, Kumkum and Sudesh Vaid, ed. *Recasting Women: Essays in Colonial History*. New Delhi: Kali for Women, 1989.

Sangari, Kumkum. "The Politics of the Possible." In *Interrogating Modernity*, ed. Tejaswini Niranjana et al. Calcutta: Seagull, 1993, 242-72.

Sathupathi, Prasanna Sree. "Conflict and Identity in Shashi Deshpande's Novels." In *Indian Women Novelists*, ed. R.K. Dhawan. Set III. Vol. 4, 12-19.

Schwalm, Helga. *Dekonstruktion im Roman: Erzähltechnische Verfahren und Selbstreflexion in den Romanen von Vladimir Nabakov und Samuel Beckett*. Heidelberg: Carl Winter Universitätsverlag, 1991.

Sheshadri, Viji and Shashi Deshpande. "Gegenwärtige indo-englische Literatur von Frauen." In *Postkoloniale Literaturen: Peripherien oder neue Zentren?*. Hrsg. Liselotte Glage und Martina Michel. Hamburg: Argument-Verlag, 1993, 95-104.

Shohat, Ella. "Notes on the 'Post-Colonial.'" *Contemporary Postcolonial Theory: A Reader*, ed. Padmini Mongia. 321-34.

Slemon, Stephen. "Monuments of Empire: Allegory/Counter-Discourse/Post-Colonial Writing." *Kunapipi*, 9, 3 (1987):1-16.

______. "Post-Colonial Allegory and the Transformation of History." *The Journal of Commonwealth Literature*, 23, 1 (1988):157-68.

______. "The Scramble for Post-Colonialism." In *De-Scribing Empire*, ed. Helen Tiffin and Alan Lawson, 15-32.

______. "Unsettling the Empire: Resistance Theory for the Second World." *Contemporary Postcolonial Theory*, ed. Padmini Mongia. 72-83.

Slemon, Stephen and Helen Tiffin, ed. *After Europe: Critical Theory and Post-Colonial Writing*. Sydney: Dangaroo Press, 1989.

Smith, M. van Wyk. "Review Article: Colonial and Post-Colonial Literatures." In *The Review of English Studies*, 44, 175 (August 1993):393-99.

Soyinka, Wole. *Myth, Literature and the African World*. 1976; Cambridge: Cambridge University Press, 1992.

Spivak, Gayatri Chakravorty. "Translator's Preface." In *Derrida, Of Grammatology*. trans. Spivak. Baltimore: The Johns Hopkins University Press, 1976 (1974), ix-xc.

______. "Imperialism and Sexual Difference." In *The Current in Criticism: Essays on the Present and Future of Literary Theory*, ed. Clayton Koelb and Virgil Lokke, 319-37. West Lafayette: Purdue University Press, 1987.

______. "Rani of Sirmur." In *Europe and Its Others*, ed. Francis Barker et al, 128-51.

______. *In Other Worlds: Essays in Cultural Politics*. New York: Routledge, 1988.

______. "Postcoloniality and Value." In *Literary Theory Today*, ed. Peter Collier and Helga Geyer-Ryan, 219-44.

______. *The Post-Colonial Critic: Interviews, Strategies, Dialogues*. New York: Routledge, 1990.

______. "Neocolonialism and the Secret Agent of Knowledge: An Interview." Interviewed by Robert Young, *The Oxford Literary Review*, 13, 1-2 (1991):220-51.

______. *Outside in the Teaching Machine*. New York: Routledge, 1993.

______. "Race Before Racism and the Disappearance of the American: Jack D. Forbes' *Black Africans and Americans: Color, Race and Caste in the Evolution of Red-Black Peoples*." In *Plantation Society in the Americas*. Vol. III, 2 (1993): 73-91.

______. "Teaching for the Times." In *The Decolonization of Imagination: Culture, Knowledge and Power*, ed. Jan Nederveen Pieterse and Bhikhu Parekh. London: Zed, 1995.

______. "Ghostwriting." In *Diacritics*, 25, 2 (Summer 1995):65-84.

______. "Translator's Preface." In *Imaginary Maps: Three Stories, Mahasweta Devi*, trans. Spivak, xxiii-xxix.

______. "Diasporas Old and New: Women in the Transnational World," *Textual Practice* 10, 2 (1996):245-69.

Sprinker, Michael. "Introduction." In *Late Imperial Culture*, ed. Roman de la Campa, E. Ann Kaplan and Michael Sprinker, 1-10.

Suleri, Sara. *The Rhetoric of English India*. Chicago: The University of Chicago Press, 1992.

Swain, S.P. "Shashi Deshpande's *The Dark Holds No Terrors*: Saru's Feminine Sensibility." In *Indian Women Novelists*, ed. R.K. Dhawan. Set III, Vol. 4, 32-40.

Thapar, Romila. *Time as the Metaphor of History*. Delhi: Oxford University Press, 1996.

Tharu, Susie and K. Lalitha, ed. *Women Writing In India: 600 B.C. to the Present. Volume I: 600 B.C. to the Early Twentieth Century*. London: Pandora Press, 1993 (first published 1991).

______. *Women Writing in India: 600 B.C. to the Present. Volume II: The Twentieth Century*. London: Pandora Press, 1993.

Thieme, John. "Editorial." *Journal of Commonwealth Literature*, 30, 1 (1995):3-4.

Tiffin, Helen. "Commonwealth Literature: Comparison and Judgement," *The History and Historiography of Commonwealth Literature*, ed. Dieter Riemenschneider, 18-34.

______. "Post-Colonial Literatures and Counter-Discourse." In *Kunapipi*. 9, 3 (1987):17-34.

______. "Post-Colonialism, Post-Modernism and the Rehabilitation of Post-Colonial History." In *Journal of Commonwealth Literature*, 23, 1 (1988):169-81.

Tiffin, Chris and Alan Lawson, ed. *De-scribing Empire: Post-colonialism and Textuality*. London: Routledge, 1994.

Trinh, T. Minh-ha. *Woman, Native, Other: Writing Postcoloniality and Feminism*. Bloomington: Indiana University Press, 1989.

Trotter, David. "Colonial Subjects." *Critical Quarterly*, 32, 3 (Autumn 1990):2-20.

Veeser, Aram, ed. *The New Historicism*. London: Routledge, 1989.

Vincentnathan, George S. "Caste Politics, Violence, and the Panchayat in a South Indian Community." In *Comparative Studies in Society and History*, 38, 3 (July 1996):484-509.

Visel, Robin. "A Half-Colonization: The Problem of the White Colonial Woman Writer." In *Kunapipi*. 10, 3 (1988):39-45.

Viswanathan, Gauri. *Masks of Conquest: Literary Study and British Rule in India*. New York: Columbia University Press, 1989.

Wägenbaur, Thomas. "Hybride Hybridität: Der Kulturkonflikt im Text der Kulturtheorie." In *Arcadia*, Band 31, 1996:27-38.

Walcott, Derek. "Caligula's Horse." In *After Europe*, ed. Stephen Slemon and Helen Tiffin. 138-42.

Williams, Patrick and Laura Chrisman, ed. *Colonial Discourse and Post-Colonial Theory: A Reader*. New York: Harvester Wheatsheaf, 1993.

Williams, Raymond. *Marxism and Literature*. Oxford: Oxford University Press, 1977.

______. *Culture*. London: Fontana, 1981.

Yegenoglu, Meyda. *Colonial Fantasies: Towards a Feminist Reading of Orientalism* (Cambridge: Cambridge University Press, 1998).

Young, Robert. *White Mythologies: Writing History and the West*. London: Routledge, 1993 (1990).

______. *Colonial Desire: Hybridity in Theory, Culture and Race*. London: Routledge, 1995.